Further praise for *The Beautiful Team*

'Jenkins' hike goes deep into pure football mythology. He dodges traffic in the Babylonian Rio rush hour, fears for his life in the crumbling chaos of the mad, bad and extremely dangerous Maracana, and drinks in the petrol fumes in goalkeeper Felix's garage. It's a poetically sketched . . . dribble down memory lane. Those who talk, and most of the team do, use their words to relive the impossible dazzle of those days and to regret the dull paint job of the modern game. Magic and loss on the samba trail.
'**** Football as erotica. Football as fairytale' *Total Football*

'By overwhelming consent, the Brazil team which won the World Cup in 1970 is the finest that football has ever seen. Jenkins decided to travel across Brazil, tracking down the members of that extraordinary side. It was a brave idea, and it succeeds quite admirably' Patrick Collins, *Mail on Sunday*

'One can only echo the sentiments of the midfield enforcer Clodoaldo, who tearfully tells Jenkins, "I want to thank you for doing this. I think it is history." The author should now be commissioned to track down Brazil's 1998 finalists. They did, after all go missing against France' *Independent*

'Read it and blot out the recollection of their successors' abject capitulation at the Stade de France.'
Nick Szczepanik, *The Times*, Best Football Books of 1998

'Gives the reader a rare insight into Brazilian football and that great team, who we have seen so often and yet know comparatively little about' *When Saturday Comes*

'A great story' *Match of the Day Magazine*

'A fascinating insight' *Total Sport*

'Packed with highly personal and often very touching memories' *Sports Collector*

Garry Jenkins is the author of four books. His fifth, *Colonel Cody and The Flying Cathedral*, will be published in October 1999. He lives in Blackheath, London with his wife and daughter.

Also by Garry Jenkins

Daniel Day-Lewis: The Fire Within
Harrison Ford: Imperfect Hero
Empire Building: The Remarkable Real Life Story
of Star Wars

THE
BEAUTIFUL
TEAM

In Search of Pelé
and the 1970 Brazilians

Garry Jenkins

Interviews and research in Brazil with Pedro Redig,
translations by Antonio Pires Soares

POCKET
BOOKS

LONDON · SYDNEY · NEW YORK · TOKYO · SINGAPORE · TORONTO

For Gabriella, meu tesorinho

First published in Great Britain by Simon & Schuster UK Ltd, 1998
This edition first published by Pocket Books, 1999
An imprint of Simon & Schuster UK Ltd
A Viacom Company

1 3 5 7 9 10 8 6 4 2

Simon & Schuster UK Ltd
Africa House
64–78 Kingsway
London WC2B 6AH

Simon & Schuster Australia
Sydney

A CIP catalogue record for this book is available
from the British Library

ISBN 0-671-01566-4

Typeset by Palimpsest Book Production Limited,
Polmont, Stirlingshire
Printed and bound in Great Britain by
Caledonian International Book Manufacturing Ltd, Glasgow

CONTENTS

ACKNOWLEDGEMENTS

Researching and writing any book involves a journey of sorts – but this one was more eventful than most. My deepest debt has to be to the members of that legendary team who gave so graciously of their time, hospitality and kindness during my travels around Brazil. Meeting each of them was a privilege. In particular I must thank Gérson and the staff at his ENITUR office in Niteroi, Carlos Alberto and the staff at his football school in Barra and Rivellino and his staff at his sports centre in São Paulo, each of whom performed services above and beyond the call of duty in linking me with other members of the Beautiful Team.

I am equally grateful to the staff at the Ministry of Sport in Brasília, in particular Luis Felipe Cavalcanti Albuquerque and Tania Ramos without whose persistent championing of my cause in difficult circumstances I would never have been allowed the time I had with Pelé.

Elsewhere in both Brazil and London I am indebted to a wide cross section of people. In Rio, I would like to thank Joaquim Redig de Campos, whose hospitality and quiet, cultivated company I enjoyed so much. Thanks too must go to his sister Maria Leticia and Onaldo Machado, both of whom contributed to making my stay in their city as dramatic as it was unforgettable. In São Paulo the elegant company of Luiza Rotbart eased the strain of life in that chaotic city. I am also particularly grateful to Alfredo Ogawa of *Placar* magazine for organising a collection of cuttings from his magazine's coverage of Mexico 1970.

In Brasília thanks are due to Gloria and Maina Pilomia de Souza, in Belo Horizonte Fernando Zagallo and Vandreia Ribeiro. Back in London I am indebted to Paula Mann at Varig Airlines, the staff at the Football Association library and at the late, lamented Reading Room at the old British Library. I am also grateful to Paula for putting me in contact with Antonio Pires Soares, whose meticulous work in translating the many hours of taped interviews was much appreciated. Thanks must go to Martyn Palmer for his general supportiveness and specific input in reading my manuscript and Ray Pask at NatWest Bank for his understanding and supportiveness.

At Aitken & Stone, my agent Mary Pachnos demonstrated her usual acumen; at Simon & Schuster I owe a thank you to Bob Kelly and Keith Barnes for their crucial early enthusiasm for the book. From then on my greatest supporters at S&S were Helen Gummer and, in particular, Ingrid Connell, a Middlesbrough fan then undergoing her own Brazilian adventure. Her expert editorial input helped guide me to a finishing line that at times seemed unreachable. If only Juninho and Emerson had been as loyal.

Of all those I have named, however, none made a greater contribution than the journalist Pedro Redig, who travelled with me around Brazil. Without his relentless work as a researcher, translator and general footballing Mr Fixit, this book would have been a very different one. Our journey was a fraught and often fractious one. Now it is time to say a simple and sincere *muito obrigado*.

As every, my final thanks must go to my wife, Cilene. This time her support extended to helping organise my travels and accommodation and spotting numerous linguistic transgressions in the manuscript. All this at a time when we were both welcoming our first child Gabriella into the world. I have already dedicated a book to Cilene. I know she will have no objection if I dedicate this one to Gabriella instead.

PROLOGUE

'Brazil's victory with the ball compares with the conquest of the moon by the Americans.'
                                    Jornal do Brasil, June 1970

Dylan Thomas couldn't remember if it snowed for six days when he was twelve or for twelve days when he was six. My memories of the weather in West Wales during the summer of 1970 are just as jumbled. My village – as it happens, a dozen miles or so west of Laugharne and the old reprobate's boathouse – might have been consumed by clouds as usual. It might just as easily have been in the grip of a freak heatwave. In truth I really haven't got a clue.

The meteorology of the Mexican cities of Leon, Guadalajara and Mexico City is another matter, however. I can remember that in Guadalajara, soon after noon on 7 June that year, the temperature touched 98°F. I know because Bobby Charlton lost ten pounds in sweat there. My recall is so tediously total that I know, during the three nights leading up to Sunday, 21 June, Mexico City suffered a series of thunderstorms so terrifying they almost turned the clock back 500 years or so. (For reasons best known to themselves, the Aztecs and their Emperor Montezuma built their capital on a vast lake.) It was only around noon that Sunday, with a sense of symbolism Montezuma's soothsayers might have appreciated, that the sun finally broke out once more in the skies above the city's fabulous Azteca stadium.

In June 1970 I was a twelve-year-old schoolboy, hopelessly obsessed with the World Cup finals. I spent as much time as my father would allow glued to the household's large, rather ungainly new colour television set. Russia v. Mexico, England v. Czechoslovakia and Rumania, highlights of Israel v. Italy, I watched the lot. What little spare time I had was spent poring over copies of *Goal*, *Football Monthly* or the old *Daily Mirror* and the dispatches of sunburnt scribes like Frank McGhee and Ken Jones.

Owing to some cunning forward planning, even demands that I get on with some homework failed to deflect me. My main school project that term was on the nations of the World Cup. With scissors and paste I had put together a guide to the sixteen participating countries on the back of a roll of old wallpaper. The roll now circled the classroom of the school's most football-minded master, a man called Dennis Jones. Each section featured a potted history, a photo of the nation's World Cup squad and a few relevant images. Italy were represented by the Pope and the Leaning Tower of Pisa. El Salvador, who had gone to war with Honduras after their qualification match, by a picture from an old World War II comic. God only knows what I used to represent Bulgaria and Morocco. Thankfully here my memory does fail me.

Football – or to be more precise, international football

– had been something of a drug since I was seven or so. It was, of course, the previous World Cup – *England's* World Cup, that had fired the whole thing off. Since then I had got terribly excited about Celtic v. Inter Milan and Manchester United v. Benfica on television. Thanks to a piece of inspired ticket acquisition by my father, I would soon see Cardiff City's 1–0 win over Amancio, Gento and the gods of Real Madrid in the quarter-finals of the Cup Winners' Cup in the unforgettable flesh along with 47,500 others at Ninian Park.

Yet Mexico marked the dawn of a new, even more exciting era, and not just because this was the first World Cup to be beamed live from the other side of the world in glorious, living colour. One man, and one team, elevated it to the realms of magic.

In hindsight it seems natural that Pelé and the 1970 Brazilians should have arrived in our living room the year after the first moon landing. Tostão and Gérson, Jairzinho and Carlos Alberto, Rivellino and Clodoaldo shared much more than their number with Neil Armstrong and his crew. They were, after Apollo 11, the second great event of the new, telecultural age. It seemed fitting that their games were transmitted from Central America via a satellite in outer space. From their opening match against Czechoslovakia it was clear they were visitors from another footballing world. (We should have guessed they'd carried out the same NASA training programmes as the astronauts.)

Brazil alone seemed to justify the extra money my father would now have to pay for upgrading his old monochrome licence. All coffee browns and ebony blacks, cobalt blues and canary yellows, their players and their playing came in shades I had never seen before. Each of their games seemed to be a drama filled with flashing free kicks, 50-yard passes and even longer-range shots. Their kit, their running, even their celebrations seemed more vivid and vibrant than anything I had witnessed before. Bobby Charlton still shook hands when he scored. Not that he was doing much of that as he melted in the Mexican heat. Pelé and company cavorted and congratulated each other like lovers at the end of a seven-year separation. Then there were the names: exotic, moody mononyms like Tostão ('the little coin'), Gérson and Jair, Clodoaldo and Rivellino. For three weeks, I was mesmerized by them. They have occupied a sun-kissed corner of my memory ever since.

Their glorious summer reached its climax on that rainy Sunday, 21 June. In the days before the Final, I had feared for them. Part of Brazil's magic, I realize now, lay in their fallibility. Their defence leaked like an old, rusted bucket. In Italy they faced the most cynical and professional side in the world. Wise men in Mexico were calling the Final a battle for football's soul, a dance to the death between the free expression of Brazil's samba football and the organizational coldness of *catenaccio*, the pincer defence that was Italy's only gift to world football. The tactical complexities were a bit beyond me back then. I saw it as a contest between a collection of inspiring if occasionally naive geniuses and a bunch of Italian hitmen. I desperately wanted Brazil to win.

They did, slaughtering Italy with the most exhilarating football ever to win a World Cup Final. Pelé got them moving, leaping like the proverbial salmon to head past Albertosi. Every Pelé goal was an occasion, but this was special – the hundredth goal Brazil had scored in the World Cup finals. Even their eccentric keeper Félix played a blinder, making one great stop from Italy's Sardinian assassin Luigi Riva. Gérson, their balding, eternally-chattering *generalissimo*, put them back ahead again after an uncharacteristic error by the young Clodoaldo had let in Boninsegna for an equalizer. Jairzinho bundled in a third to become the first player ever to score in all matches in the finals, then Carlos Alberto scored the fourth, a weave of interpassing started by the now redeemed Clodoaldo and the best goal of the lot. In years to come the phrase would pass peacefully into the obscurity reserved for the very worst sporting clichés. On 27 June 1970, however, it seemed as if the game of football truly was the winner.

The final whistle brought bedlam. Much had been made of the intimidating moat keeping the Azteca hordes at bay. Suddenly it seemed as if even the Brazilian fans could walk on water. Thanks to the miracle of colour television, I saw Tostão stripped down to a pair of blue underpants. Pelé was lost under the biggest sombrero in Mexico. The presentation was delayed by fifteen minutes as the players fought their way through the throng.

As Carlos Alberto lifted and kissed the Jules Rimet trophy we knew we would never see the old trophy again. Brazil had won it for the third time. It was theirs to take home back to Rio and keep. What we did not know was that we would not see football like this again. As the sun set on the Azteca that afternoon, so too a golden sporting age faded, never to return.

By the time Brazil came to defend their world championship in West Germany four years later, Pelé, Gérson and Tostão had all retired. Jairzinho returned, more muscled and sporting an Afro haircut straight from the *Shaft* movies of the day, but his rampaging runs were no more. Rivellino still fired in a free kick or two, but he was also reduced to squaring up to Billy Bremner of Scotland. It seemed as if the gods had fallen off their pedestal.

The freewheeling, fantasy football had gone, replaced by a pragmatic, European style. Europe – in the free-thinking form of Johann Cruyff and Holland – reverted to historical type and once more played the *conquistadores*. Cruyff and co. were a sight to behold. But Brazil were a heartbreaking shadow of their former extraterrestrial selves. After that, despite a brief return – naturally enough in a team led by Socrates – to the old philosophy in 1982, the *real* Brazil disappeared. So too, for me anyhow, did some of the magic of the World Cup.

Brazil finally won the crown again in 1994, sending the most passionate football nation on earth into deliria. I was in California when it happened and witnessed the scenes in Pasadena as the samba beat out. But it wasn't the same. Theirs was a triumph of tactical nous and modest flair. Even Brazil's most ardent fans do not claim the heroes of that win deserved a place on football's Olympus. Talk of Bebeto and Romario, Dunga and Rai and grown men will nod in respectful acknowledgement. Mention Pelé and Tostão, Gérson and Jairzinho and you may see those same grown men cry. The wounds inflicted by the Ronaldo affair and the nation's pathetic capitulation to France in the 1998 final only deepened their sense of loss.

Almost thirty years on, the shadow cast by the 1970 Brazilians seems longer than ever. This isn't just senti-ment, the statistics bear me out here. Videos of their campaign remain bestsellers. Few of football's legion of new writers can resist referring longingly to their greatness. Even the best of the older ones, Hugh McIlvaney, admits they 'may have represented the highest point of beauty and sophistication the game is destined to reach'.

In the years since their triumph, FIFA and its potentates have moulded football into a global obsession and a multi-billion-dollar business. Yet like the multinationals it now conspires with, the game's ruling body profits from a product as humdrum and homogenized as a Big Mac or a Diet Coke. As the game has got bigger so its teams and its players seem to have shrunk with it. When Péle opened Euro 96 at Wembley, there was hardly a dry eye in the house. Perhaps we were crying for our lost footballing selves?

Over the years I had often wondered what had happened to those heroes of twenty-seven summers ago. Only Pelé, now Brazil's sports minister, remained a world figure. Carlos Alberto joined him at the New York Cosmos, but I had seen or read nothing on the rest of that magnificent eleven. All manner of tales had drifted my way as time went by. How the team and its stars had been exploited for political ends by the then military dictatorship. How, mainly for political reasons, Pelé, Gérson and Carlos Alberto had refused to defend their title in Germany even though they were fit to play. How the intellectual Tostão had walked away from fame and football to become a near recluse. How one or two had tumbled into the sort of booze-hazed half-life that had put paid to the careers of geniuses like George Best and Garrincha.

In the spring of 1997, with the last World Cup of the century approaching, I set off to find them. The search would take me on a journey of 12,000 miles and to four major Brazilian cities and one minor one. A little of what I had heard turned out to be the truth, or close to it, at least. Most of the mythology turned to the disreputable dust I had always hoped it would. Instead I discovered a collection of stories that were sometimes colourful, often crazy but always compelling. This then is the story of that journey. Much more importantly, it is the story of that bewitching, beautiful team . . .

The Road To the Azteca

THE SQUAD

Ado
(Eduardo Roberto Stinghero)
Goalkeeper, Corinthians, São Paulo.
Age: 23.

Félix
(Félix Mialli Venerando)
Goalkeeper, Fluminense, Rio. Age: 32.

Leão
(Emerson Leão)
Goalkeeper, Palmeria, São Paulo.
Age: 20.

Baldocci
(José Guillermo Baldocci)
Defender, Palmeiras, São Paulo.
Age: 24.

Brito
(Hercules Brito Ruas)
Defender, Flamengo, Rio. Age: 30.

Carlos Alberto
(Carlos Alberto Torres)
Defender, Santos. Age: 26.

Everaldo
(Everaldo Marques da Silva)
Defender, Grêmio, Porto Alegre. Age: 25

Fontana
(José de Anchiera Fontana)
Defender, Cruzeiro, Belo Horizonte.
Age: 30.

Joel
(Joel Camargo)
Defender, Santos. Age: 25.

Marco Antonio
(Marco Antonio Feliciano)
Defender, Fluminense, Rio. Age: 19.

Piazza
(Wilson da Silva Piazza)
Defender/midfield, Cruzeiro, Belo
Horizonte. Age: 27.

Zé Maria
(José Maria Rodrigues)
Defender, Portuguesa, São Paulo.
Age 20.

Clodoaldo
(Clodoaldo Tavares Santana)
Midfield, Santos. Age: 21.

Gérson
(Gérson de Oliveira Nunes)
Midfield, São Paulo. Age: 29.

Paulo Cézar
(Paulo Cézar Lima)
Midfield/ attacker, Botafogo, Rio.
Age: 21.

Rivellino
(Roberto Rivellino)
Midfield/ attacker, Corinthians, São
Paulo. Age: 24.

Dario
(Dario José dos Santos)
Attacker, Atlético Mineiro, Belo
Horizonte. Age: 23.

Edu
(Jonas Eduardo Américo)
Attacker, Santos. Age: 20

Jairzinho
(Jair Ventura Filho)
Attacker, Botafogo, Rio. Age: 26.

Pelé
(Edson Arantes do Nascimento)
Attacker, Santos. Age: 29.

Roberto
(Roberto Lopes Miranda)
Attacker, Botafogo, Rio. Age: 26.

Tostão
(Eduardo Gonçalvez de Andrade)
Attacker, Cruzeiro, Belo Horizonte.
Age: 21

QUALIFICATION FOR MEXICO

| Bogotá, 6 August 1969 | Colombia | 0 |
| **Brazil** | 2 | |

(Tostão 2)

| Caracas, 10 August 1969 | Venezuela | 0 |
| **Brazil** | 5 | |

(Tostão 3, Pelé2)

| Asunción, 17 August 1969 | Paraguay | 0 | **Brazil** |
| | | 3 | (Mendoza o.g. Edu, Jairzinho) |

| Rio, 21 August 1969 | **Brazil** | 6 |
| Colombia | 2 | |

(Tostão 2, Pelé,   (Mesa,

Gallego   )

Edu,Rivellino,
Jairzinho)

| Rio, 24 August 1969 | **Brazil** | 6 |
| Venezuela | 0 | (Tostão 3, Jairzinho, |

Pelé 2,

1(pen))

| Rio, 31 Augus | | 1 |
| Paraguay | | |

GROUP ONE
(Mexico City)

Mexico	0	Russia	0
Belgium	3	El Salvador	0
Russia	4	Belgium	1
Mexico	4	El Salvador	0
Russia	2	El Salvador	0
Mexico	1	Belgium	0

	P	W	D	L	F	A	Pts
Russia	3	2	1	0	6	1	5
Mexico	3	2	1	0	5	0	5
Belgium	3	1	0	2	4	5	2
El Salvador	3	0	0	3	0	9	0

GROUP TWO
(Puebla/Toluca)

Uruguay	2	Israel	0
Italy	1	Sweden	0
Uruguay	0	Italy	0
Israel	1	Sweden	1
Uruguay	0	Sweden	1
Italy	0	Israel	0

	P	W	D	L	F	A	Pts
Italy	3	1	2	0	1	0	4
Uruguay	3	1	1	1	2	1	3
Sweden	3	1	1	1	2	2	3
Israel	3	0	2	1	1	3	2

GROUP FOUR
(Leon)

Peru	3	Bulgaria	2
Morocco	1	West Germany	2
Peru	3	Morocco	0
Bulgaria	2	West Germany	5
Peru	1	West Germany	3
Morocco	1	Bulgaria	1

	P	W	D	L	F	A	Pts
W. Germany	3	3	0	0	10	4	6
Peru	3	2	0	1	7	5	4
Bulgaria	3	0	1	2	5	9	1
Morocco	3	0	1	2	2	6	1

GROUP THREE (Guadalajara)

| England | 1 | Rumania | 0 |

Czechoslovakia 1

(Petras)
Viktor, Dobias, Horvath, Migas,
Hagara, Hrdicka, Kuna,
Vesley (F), Petras, Adamec, Jokl.
Subs: Kvasnak, Vesley (B).

Brazil 4

(Rivellino, Pelé, Jairzinho 2)
Félix, Carlos Alberto, Brito, Piazza,
Everaldo, Gérson, Clodoaldo,
Rivellino, Jairzinho, Tostão, Pelé.
Sub: Paulo Cézar.

| Czechoslovakia | 1 | Rumania | 2 |

England 0

Banks, Wright, Cooper,
Mullery, Labone, Moore, Lee,
Ball, Charlton, Hurst, Peters.
Subs: Bell, Astle.

Brazil 1

(Jairzinho)
Félix, Carlos Alberto, Brito, Piazza,
Everaldo, Paulo Cézar, Clodoaldo,
Rivellino, Jairzinho, Tostão, Pelé.
Sub: Roberto Lopes.

Brazil 3

(Pelé 2, Jairzinho)
Félix, Carlos Alberto, Brito, Fontana,
Everaldo, Paulo Cézar, Piazza,
Clodoaldo, Jairzinho,
Tostão, Pelé.
Subs: Marco Antonio, Edu.

Rumania 2

(Dumitrache, Dembrowski)
Adamache, Szatmarani, Lupescu,
Dinu, Mocanu, Nunweiller, Dumitru,
Neagu, Dembrowski, Dumitrache,
Lucescu. Subs: Raducanu, Tataru

| England | 1 | Czechoslovakia | 0 |

	P	W	D	L	F	A	Pts
Brazil	3	3	0	0	8	3	6
England	3	2	0	1	2	1	4
Rumania	3	1	0	2	5	2	
Czechoslovakia	3	0	0	3	2	0	

QUARTER FINALS

SEMI FINALS

Russia   0

Uruguay   1

Uruguay   1

(Esparrago)

(Cubilla)
Mazurkiewicz, Ubinas,
Ancheta, Matosas, Mujica,
Montero, Maneiro, Cortes,
Cubilla, Fontes, Morales.
Sub: Esparaggo.

Brazil   4

(Rivellino, Tostão, Pelé, Jairzinho)
Félix, Carlos Alberto, Brito, Piazza
Marco Antonio, Gérson, Clodoaldo,
Rivellino, Jairzhino, Tostão, Pelé.
Subs: Paulo Cézar, Roberto Lopes.

Brazil   3

Peru   2

(Clodoaldo, Jairzinho, Rivellino)
Félix, Carlos Alberto, Brito,
Piazza, Everaldo, Gérson,
Clodoaldo, Rivellino,
Jairzinho, Tostão, Pelé.

(Gallardo, Cubillas)
Rubinos, Campos, Fernandex,
Chumpitaz, Fuentes, Challe, Mifflin,
Baylon, Leon, Cubillas, Gallardo.
Subs: Sotil, Reyes.

Mexico   1

(Gonzalez)

Italy   4
(Domenghini, Riva 2, Rivera)

Italy   4

(Boninsegna, Burgnich, Riva,
Rivera)

England   2

(Mullery, Peters)

West Germany   3

West Germany   3

(Beckenbauer, Seeler, Muller)

(Schnellinger, Muller 2)

THE FINAL

(Azteca Stadium, Mexico City, 21 June 1970)
Referee: Herr Rudi Glockner (East Germany)

Brazil   **4**

(Pelé, Gérson, Jairzinho, Carlos Alberto)
Félix, Carlos Alberto, Brito, Piazza,
Everaldo, Gérson, Clodoaldo, Rivellino,
Jairzinho, Tostão, Pelé.

Italy   1

(Boninsegna)
Albertosi, Burgnich, Facchetti, Domenghini,
Cera, Mazzola, de Sisti, Rosato,
Boninsegna, Bertini, Riva.
Subs: Juliano, Rivera.

CHAPTER I

Papagaio

> 'There are two types of football, prose and poetry. European teams are prose, tough, premeditated, systematic, collective. Latin American ones are poetry, ductile, spontaneous, individual, erotic.'
>
> Pier Paolo Pasolini

At junior school in the southern Brazilian city of Niteroi, the young Gérson de Oliveira Nunes was known as *papagaio*, the parrot. A lean, rugged, square-shouldered boy, he was never short of an opinion, particularly on the football pitch where he already cut a confident and commanding figure. The fact that his words could never match the eloquence of the sublime left foot he possessed did little to quieten him. The reputation for rampant verbosity remained with him throughout sixteen years as a professional with Flamengo, Botafogo, São Paulo and finally Fluminense. So too did the nickname.

1

On a hazy Friday morning in an office not so many football pitches away from where he grew up, the *papagaio* is still in full flight. 'With that team we would have won three World Cups,' he says, extending then counting off the digits of his right hand. 'There was no one like Pelé, there was nobody like Tostão, Rivellino, Jairzinho – there wasn't.'

Arranged on a large, boardroom desk in front of him are a collection of thin, plastic, thimble-size cups in which we have been drinking *cafezinho*, Brazil's sweet, viscous version of espresso coffee. For the past hour or so Gérson has been using the cups as makeshift visual aids, moving them strategically around the table, like chess pieces. With the aid of nine of them he is re-enacting the endgame that reduced the world's best teams to a state of hopeless resignation three decades earlier.

'Sometimes they had two players to mark Pelé, so there was one of us without a marker,' he says, moving three cups to the margins of the table. 'Then two more were needed to mark Jairzinho, so there was one more free,' he goes on, clearing three more. The liberated triumvirate of cups that remain represent himself, Rivellino and Tostão. He looks at them, then at me, smiles and outstretches his upturned palms as if to signal checkmate: 'Our team was the best. Those who saw it, saw it. Those who didn't will never see it again.'

There could be no more fitting a place to begin my journey than on the cluttered surface of Gérson's boardroom battleground. Brazil may have planned their assault on Mexico 1970 with more sophisticated tools than miniature coffee cups. Yet then, as now, Gérson was its tactician supreme. Inside his balding head beat the brain of the beautiful team.

For many, Gérson's influence was even greater than that of Pelé. Watch closely the videos and you cannot fail to be struck by how many of the Brazilian moves flowed through him. Time after time he would pick the ball up around half-way and launch one of his fiendish, flighted passes into the opponents' half. Time after time the ball would fall at the feet of the man all Brazil called *furacão* (the hurricane), Jairzinho, or on the chest or head of the man they called simply *o rei* (the King), Pelé. In each case the ensuing contest would bear a striking similarity to a race between a Ferrari and a Fiat Panda.

Above all, the tapes remind you of how Gérson utterly dominated the later stages of the Final. Somehow the Italians barely bothered to mark him as he lurked deep in the first half. As Hugh McIlvaney memorably wrote, it was akin to handing an arsonist a box of matches and a can of petrol. Sure enough Gérson set fire to the game in the second half, scoring with a magnificent shot and setting up another with a perfect long pass to Pelé to set up Jairzinho for the third. As the world packed its bags and left Mexico, he was the first name on everyone's team of the tournament.

For all his greatness, however, he remained something of a mystery. On the pitch we saw him coaxing and cajoling, directing and dictating. Yet off it Gérson preferred to stay in the background, the brooding, enigmatic genius. During his rare appearances at the Brazilian press conferences at their Guadalajara retreat, the exotic sounding Suite Caribes, he offered glimpses of a combination of

3

Henry V and Hamlet. Gérson talked the language of the battlefield rather than the football field. 'Their defence will not be so naive. They will not play a straight line across the field like old-fashioned soldiers,' he predicted before Brazil's match against England, after unpicking Czechoslovakia's defence with almost nonchalant ease in Brazil's opener. Only one match into the campaign Gérson had been in no doubt: 'This is the match that stands between us and our third World Cup.' There seemed to be an air of steel-shuttered self-confidence and almost moral certainty about him. Three decades on, it turns out little has changed.

After weeks of often frantic transatlantic telephoning and faxing, Gérson is the first of the team to agree to an interview. His suggestion that we meet at his office in Niteroi at 9 a.m. on a Friday morning sounds more like an order than an invitation, but who cares? One down, nine to go. Twenty-seven years on from the 1970 finals, all but one of the first-choice eleven – Everaldo Marques da Silva, the sturdy left-back who played in all but one of the matches in Mexico – are alive and well. Everaldo, a star at the Gremio club in the extreme southerly state of Rio Grande do Sul, died in a car crash shortly after the triumph. His loss was mourned all over Brazil.

Ask a Carioca to sum up his city and he will undoubtedly quote you the line that goes: 'God spent six days making the rest of the world, then saved the seventh for Rio.' I met Gérson on my second day in the city. By then I was still not convinced God didn't sub-contract the last day's work to the Devil.

Arrival in any new country is a moment of sensory over-load. You emerge from the hermetically sealed blandness of your aircraft into a firing squad of sights and sounds, unfamiliar aromas and unfathomable atmospheres. Nothing can prepare you for the barrage. It is, I suppose, why nowhere ever conforms to your expectations when you get there. Rio certainly didn't. I arrived on my first visit there to find the world's once legendary party town fast asleep. In the Babylonian gridlock of the main route into the city, the Avenida Brasil, everyone – even the drivers – seemed to be catching forty winks.

Much was as I had expected, however. If that over-used phrase 'city of contradictions' properly fits one city on earth, that city is Rio – home to contradictions crueller and crazier than anywhere else on earth.

I had known it was a city where the impossibly poor and the Croesus rich live side by side, where the First World and Third World nervously co-exist. What I did not realize was that the poor have the best views. The beachfront condominiums of Ipanema and Copacabana – Central Park West or Mayfair with a view of paradise from the verandah – are among the most expensive and beautifully appointed pieces of real estate in the world. Yet the most breath-taking vistas of all are reserved for the dwellers of the tumbling slums, the *favelas*, that light up the mitre-shaped mountains like Christmas trees at night.

Rio is set in the most staggeringly beautiful landscape on earth, a sun-drenched Shangri-la of sugarloaf peaks and imperious bays. Scratch its surface, however, and you find its street-crimes and street-children, victims ready to victimize any tourist, or *gringo*, who dares to walk alone. The gangs congregate around the famous Copacabana

5

Palace Hotel, but their spirit is everywhere. On my first night, an enchantingly pretty little girl in pigtails and an angelic white Confirmation dress approached the open window of my once-more gridlocked taxi. The driver, a decent man, asked her why she was not at home? 'My parents say I must work here until midnight,' she replied sweetly. I don't know what her work involved, nor do I ever want to.

'In Rio misery always existed, and was always over-looked,' the visionary architect of the nation's capital, Brasília, Oscar Niemeyer, once said. Perhaps the greatest irony of all is that the figure overlooking this callous, chaotic, compelling place is Jesus, His vast, concrete arms outstretched high up on Corcovado. Far below Rio's omnipresent, sadly symbolic statue, it has to be said, Christian love seems distinctly thin on the ground.

Rio's smaller, more sedate little sister, the city of Niteroi stands on the other side of Guanabara Bay. Rather than tackling the drive across the vast new $4 billion Niteroi bridge, I take the 4 reals (£2.50) ferry ride across from Rio's new commuter port, a few miles from the end of Copacabana beach. As the ferry glides its way across the bay, the pale, pastel peaks of Barra da Tijuca and Corcovado and the penthouses of Botafogo shimmer on a baking hot morning behind me. From here, at least, I can see what the locals mean about God and the seventh day.

A short drive from Niteroi's ferry terminal, Gérson's office overlooks the Praia Saca de São Francisco, one of the string of dazzling, white-sanded beaches that stud the city's jagged coastline. Across the road is a ritzy private members' club, Clube Praia Saca de São Francisco. With its Chanel-clad joggers and air of un-Rio-like relaxation, the beach lives up to its laidback Californian name. The calm is less apparent inside Gérson's office, where a small army of people are preparing for a regatta at the weekend.

By Brazilian standards Gérson is a paragon of punctuality. He pulls up in his claret Volkswagen a mere twenty minutes late. He is instantly surrounded by a group of others who have been waiting to see him. One turns out to be a potential sponsor for his driving passion, Projeto Gérson, a scheme to provide underprivileged kids with free sports tuition. Gérson deals with them all in a brusque, businesslike manner. As he does so he shepherds me to an inner sanctum and I begin with the first run out of what will become my standard Portuguese apology. *'Desculpe, eu falo muito poco Portuguese. Eu sou um grande admirador de voce.'* Please excuse me, I speak very little Portuguese but I am a great admirer of yours. He responds with an *obrigado*, thank you, and offers a seat at a large table and the first of many *cafezinhos*.

In the flesh Gérson is part *papagaio*, part *pega*, a magpie. Gold jewellery drips off him – a chunky chain hangs around his neck, two equally weighty bracelets around his wrist. Throughout he seems intense, watchful and wary. He has long since given up the battle with baldness. His polished head accentuates the nobility you noticed even back in Mexico. You look at Gérson and suspect he probably commanded Roman legions in a previous life.

Today he is sports secretary for the city hall in Niteroi. His always outspoken opinions on the state of modern Brazilian football have made him a popular presenter on the Bandeirantes television channel. 'When I was a boy I would go to watch Garrincha or Didi. Today you go for what?' he says, a look of mock bafflement on his face.

'There are one or two players but they get the ball and someone comes and punches them.' It is hardly a chore for him to cast his mind back to an earlier, more elegant footballing age.

Gérson arrived at Mexico with much work to do. He was twenty-nine, approaching the end of a career that had somehow failed to fulfil its early, infinite promise. Even more than for Pelé, 1970 had represented his last realistic chance to stamp his greatness on the world game.

He was born on 11 January 1941, to a family with football in its veins. His father Clovis Nunes and his uncle were both professionals in Rio. The legendary Zizinho, with Ademir and Jair part of the free-scoring Brazilian forward line of 1950, was a close friend of his father's and a familiar face at the Nunes household. When the teenage Gérson announced his intention of becoming a footballer too, he found few obstacles put in his way. 'I did not have lots of problems in that respect,' he smiles.

As a boy his heroes had been Zizinho and Danilo and Jair. At his first club, Flamengo, across Guanabara Bay in Rio, however, he found himself cast in the same mould as the most influential midfield player of Brazil's first gilded age, Didi. The young Gérson combined speed and ferocious shooting power with the intelligence and ability to control a game from the midfield, the *meio de campo*. One of his greatest assets was his ability to switch defence into attack with one long, laser-like pass – or *lançamento* – from deep in his own half. Soon he was being talked of as a successor to Didi.

Even in adolescence, Gérson resisted the comparison. He was his own man, the original Gérson not the next Didi, although he admits he had an affinity with him. 'His style of play was very similar to mine,' he nods. The suggestion that he modelled himself on him meets with a pursing of the lips and a stern, shrugged 'No'.

Gérson's first five years in the game represented an almost seamless rise through the ranks. Within a year of making his professional debut for Flamengo in 1958, he was in the Brazilian 'amateur' team in the Pan-American Games. A year later he was a lynchpin of the side at the Rome Olympics. By 1961, with Didi in decline, he was the playmaker at Flamengo and had starred in the Brazilian side that won the inter-South American competition, the Oswaldo Cruz Cup. He had also been recruited into the full national squad to defend the World Cup in Chile by the new national coach Aimore Moreira.

By now Gérson had made the short journey from Flamengo to Botafogo, also in Rio, home to the most natural talent of all, his boyhood idol Garrincha. His dreams of combining with the bandy-legged 'Little Bird', along with Pelé and Didi, in Chile were dashed when he suffered a serious knee injury. Forced to undergo surgery, he couldn't get himself back into Moreira's squad. It would be one of many injuries to blight his career.

'We'll be waiting at the airport, Thursday'
England 1966

For Gérson – like Brazil itself – the journey to Mexico had begun 6,000 miles from paradise, amid the grim, grey land- scape of industrial, middle England and a train journey from Liverpool Lime Street to London Euston four years earlier. He had been among the haunted Brazilian faces that had stared out of a first-class compartment, struggling to come to terms with their humiliating early elimination from the 1966 World Cup. To the crowds of pressmen and autograph-hunters that greeted them at Euston, the besuited Brazilians bore the look of men on their way to their own execution. In a way many of them were.

For the best part of a decade they had, even more than Puskas and his magnificent Magyars, been the dominant force in the World Cup. Their win in Sweden in 1958 was – and remains – the only one football's European and South American superpowers have registered on the 'away' continent. When they triumphed once more in Chile, four years later, the continental cradle of the game was on the verge of conceding permanent defeat to what appeared to be a naturally superior breed of footballer. For the Europeans, the 'athleticism and flexibility' of the Brazilians became the subject of serious, and at times, obsessive study. Karel Kolsky, the great Czech coach of the period, concluded that the Brazilian player needed only 60 per cent of the training the European needed to maintain good physical condition.

If Kolsky's words were meant to instil an air of false security they worked. In 1963, Aimore Moreira summed up the superiority complex his nation now seemed to nurture: 'Brazilian football is played by men who, in this sport, excel above all others in the whole world. The Brazilian can change, move, improvize, within a fraction of a second. By contrast, the European is stiffer in action, and pursues a tactically monotonous game,' wrote the coach. 'One imagines then, what happens when the

Brazilian, being a born footballer, comes into a team well trained, coached and organized. He wins World Championship titles without greatly over-extending himself. Brazil has always had great players, our game only lacked organization. Now we have that, also, and so long as we remain well organized I cannot conceive of Brazil back-sliding from her prominent position in world football.'

Stiff and monotonous they may have been, but in England in 1966 the Europeans brought the Brazilians crashing to earth – in Pelé's case literally. Fitter, faster and tactically more sophisticated, England, West Germany, Portugal and Hungary were ready to prove Voltaire's argument that 'God favours the big battalions'.

Brazil's back-to-back wins had infected a natural confidence with a hint of arrogance, an unnatural discipline with a streak of complacency. By 1966 Gérson had finally inherited the mantle of Didi at the heart of a team now guided by the Buddha-like figure of Vicente Feola. Feola's preparations had bordered on the chaotic. He had refused to prune a vast squad of forty-four players, rebuilding his team almost game by game as he dithered about who should and shouldn't travel to England. In the end Gérson found himself in the middle of a footballing anachronism, one of a collection of brilliant newcomers overshadowed by the giants of what turned out to be a bygone era. Feola's final choice made a mockery of all his experiments. Not only were double champions Gilmar, Djalma Santos and Garrincha still there, the coach even recalled the veterans Bellini and Orlando, the central defenders from the 1958 side. His reverence for the heroes of the past two campaigns 'bordered', as Brian Glanville elegantly

11

put it, 'on gerontophilia'. Eight of his first-choice side were over thirty.

Gérson, along with a nucleus of other younger players including the seventeen-year-old sensation from Cruzeiro, Tostão, Jairzinho of Botafogo and Brito of Vasco da Gama, found the job of bridging the generation gap an impossible one. 'It was a very strange team. Those players came to 1966 when they should not,' Gérson says, referring to the old guard with a shake of his head. 'They were double champions – but the team was in need of renovation.'

Feola, like all of Brazil, simply trusted that the stellar survivors of Sweden and Chile would paper over the cracks. In the first game against a lacklustre Bulgaria, Pelé and Garrincha duly obliged, scoring a goal each from direct free kicks. Against Hungary at Goodison Park, however, age – and a new, invigorated European style – finally caught up with Brazil's dinosaur heroes. Along with Tostão, Gérson came in for his first game of the tournament, replacing Denilson of Fluminense. The youthful enthusiasm they added was soon being undermined by the ponderousness of the defence. Albert, Bene and Farkas ran riot, Pelé and a tired-looking Garrincha were shackled by tough tackling and Hungary won 3–1, sending shock waves through the population back in Brazil.

By the third match against Portugal a panic-stricken Feola had made another seven changes, finally replacing the old legs with the new. By now, however, Brazil's lack of continuity could not have presented a starker contrast to the well-oiled cohesion of Portugal and their stars Coluna, Torres, Simoes and Europe's own Pelé, Eusebio. While the prototype was exiled to the margins of the game by more brutal tackling, the Mozambique-born model ran riot. Brazil were two-down within twenty-five minutes, both goals the result of the defence's inability to deal with crosses. Rildo's second-half goal offered faint but false hope and Eusebio sent them on their way home with a final goal. Gérson was one of the forlorn party that arrived by train at Euston on their way to Heathrow.

Back in Brazil grief quickly gave way to anger. In Rio and elsewhere crowds gathered in the streets burning effigies and carrying gallows. Their placards carried drawings of Feola, the President of the Brazilian footballing authority, the CBD (Confederação Brasileira de Desportos), João Havelange and others they blamed for the humiliation, walking towards the nooses. The banners read, '*Morte para a Comisão – vamos espera – los na quinta no aeroporto.*' 'Death to the commission – we'll be waiting for you at the airport, Thursday.'

The Europeans who imagined they were watching the Brazilian era drawing to a close would have done well to listen to the words of warning issued by the team's official medical chief and unofficial godfather, Dr Hilton Gosling, however. Asked about the future for Brazil as his team slid away from Euston he smiled knowingly: 'They will start working very hard for the next World Cup.' Gérson would return to the tournament, a member of the best prepared team in the history of Brazilian – perhaps even, world – football.

Gérson watched England win the World Cup back home in Niteroi. He admired Bobby Charlton, England's balding maestro of the *meio de campo*. 'An exceptional player,' he says. 'It was a good team, playing at home. They also played a more classic football than England played before 1966. It was not the football of force, of crossing, they had talented players.' In his heart, however, Gérson was not ready to concede parity with the new powers of European football. He would have to wait four more years to prove his point.

In the aftermath of the *fracasso*, the shame of 1966, Brazilian football had demonstrated its other great genius by ripping itself to shreds internally. As chaos reigned at the CBD, Pelé swore never to play in a World Cup again. 'There is only one way to describe Brazil's 1966 World Cup effort,' he fumed then, and has done ever since. 'And that is to declare that from beginning to end it was a total and unmitigated disaster.' Havelange, already the most acute political mind in the world game, persuaded him back into the fold with a promise of greatly improved preparation and a quite extraordinary appointment as the new coach.

João Saldanha had been a moderately successful coach at Botafogo in Rio, but had made his most noticeable mark on the Brazilian game as its most popular, outspoken and intelligent radio commentator. To the Brazilian masses his appointment seemed a symbol of a return to the age of adventure and enlightenment. To the rest of the world it was a signal that the sleeping superpower had finally lost its grip on footballing reality. With his emaciated, often haggard features and fifty-a-day cigarette habit, Saldanha looked emotionally incapable of handling the strain of ten minutes on a training pitch let alone a World Cup campaign in the bearpit that was the Brazilian dugout.

Gérson, however, saw a kindred spirit. 'We are very close friends and I am suspicious of talking about him because I can only say good things about him,' he cautions. Gérson saw Saldanha much as Sancho Panza saw Don Quixote. He may have been mad, but at least he had the courage to dream. Gérson had seen two managers, Moreira and Brandão, come and go before Saldanha's appointment. 'Nobody would take responsibility for the Brazilian team. It had been trainer in, trainer out, confusion. He arrived and decided what everybody else had been afraid of deciding – the team.'

Saldanha had demanded complete freedom – *carta branca*, as he called it – to choose his own team. His philosophy was plain. 'What I want is goals,' he told Gérson and the other attacking geniuses he intended basing his campaign around. Saldanha built his side around a *meio de campo* of Gérson and Piazza of Cruzeiro, with Jairzinho of Botafogo as an attacking right winger, Tostão as the key supply link up front and Edu of Santos as the left-sided attacker. Pelé, coaxed back into the squad by Havelange, would be the formation's main attacking force at centre-forward.

At first Saldanha seemed able to cope with his new, goldfish-bowl existence and the frequent banality of the Brazilian press. Early in the summer of 1969, Gérson sparked a mass brawl when he lashed out at La Torre of Peru in a 'friendly' at the Maracanã. It took the officials forty minutes to cool tempers, by which time Peru had retreated to the dressing room from where they refused to come out. Only the personal intervention of João Havelange teased the visitors back into the lion's den. Having led 2–0, Peru lost 2–3. Afterwards Saldanha said he drew great comfort from the match. He was pleased that his Brazilian side contained no women!

15

'He did not lose his humour. If a journalist came up to him and asked him what he thought about the grass on the pitch he would say "I don't know, I haven't tried it yet",' smiles Gérson.

By the end of August, Saldanha had even more cause to indulge his surreal sense of humour. 'We won the World Cup eliminators with ease,' says Gérson. Brazil's qualification campaign was condensed into a miniature version of the World Cup finals themselves. It began on 6 August 1969, with a comfortable 2–0 win over Colombia in Bogotá. Saldanha's gamble of playing Tostão and Pelé together paid off as the Cruzeiro man scored both goals, the first pouncing when Colombian keeper Lagarcha could only parry a 30-yard Pelé free kick. Four days later, against Venezuela, in Caracas, Tostão was the hero once more, breaking seventy-seven minutes of deadlock with a brilliant solo dribble and shot. In the final quarter of the game Pelé scored twice and Tostão completed a hat trick in an unlikely 5–0 thrashing.

By the time they took the pitch in Asuncion seven days later, the match against Paraguay, who had also twice won away from home, had the look of a qualification decider. After a goalless and virtually chanceless first half, the breakthrough owed as much to luck as inspiration. Left-back Valentin Mendoza, harassed by Jairzinho, slashed at the ball in an attempt to clear his lines. The Paraguayan keeper Aguillera could only look on helplessly as the sliced kick ballooned over him into the goal. The fluke broke the Paraguayan resistance and three minutes later Jairzinho scored himself. Edu added a third on the final whistle to flatter Brazil with a 0–3 scoreline. The goals took Brazil's tally to ten in three matches, but more importantly saw off their only real challengers.

Four days later on 21 August they were back at the Maracanã facing Colombia in the first of three matches to be squeezed into ten days. When Pelé set Tostão up for the first it looked plain sailing but Colombia equalized when Mesa dispossessed a sleepy Gérson and beat Félix, the small Fluminense goalkeeper Saldanha had selected in all the qualifiers to date. The visitors almost took the lead moments later when Félix was caught off-guard by a speculative long shot. By the second half the Colombian keeper Lagarcha had left the pitch with a damaged hand and been replaced by Quintana. Rather than weakening their defence, the reserve went on to turn in one of the best performances of the year at the Maracanã.

There was little he could do when Segovia mistimed a tackle on Tostão leaving him with another, short-range shot to score. He was equally powerless when an Edu free kick hit a defender's leg and deflected into his goal for the third. After Colombia clawed their way back into the match with an astonishing 40-yard shot from Gallego, however, he pulled off a string of magnificent saves. For a while Colombia threatened to draw level. Pelé extended Brazil's lead but was then replaced by Paulo Cézar of Flamengo. At the same time Saldanha substituted Gérson with Rivellino, the rising star of Corinthians in São Paulo. The modifications did the trick as Rivellino scored four minutes from time. Jairzinho rubbed salt in with a sixth at the death. If it had not been for Quintana and the post, Brazil could have hit double figures. The Colombian was given a standing ovation by the Maracanã as he left the pitch.

17

The hard-fought win put Brazil within one game of qualification. Within three days they had booked their place in Mexico. In front of a crowd of 123,000, Tostão got off to a flier in the return against Venezuela, scoring in the seventh, twenty-first and twenty-fourth minutes for one of the fastest hat tricks ever seen in international football. Pelé's passing had contributed to each of the goals and he was again the provider in the thirtieth minute when Jairzinho scored. In injury time in the first half, he added his own name to the score sheet with a penalty. With a 5–0 lead going into the second half, Brazil understandably relaxed. Venezuela even managed to hit the post as they were given a free rein. Pelé rounded off the win with the best goal of the game, a weave of inter-passing with Tostão and Jairzinho which ended with a stunning shot past Fazano.

By the time the stubborn Paraguayans came to Rio on 31 August there was no spoiling the party. A vast 183,000 crowd packed the Maracanã. Paraguay once more mounted admirable resistance. But it was Pelé who had the final say in the group, pouncing when Aguillera failed to hold on to a ferocious shot from Edu. Within Brazil there was a sense that the good times were ready to roll once more. Saldanha had suffused style with organization and in Pelé and Tostão unearthed a goalscoring partnership that promised to outshine anything even Brazil had seen before.

Not everyone was impressed. The urbane Eric Batty of *World Soccer* summed up the sceptic school of thought in Europe: 'I cannot help feeling that a team drawn from the Cumberland town my family comes from wouldn't give Venezuela a good run.'

There were plenty who saw the tide once more turning in Brazil's favour, however. Brazilian clubs had swept all before them when they crossed the Atlantic to Spain in the summer. Even without their World Cup stars, Palmeiras had won the Copa Carranza, beating Real Madrid in Cadiz, Corinthians the Copa Del Sol in Málaga, and São Paulo the Copa Colombino in Huelva. Real Madrid's canny Miguel Munoz was among those who thought Saldanha's side had 'many probabilities of becoming world champions'. So they did. Saldanha, however, would not be there to lead them.

Of all Brazil's 110 million amateur managers, none harboured such grandiose hopes for the national team as the President, General Emilio Garrastazu Médici. Unlike his predecessors at the helm of the nation's military dictatorship, Castelo Branco and Costa E Silva, Médici had not been a major figure in the coup that had ended democratic rule in 1964. A soldier's soldier, he had only accepted the post out of duty and the fact that he was the only four-star general who could hold the army's warring factions together. He took over in October 1969.

He was as astute a politician as the military had produced, however. If Médici had one supreme gift it lay in his understanding of the media and the emerging power of television in particular. By 1970 his propaganda body – AERP, Assessoria Especial de Relaçoes Publicas – had transformed his face into the most famous in Brazil after Pelé.

In his ongoing war with the nation's dissidents and terrorists, Médici understood television's power as a weapon of mass manipulation. In the early months of his presidency he had used statistics claiming that terrorism had been quelled and economic growth was at ten per cent to launch an advertising blitzkrieg. Catchphrases like 'You build Brazil', 'Nobody can hold this country back', 'Brazil count on me' flashed on television screens with almost subliminal frequency. Amid the barrage, the dissenting voices of popular artists like Gilberto Gil and Caetano Veloso – exiled in London – became more and more marginalized.

Médici was not the first politician to detect football's position as Brazil's opiate of the people. 'While there is *cachaça*, samba, carnival, *mulata* [dusky skinned women] and football championships there will be no rebellion in Brazil,' the supposed 'opposition' MDB party leader Ulysses Guimaraes opined. The fact that, unlike many of his patrician political colleagues, Medici was a genuine football fanatic made his intervention all the more inevitable.

Médici was a familiar figure at the Maracanã where he would sit on the terraces without bodyguards, cheering on his favourite side Flamengo. He had already begun influencing club policy and was instrumental in negotiations that would soon bring his favourite player, the flamboyant striker, Dario to Flamengo from Atletico Mineiro. (When Dario didn't work out, Médici organized a meeting with the directors to suggest the extravagantly gifted Paulo Cézar be brought over from Botafogo to help him. This move too was soon under way in the wake of Mexico.)

João Saldanha was hardly going to be the favourite of the right-wing militarists. He had been an outspoken Communist sympathizer in his youth. Yet as his managerial career entered its most crucial phase he did little to make life easy for himself.

Soon after his arrival in power, Médici had invited the team for lunch at the Presidential Palace. Saldanha refused to alter the training schedule to allow the players to go. It was in March 1970, as Brazil played Argentina in a warm-up in the southerly city of Porto Alegre, that he committed his gravest error of judgement, however. Saldanha was asked by an Argentine reporter why he had not included Dario in his side? Irritated by the question, the manager said that he thought Roberto of Botafogo and Tostão were better. When reminded that Dario was Médici's favourite, Saldanha shot back: 'I don't choose the President's ministry and he can't choose my front line.' His reply proved as succinct as it was suicidal.

His occasionally irrational and outspoken behaviour did little to foster loyalty within the clubs and the ruling CBD. In the wake of the triumph in the *eliminatorias*, Saldanha had travelled to Europe where, as well as watching football he had talked about it endlessly on television stations all over the continent. He came back convinced he needed heavier men in defence to stand up to the 'brutal play and lenient referees' he expected to encounter in Mexico. His first-choice keeper Félix was dropped in favour of heavier goalkeepers – Ado of Corinthians and Leao of Palmeiras. Two hard-tackling defenders, Baldocchi of Palmeiras and the teenage prodigy Marco Antonio of Fluminense were drafted to add steel. Before his European trip Saldanha's defence had averaged 163 lbs and 5ft 8in. Suddenly that had been bulked up to 168lbs and 5ft 11in. But as his team's size increased so its confidence and effectiveness diminished – disastrously.

*   *   *

Saldanha had been at the Hotel Maria Isabel in Mexico City on 10 January 1970, to witness the draw for the finals that June. The list of sixteen qualifiers included its fair share of makeweights, notably Israel, Morocco and El Salvador, but also Russia, Bulgaria and Sweden, none of whom were fancied to cope with the heat and the quality of the competition from the likes of England, Italy, West Germany and Czechoslovakia.

Saldanha's paranoia about the more physical European sides had by now taken immovable root. 'The finals will develop into a brawl if we are not vigilant and the European teams with the best boxers and wrestlers will win it,' he had said to FIFA's embarrassment at an official function in Mexico. The draw only pushed him nearer the abyss.

As the names were drawn out of the hat, Brazil found themselves placed in group three at Guadalajara, Mexico's second largest city, 360 miles west of the capital. The 71,000 capacity Estado Jalisco had the reputation for having the best playing surface in Mexico and the hottest atmosphere. As the other three names were drawn, it was Saldanha's temperature that went rising with it. The group would include England, the reigning world champions, Czechoslovakia, one of the most impressive sides in qualification, and Rumania, fast emerging as a real force at European club level. Saldanha had no argument with the journalists who quickly christened it the Group of Death. To many it was no coincidence that Saldanha effectively signed his own death warrant three months later.

The two matches Brazil played against Argentina in March marked the beginning of the end. After Brazil lost the first 2–0, leaving the Maracanã to boos and whistles, the Argentine defender Roberto Profumo could hardly contain his glee. 'This is the poorest Brazilian team I have played against and they will have a job to get anywhere in Mexico unless they improve greatly,' he said. (Only Pelé rose to the bait, replying, 'I am glad to see Argentina is returning to play soccer without the need of kicking opponents and imposing rough play.') Saldanha's defensive changes had thrown his team out of synch. Against the aggressive Argentines, Gérson and Piazza had been unable to hold the midfield. Afterwards Saldanha complained that Pelé, playing along with Dirceu Lopez of Cruzeiro up front, hadn't followed his instructions by dropping back to help them.

In the return Brazil scored in two minutes. Brindisi soon equalized, however, and the game looked a certain draw when Pelé scored the winner five minutes from time. The revelation of the match was the nineteen-year-old Clodoaldo of Santos. He had brought vibrant new life to the midfield when he came on in place of Piazza. If Saldanha had rediscovered his team, however, it was too late.

Of all the enemies he had made with his erratic behaviour, none proved more dangerous than Pelé. In the eliminators, he had gone along with Saldanha's enthusiasm and free-thinking. Then, as the manager's lack of experience at the highest level was suddenly exposed, his support dis-appeared. When a by-now-desperate Saldanha announced that he was considering dropping Pelé for the next warm-up game against Chile, the manager had made his final, fatal mistake. He was removed on the grounds of 'emotional instability' within days.

Gérson recalls the March morning when Saldanha gath-ered the team together before a training session. 'He asked for a meeting with everybody and said: "I have an appointment with the CBD and I don't think I'm coming back. I came to say goodbye, thanks a lot".' The players went ahead with the morning session. 'At lunchtime we had the message that he was not the trainer any more. Nobody knew what was happening. Everybody was lost,' says Gérson.

Theories still abound on precisely why he was removed only weeks before his team were due to travel to the Mexican retreat at Guanajuato, sixty miles east of Guadalajara, where he had planned to spend two months knocking his final team into shape. The Dario/Médici affair undoubtedly undermined Saldanha's position. There was no question either that the manager's state of mind could occasionally verge on the dangerously unstable. 'Sometimes he lost control. He had a *pavio curto*, a short fuse,' says Gérson, shaking his head.

In 1967, when Botafogo won the Rio championship, Saldanha had accused the former international goalkeeper Manga, of the Bangu side, of taking a bribe to lose the Final. When Manga confronted him days later, Saldanha had pulled out a pistol and fired two shots. Luckily Manga had already started running. Only a week before his dismissal, Saldanha had left the national team HQ in Rio and headed for a hotel where he knew the Flamengo side was gathered. Flamengo's manager Yustrich had called Saldanha a coward in a radio interview. Saldanha walked into the hotel once more waving his pistol in the air and demanding to know where Yustrich was hiding. Luckily his prey had already left the building. As he lost the support of players, public and press alike, Saldanha had regularly challenged journalists to fist fights on the training pitches of Rio. 'If a fan said something that Saldanha didn't like, then he went for the fan, ready to beat him up,' Pelé complained later. To many in Brazil, the manager's wounds seemed blatantly self-inflicted.

Whatever the truth, in the vacuum the job became a poisoned chalice. Two senior coaches, Dino Sani and Oto Gloria, turned down the job, neither man interested in being immortalized as a kerosene-soaked effigy. In the end the CBD turned to the heroes of Sweden and Chile once more for its inspiration.

Mario Zagalo was already a World Cup winner twice over as a player. Born in the north-east of the country, in the state of Alagoas, but raised in Rio de Janeiro, the young Zagalo had played barefoot on the open fields of the Professor Gabiso Street district that was to be home to the legendary Maracanã. It was in his boyhood *peladas*, or kick-arounds, that he picked up his nicknames – *home de sorte*, lucky stalk, or *formiginha*, little ant, because he worked so hard. The moment in the 1958 Final when the winger had made an unexpected – and highly un-Brazilian at the time – goal-line clearance to stop Sweden going 2–0 ahead typified his industry. 'Zagalo showed us that footballers must have two shirts – a defender's and an attacker's,' his admirers said of him. It would be his greatest gift to the side he was now taking over.

Zagalo's style could not have presented a starker contrast to the ranting, raving Saldanha. Pelé called him the 'calmest person I have ever known'. (He also said of him: 'He was a firm believer in the old proverb that a shut mouth catches no reindeer', whatever that may mean!) In Scandinavia in 1958, some had wondered whether Zagalo was actually a Swede in disguise. He also enjoyed advantages Saldanha would never have earned. As a veteran of two World Cups, Zagalo understood the physical sacrifices his players would be required to make. He also understood the pressures of carrying the hopes and dreams of 110 million Brazilians. Zagalo's typically terse comments when he took over spoke volumes. 'I am happy to serve. I could not refuse it, even knowing the obstacles I shall have to face. I am not afraid of the situation.' He would be as good as his word.

'*The smoking generalissimo*'
The Road To Guadalajara, March-June 1970

Predictably Gérson is convinced the team was good enough to win regardless of its manager. 'Yes, we would have won with Saldanha,' he says without equivocation. Even he will not deny the blend of tranquillity and toughness Zagalo brought with him, however.

For all his claims that he would not interfere directly in the team's preparations for Mexico, it was not difficult to detect Médici's hand at work in the new-look structure Zagalo inherited. A retired army captain and military physical training expert, Captain Claudio Coutinho, was appointed to oversee the squad's fitness. Other military figures, including the imposing Admiral Jeronimo Batsos, appeared on the periphery too. For a generation the world had wondered at the military precision with which Brazil planned its World Cup campaigns. In 1970 the phrase was more apposite than ever.

Brazil's approach to the preparation of its team had revolutionized sports science in the 1950s. In Sweden they had employed a staff of dieticians, masseurs and even a psychologist to prepare their team. The psychologist assessed each player by getting him to draw pictures of a man. The more intelligent players like Zagalo drew well-rounded portraits. The uneducated Garrincha scratched out a crude matchstick man. Manager Feola didn't need a shrink to tell him the Little Bird saved his artistry for the football pitch. Most of the psychological advice was discarded.

Underwritten by the limitless funds of the CBD and, if necessary, Médici's government itself, the 1970 campaign would take this scientific approach even further. To the rest of the world the Brazilian approach had often looked like rocket science. This time it actually was. Amid some secrecy, Captain Coutinho had spent time at NASA in Florida, studying the training programmes America's Apollo astronauts had been put through. He returned with a fitness regime based on the Americans' Cooper Test, in which players' physical condition could be monitored and measured with accuracy.

At the squad's main training ground, at the Retiro Dos Patos in Rio, every member of the squad was tested for speed, endurance, lung capacity and physical strength. Coutinho's ever-present clipboard became the repository for a sea of statistics. His collection of counts and coefficients formed the basis for individually prepared programmes designed to help each man acclimatize to the Mexican altitude and to the physical requirements that would be expected of him in the World Cup. Their progress would be measured every step of the way to Guadalajara.

Gérson had listened intently to what Coutinho had to say when he returned from America. 'He showed us a film, he gave us a technical explanation that we found feasible and then we did a pilot test. It was serious work,' he smiles. As one of the few survivors of 1966, Gérson had seen at first hand the advantage the Europeans had in fitness and physical strength. 'We knew we needed to do something to improve our physical condition. In 1966 we had good physical condition, but not as good as theirs,' he explains. For a generation Brazil had relied on its natural advantages. Physical fitness had come a poor second. 'It was eighty per cent technique and twenty per cent physical condition,' says Gérson. 'We knew how to play, they knew how to run,' he adds with an arch of an eyebrow. In their preparation for Mexico, technique and fitness became the twin religions of Brazil's new breed of footballer.

Gérson confesses he had greater obstacles to overcome than most. Off the pitch he was rarely without a cigarette in his hands. He could barely make it through forty-five minutes without a drag on his favourite Vila Ricas. (He would later advertise them on television.) At his club Botafogo and on the Brazilian team, a member of the coaching staff was under instruction to be waiting with a lit cigarette ready at half and full-time. 'I used to smoke three packs a day,' he grimaces. The medical staff knew they could not force him to quit at such a tense time in his career. 'They asked that we smoked less, particularly because of the altitude, so it would not have so much effect,' he says. Some were successful, others were not. The reserve defender Fontana made a public announcement that he had quit in the run up to Mexico. 'I want to be well in the Cup,' he told the Brazilian people. Carlos Alberto reduced his habit to two a day, 'one in the morning and one in the evening'. Along with another chain-smoker, Félix the goalkeeper, Gérson has to admit his World Cup was less than a success in this respect. It was not until years after he had retired from the game that he was able to give up.

It had been the average Brazilian footballer's weakness for other vices that had given rise to the *concentração*, the rigidly disciplined training camps at which both clubs and international sides prepared for major matches and tournaments. In the 1950s and 1960s, the working-class players who dominated the game lived a life of bohemian over indulgence. No one personified the problem as powerfully as Garrincha. One of the greatest natural talents the game had ever seen, he was also an incurable alcoholic and womanizer. According to legend he drank a bottle of *cachaça* every day of his adult life. As a result he rarely knew where he was in the world let alone who the opposition were. After winning the 1958 World Cup in Sweden he supposedly wandered around confused by all the excitement asking, 'Is it the end?' His sex life, the subject of scandal when he left his wife for a famous singer, was equally chaotic. At the end of his career he returned to the poverty from which he had emerged and drank himself into an early grave.

In such a climate, curfews, alcohol bans and isolation from wives and families had long since been accepted as a necessary evil for concentrating the more wayward players' minds. Yet the parallel with razor-wire and search-lights was never more appropriate than at Guanajuato where the squad arrived at the beginning of May 1970. Gérson and his colleagues found themselves garrisoned in a castle, isolated from the rest of the world, far from the centre of the small town. The foundations for the glories to come were laid there with a combination of science, sweat and the occasional strong word from the *papagaio*.

On the training pitch there was no doubting Gérson was the *generalissimo* who would direct the forthcoming campaign. His left foot was central to the tactics developed by Zagalo and senior players like Carlos Alberto, Piazza and Pelé. At the heart of the Brazilian game-plan would be a series of strategies designed to create space for its fastest front men, Jairzinho and Pelé. Under Coutinho and his Cooper Tests, Pelé was returning to the best physical condition of his life. Even if, at thirty, his pace had begun to desert him, he was still among the quickest players in the world. As Zagalo put it: 'A bad phase for Pelé is the best phase for any other player.' In Jairzinho, however, Brazil probably had the fastest footballer of all.

Gérson's days were dominated by exercises in which he would practise the variety of long balls he would need to use in Guadalajara. He would land his elegant *lançamentos* on small athletics hurdles placed in the semi-circle at the edge of the penalty area. Pass after pass would be pumped towards the hurdles. He would work from 20, 30, 40 and 50 yards away, positioning himself in the centre circle and deeper inside the defensive half of the pitch. Gérson would work before and after the full training sessions, drilling sometimes hundreds of balls into the air with the meticulousness of a golf pro working his way through his bag of clubs.

During full training sessions, Pelé and Tostão, Jairzinho and Rivellino, as well as the reserves Roberto, Paulo Cézar and Toninho, would feed off Gérson's deliveries. Soon a kind of telepathy was forming, with Jairzinho and Pelé in

particular. Whenever Gérson saw Jairzinho take two steps
back towards him drawing a defender with him, he would
know to launch an immediate probe. He had learned that
before the ball had left his foot the winger would have
turned in anticipation and be cruising effortlessly past the
defender already. He developed a similar understanding
with Pelé. 'I knew what they were going to do, we arranged
all that before,' he says matter-of-factly, his *cafezinho* cups
helping him illuminate his points as he speaks.

Gérson's influence extended way beyond the black-
board and the training pitch, however. With Pelé and
Carlos Alberto, he formed what the Kojak-like figure of the
masseur Mario Americo called the *cobras*. The trio would
sit long into the night in Pelé's room discussing the performance and morale of the younger and less experienced
players, approaching Zagalo and the technical committee
when they felt strongly on a subject.

These three had already gone to Zagalo with their idea
of the first eleven in the run up to the final friendly match
before leaving Brazil, against Austria at the end of April.
After a confidence-boosting performance, the formation
became Zagalo's favoured choice too. Gérson downplays
his influence with a smile. 'It was a friendly conversation.
We didn't order him to do anything but we tried to help
Zagalo to solve the problems that he still had, to select the
best team or the one that could become the best one.'

When the squad had first arrived in Mexico, the *cobras*
went to the Brazilian's chief of staff, Antonio do Passo,
asking to be allowed to officially address the squad. The
trio were not convinced that the younger players realized
the magnitude of their mission. Do Passo spoke to the
players before handing over to the three men. Gérson's

31

message was simple. 'We were not there on holiday or to go shopping,' he recalls with a shrug.

Gérson was vocal in his opinions on how the players should handle the pressure, particularly from the fickle Brazilian press. 'Paulo Cézar cried a lot after the game we played against Bulgaria. We were criticized a lot, but I had to rebuke him.' The *cobras* increasingly took over the public relations duties. Gérson made no effort to disguise his contempt for those who had been critical of the team. He had come in for flak himself, accused by some of making the team too slow and being pedestrian in his play.

'There are a lot of people among the journalists who are trying to promote themselves. They don't know anything about football. When I stop playing I will be a radio commentator only to show that these guys don't understand anything,' he complained at the time. (Typically, it was no idle boast. Within three years of Mexico he joined a Rio radio station.) Unlike others, he positively thrived on the criticism. 'It is something that gives us a lot of motivation,' he told the assembled media. 'Brazil will only lose the Cup if they break the leg of Pelé, the arm of Tostão, the knees of Gérson, the head of Rivellino or if they kill all our team,' one journalist reported Gérson as saying.

Brazil's minute attention to detail was by now the subject of envy – and occasional ridicule – among the rest of the footballing world. Once more nothing was overlooked. Impressions were taken of every player's feet so as to discover the precise areas where his weight was distributed. Hand-made boots would then be studded accordingly. At first the Brazilian strip for the tournament had once more included their traditional green collar. In the Mexican heat, however, the collars had grown heavy with sweat. A new, round-necked strip was designed instead. To avoid friction or inhibition of movement, each player's shirt and shorts were hand-tailored. Ten days before heading to Mexico, the team's eating and sleeping schedules were altered to coincide with the Central-American time-zone. At the same time the Brazilian team chef began cooking in Mexican oils and with Mexican fruit and vegetables. No end of science could protect the best-prepared squad in Brazilian history from the realities of footballing life, however.

It was fifteen days before the first match in Mexico that Gérson discovered the price he would have to pay for pushing himself through this relentless regime. During another training session he broke down holding his right calf. He limped off and took a limited part in training over the following days. 'I felt my leg pulling. I had some treatment but then I could not make some movements. I only did a little swimming and some sit-ups after that,' he explains. Gérson was so central to Zagalo's strategy that to begin their campaign without him was almost unthinkable. In the fraught run up to the kick-off, the Brazilian press speculated that Mario Americo even massaged the right leg while Gérson was asleep.

He played against the Czechs in the opening match with a support on his leg. He left the pitch ten minutes before the end but not before he had supplied the bullets with which Pelé, Jairzinho and Rivellino secured their 4–1 win. His euphoria was short-lived. The next morning he woke up with a livid haematoma bruise on his right leg.

Privately Zagalo knew he needed his playmaker for the later stages. With two points safely won – and with the group already shaping up as a straight shoot-out with

England – he decided not to risk Gérson against the reigning world champions. 'He said: "I'll leave you out of this game against England. If we lose to England you play against Rumania. If we win against England, you are also free for the other game because I'd rather have you playing in the second phase than in the first one".' If the decision saved his leg, it did little for his lungs or his nervous system. Gérson admits he found the process of watching the matches so painful it was almost unbearable. 'You wear yourself out more than when you are playing,' he says.

Gordon Banks' miraculous save from Pelé ten minutes into the match must have accounted for half a pack of Vila Ricas on its own. 'It only happens once in life and once in death,' he says, shaking his head at the memory. To many Brazilians England were the only team to fear in the tournament. When Bobby Charlton visited the Suites Caribes and spent time talking with his Brazilian counterparts afterwards, many of them expected to be reunited with the Manchester United man within a fortnight in the Final at the Azteca. Gérson was not so sure. 'They were a team to be respected. But technically speaking they were not as good as us,' he says with conviction. His respect for Charlton, Bobby Moore and Gordon Banks is limitless, however. Would they have made it into the Brazil side? 'Yes, without doubt,' says Gerson. As we wonder who Charlton might have replaced he shakes his head and smiles. 'Then Zagalo would have had a problem.'

Gérson continued to rest his leg and missed the Rumania game on the following Wednesday. He returned to pull the strings in the quarter-final against Peru and the semi-final against Uruguay. In the heat of the battle Gérson was the

Napoleon of Niteroi, constantly hectoring and organizing his team-mates. 'It was said that I was Zagalo's coach on the pitch,' he concedes. 'I think a midfield player can see a little bit more.'

Off the pitch, even the autocrat deferred to the squad system's more democratic principles, however. One of the original squad members, Rogério, and coaching assistant Carlos Alberto Parreira ran along the touchlines with cameras during all three matches at Guadalajara. Afterwards they would analyse their performances using blown-up slides. Everyone's opinion was forthcoming. 'Speaking is not the only important thing,' Gérson says with another ironic arch of an eyebrow. 'You must listen as well, you are not always right.'

The most passionate debates reflected the arguments that had riven all Brazil since 1966. To most Brazilians, football now offered three distinct philosophies: *futebol-força*, the power game played by strong European sides like West Germany and England; the pragmatic *futebol de resultados*, the win-at-all-costs school exemplified by the Italians; and *futebol-arte*, the beautiful, expressive style Brazil's win in Sweden had first introduced to the world. As a survivor of the shame of 1966, Gérson was one of the team's unreconstructed pragmatists.

'What is important is to win. It does not matter if you play in a wonderful way and lose,' he explains simply. In his heart, though, Gérson, like Pelé and Zagalo, looked for ways in which Brazil could succeed with a cocktail of all three philosophies. 'Of course if you can play in a wonderful way and win, that's great, that's the philosophy.' The Final against Italy provided Gérson with the perfect platform from which to expound his thinking.

35

Gérson was much happier to be playing the tactically rigid Italians than the more flexible Germans, whom they had beaten 4–3 in extra time of a pulsating semi-final. 'It would have been much more difficult for us to confront the German system and their talented players,' he admits.

He does not agree with the arsonist analogy when I put it to him. 'If I had done that, the midfield would not have worked,' he says with a frown. To Gérson's mind, Italy gifted him the space in which he operated by playing a two-man midfield of de Sisti and Mazzola. The selection dilemma between Mazzola and his great rival Gianni Rivera had divided all Italy in the run up to the Final. Mazzola was given the nod leaving the A.C. Milan captain and European Footballer of the Year on the bench. Once more the *cafezinho* cups illustrate the simple mathematics that worked in Brazil's favour. 'They had 4–2–4, we had 4–3–3 and sometimes 4–4–2. They should have played with Rivera,' Gérson says.

The first half had finished even after Pelé's opening goal had been cancelled out by Boninsegna, capitalizing on a horrendous mistake by Clodoaldo. As if sensing his time had come, Gérson returned from his half-time cigarette and took control of the rest of the match.

In the decades that have passed, Brazil's performances in Mexico have been compared to a form of footballing jazz, improvized and extemporized to some secret, shared rhythm. In reality, their games were masterpieces of classical musicianship. If Pelé, Tostão, Rivellino and Jairzinho were the team's lead violinists, Gérson was its conductor. The latter stages of the Final against Italy represented his command performance.

By now the carefully choreographed theory of Guanajuato

had translated itself into a thrilling reality. One of the tactics developed there had been to pull the play to the left side of the pitch to take advantage of the speed of Carlos Alberto, their one genuine attacking full-back. Tostão, Rivellino, Gérson and Pelé would suck the opposition defence across the pitch before then spreading it wide. 'We couldn't do the same thing with the other side because Everaldo was not like Carlos Alberto, he was more a marker,' says Gérson. Early in the second half, Carlos Alberto roared down the flank before putting in a cross that missed Pelé's toe by inches. He would have better luck later in the match.

Ultimately, however, Gérson turned the Final with a rare moment of individualism. The game was still evenly poised when, in the sixty-fifth minute, he sent Everaldo away on the left with a wonderful blind pass. When the ball worked its way back to him via Jairzinho, Gérson dragged it around an advancing defender. From twenty yards out he hit an angled, one-iron shot that was as low in its trajectory as it was lethal in its placement. Albertosi flailed but failed to get near it. It was Gérson's one and only goal in Mexico.

He ran towards Zagalo and the bench, arms outstretched and preaching in celebration. 'You become a professional, reach the Brazilian team and then become a World Champion,' he says when I ask him about his emotions at that moment. 'It is indescribable.' Of all his goals, was it the finest? 'It was,' he says. 'And it was certainly the goal that made the greatest impression.'

It was definitely that. His goal inspired him to reach greater heights. Within five minutes he had swung the most influential left foot at the Azteca once more to

37

place an exquisite cross on Pelé's head. The meeting of Pelé's mind and Gérson's left foot was by then overwhelming Italy. It was if they were part of the same disjoined body. Rather than finishing it off himself, as he had done in an almost identical move against the Czechs five games earlier, Pelé nodded the ball down for the inrushing Jairzinho to score. Such was his perfectionism Gérson asked Pelé afterwards why the pass had not been good enough for him to score as he had done previously?

When the final whistle went Gérson recalls running for the tunnel. He sat down there, on his own as far as he can remember. In the dressing room afterwards he broke down. Images of his implacable features wreathed in tears were among the most touching of the photographs to emerge in the days and weeks that followed. 'I'm very emotional,' he says simply, almost apologetically. 'Yes, I cried.'

Afterwards Gérson went into the Italian dressing room. He exchanged shirts with Giacinto Facchetti, but it was not the yellow No. 8 he had worn through the heat of the Final. Signed by all his colleagues, it remains his proudest footballing possession. I wonder how he feels now, rekindling the memories of that day. 'It is indescribable,' he says again, solemnly. His voice is faltering, he offers an apologetic shrug. For the first time this morning, the *papagaio* is lost for words.

Gérson returned with the rest of the side to a hero's welcome. He arrived back in Niteroi, his status as the city's favourite son now assured. He played briefly in São

Paulo but has effectively remained rooted in his boyhood community his entire life.

Gérson's performance in Mexico drew the attention of the lira-laden Italian clubs once more. They had first approached him back in 1961 after his impressive displays in the Olympics. He would have made enough to 'bring Niteroi with him and put it in the back garden'. Yet a move to Europe never seriously entered his head.

Gérson was called up for the 1974 squad and what would have been his third World Cup. Now thirty-three, with his fitness fading and thoughts of retirement in his mind, he didn't accept the call. The theories I had heard about politics influencing his decision were rejected with a stern shake of the head. He will not deny the team provided Médici and the AERP with the PR opportunity of a lifetime. 'We knew about all the problems that Brazil was going through, because we participated in them as well,' he says, his features hardening. He scowls at suggestions that the team were somehow exploited by the regime, however. 'Our obligation was training and playing. We were there to play football not to be manipulated. If we had felt that way we would have left everything and gone away.' His decision not to travel to West Germany was purely a footballing one, he says. Memories of Feola, Goodison Park and the grand old men of Sweden and Chile simply strengthened his conviction that it would be a campaign too far. 'It was too much for me. I had played in the Brazilian championship which was very wearing. I was out of condition and I was already thinking about stopping.'

When he finally retired, Gérson followed the example of his father who had moved from football to being a local government inspector, *fiscal da prefeitura*. Today he is a sports secretary for the Niteroi city authority. In addition he shows me a leaflet for Projeto Gérson, the charity he has set up to provide a form of education for the poor and homeless of Niteroi. To the jaded European eye, marriages of politics and charity always seem somehow dubious. Yet it is hard to find a false note in Gérson's genuine passion for his cause, which he promotes independently from his role at Niteroi city hall. He has been fighting, often in vain, for eight years to establish the project properly.

Sitting here in Gérson's office overlooking the Praia Saco de São Francisco it is hard to believe Niteroi's beauty is only as skin deep as its neighbour across Guanabara Bay. The uncomfortable truth is that poverty has driven hundreds of its children on to the streets.

'The idea is to get children who are not studying to practise football then enrol in a school. To give food to those children, and in the best way remove them from the streets,' he says. His frustration at the lack of support he is getting from business is palpable. 'For the children, everything is free; the difficult part is to convince the private sector to participate.'

It is when he begins to talk about the children that his guard falls for the first time. Suddenly his features soften, his voice drops below the barrack-room level at which it has been pitched for most of the morning. 'We cannot plan anything in our lives because we do not know if we are still alive tomorrow,' he says quietly, a sadness now filling his voice. It turns out his words are the legacy of his own personal tragedy.

As he has done every 8 May for the last few years,

Gérson spent the previous day in church with his family. The date marked the anniversary of the death of one of his two daughters. Together the family lit candles in her memory. Gérson, a deeply religious man, admits he was 'bewildered' by the loss.

Whatever anger and emotion he felt, he does not believe it has a place in public – or in the face of God. 'What we feel inside is important, inside. Outside is different,' he says, examining his fingers as he speaks. 'A man must be at peace with God, even if his family is dead in front of him he must be there with his face clean,' he says before cutting himself off. 'It is a little bit complicated. But we have another daughter, another grandson. We have to get on with our lives. We are Catholic, very religious, so we understand it in a different way. Our life is not really here, it is there,' he says, indicating to a distance I assumed he sees as the other side. 'It's difficult, complicated.' I do not intrude further into his grief.

Soon afterwards, our interview over, we walk to the Praia Saco de São Fransisco where Gérson agrees to pose for a few photographs. The beach and its network of football pitches and volleyball courts is all but deserted in the midday sun. A single coconut vendor is sitting in the shade of a tree. He uses his machete to slice a huge, green husk open then offers it to us.

By now the morning haze has cleared and Rio in the distance looks even more alluring. As I stand there in awe of the scene, I catch Gérson looking out to sea, as if it were his first visit here too. At that moment I understand why he has never uprooted himself from Niteroi.

His show of sentimentality is brief. Back in his office Gérson and his staff are gracious with their telephones

41

which are soon ordering a taxi back to the ferry. As we say our goodbyes he closes the door on his boardroom and begins the next phase of his working day with a mass dressing-down of his staff. It is audible half-way down the hall. It is translated back to me as 'Haven't you people got any work to do?' Judging by the fearful look on the face of the *papagaio*'s staff as they emerge from his office moments later, it is safe to assume there is an expletive or two missing.

CHAPTER II

O Capitão

The brash, new suburb of Barra da Tujica is a world removed from the faded grandeur of old Rio, ten miles or so along the coast. A wannabe Miami of drive-in *hipermercados* and duplex developments mushrooming along a strip of land on the edge of an endless, white-sanded beach way out west of Ipanema, it is an affluent symbol of a booming and buoyant Brazil. It is here that multi-millionaire playboys like Romario come for a game of foot-volleyball. It is here and not Ipanema or Copacabana that Rio's really beautiful people parade themselves at the weekend.

On a mini-football pitch at the Clube Aeronautica, a disused airfield two or three miles inland from the Barra beach, however, the hunger on the faces of the five-year-olds is no different from that of the boys playing their kick-around *peladas* on the streets of the city's most infamous *favela* – Rocinha, half-way back down the road to Rio. They clatter into each other without fear. Extravagant flicks and long shots fly everywhere. Anything is attempted in an effort to catch the eye of the watchful figure standing on the touchline.

43

'Boys in Brazil have always wanted to be football players,' says Carlos Alberto Torres, his arms folded in concentration, his face wreathed in a smile as he watches the lawyers' and accountants' sons run themselves ragged to impress him. 'The difference today is that even those parents who have money can see it is one of the most lucrative professions in the world.'

For the 70 reals (around £40) a month their middle-class parents pay, these boys play three of these sessions a week. To judge by the numbers swelling the pitches, the prospect of having their sons coached by one of the living legends of Brazilian football would seem cheap at ten times the price. Like the school's father figure and his coaching staff, the boys are kitted out in the same, smart designer strip – colour coded according to their age-group or position. Each tracksuit, polo shirt, shirt or stocking bears the school's distinctive logo – a drawing of a smiling Carlos Alberto raising the World Cup in 1970.

The search for a corporate identity must have been among the shortest in Brazilian business history. Wherever he travels in Brazil, Carlos Alberto is referred to simply as *o capitão*, the captain. The slogan adopted for his new school says simply: *O capitão esta agora na Aeronautica*. 'The captain is now at the airport.'

Carlos Alberto is one of the finest attacking defenders Brazil has ever produced. He had his frailties in defence, yet the sight of him on one of his long, loping cavalry charges into the opposition half was among the most thrilling in the game. In a magnificent twenty-year career, he played close to a thousand competitive matches, first in Brazil then, with his friend Pelé, at the New York Cosmos during American soccer's heady salad days in the late 1970s. Yet for most of us his reputation rests on our memory of one match. He has worked in Japan and Cameroon. Mention his name in Yokohama or Yaounde and it will be the one they recall as well.

If Gérson had been the colossus of the Final against Italy, it was Brazil's imperious No. 4 who dominated its closing moments. The Italians had all but given up when he appeared unmarked on Pelé's side in their penalty area at the end of a move begun by Clodoaldo's uncharacteristic dribble. At Santos he had found himself in such positions a hundred times before, yet his friend and former next-door neighbour had never been quite so generous with a pass. Pelé rolled the ball into his path with all the care of a father coaching his two-year-old son. Carlos Alberto could do nothing but meet the ball perfectly in his stride. There was even something beautiful about the way his raking, right-foot shot disturbed the looseness of Albertosi's netting. As Carlos Alberto danced deliriously behind the goal, 110 million Brazilians began their *batucada*, beating the drums for the biggest party in the nation's history.

In the mayhem that followed the final whistle, it took him another fifteen minutes to fight his way back to the dressing room then up to the stands and the handshake of Mexican President Gustavo Díaz Ordaz. Photographs of Carlos Alberto's broad, toothy smile as he held the trophy aloft made the front pages of newspapers on five continents the next morning. His grip on immortality has never loosened since.

The last man to raise the Jules Rimet trophy was one of the first to agree to talk to me. He had, by an extraordinary chance, been told about my plan to find the 1970 side during a conference in Frankfurt a month or so before I left London. He gave his card to my sister-in-law, also attending the conference, who passed on the message that I should give him a call in Rio. He proved as good as his word, agreeing to talk on a Friday afternoon at the school.

Carlos Alberto spent six years in New York at the end of the 1970s but any hopes I might have had that we could talk in English were quickly dismantled. As we are introduced he mimics my Portuguese apology with a wink. 'I am sorry I speak *muito poco Ingles*,' he says. Over the course of the two days I spend in his company, however, he proves an Emeritus Professor of Linguistics, a specialist in the international language Brazilians call *futebol*.

Even Pelé, who has never coached, lacks the coalface credentials that his friend has acquired playing and administrating in America, coaching in Nigeria and acting as an unofficial manager for his son Alexandre, now playing in Japan. The changes he has seen extend far beyond the overactive five year olds dreaming of becoming the new Romarios and Ronaldos of Brazil under his paternal eye. 'What my son earns today I never earned in all my life,' he says, shaking his head in quiet disbelief. It was not so long ago that his own father was wearing the same expression, of course.

Carlos Alberto was born on 17 July 1944, one of twin brothers. His twin Carlos Roberto Torres, today a shorter, more pugnacious-looking version of Carlos Alberto, works with him at the football school. With their brother Jose Luis and sister Maria Helena the Torres twins grew up in the old

46

Rio suburb of Vila da Penha. They had none of the benefits on offer to his pupils at Barra. 'I came from a modest family; my father Francisco was a public employee in the city hall of Rio. I had nobody that could give me instruction as we are doing here,' he says, surveying the pitches. 'But maybe it was good for me somehow because I had to learn by myself.'

His father knew that education was the key to a better life for his children. Francisco would come home from his office job, eat a meal then head back out into the Rio streets to spend the night as a taxi driver. 'He made a big effort to earn a little more for us,' says Carlos Alberto. He too was working by the age of fourteen, saving money each month to go to the local cinema in Vila da Penha. 'I liked cowboy films,' he smiles. Bright and diligent, Carlos Alberto shone at the junior Escola Grecia and then Colegio Souza Aguiar in Vila da Penha, before moving on to college at the local Educandario Santa Fatima.

All three of the Torres brothers played football. It was the bigger, faster, more physical Carlos Alberto who was spotted by coaches from Fluminense. He began playing as a *juvenil*, or junior, at the age of fifteen. The decision to play for the famous red, white and green stripes flew in the face of his passion for their arch-rivals, the red and blacks of Flamengo. His boyhood idols were Didi and Nilton Santos, the black rock at the heart of the national team's World Cup defence. He still calls Santos, the bulwark in Sweden and Chile, 'the biggest phenomenon in football history'.

Yet the money he earned playing twice a week for the *juvenil* side was simply too good to be missed. With his father's encouragement, he had soon quit his job as an office boy and committed himself to football. 'I earned

47

as much as I did working the whole week in my other job.'

If Brazil's raw materials were the finest in the world, it was its apprentice system that ensured its rough diamonds were polished into the most perfect of jewels. As a *juvenil*, Carlos Alberto trained with the professionals and had professional coaching. Vast crowds would watch even the preliminary games he played in. If a professional was injured he would be drafted in as temporary cover. When it came to the leap to the first team he was ready. By the time he was eighteen Carlos Alberto had established himself as the right-back in the Fluminense first team. He had been drafted into the Brazilian national squad before his twentieth birthday.

Carlos Alberto made his international debut marking Bobby Charlton at the Maracanã during the 1964 Nations Cup between Brazil, England, Portugal and Argentina. The familiarity of the ground and the crowd helped him subdue both his nerves and a Charlton at the peak of his powers. Brazil won the game at a canter, 5–1. 'I felt calm and I played very well,' he says quietly. He would come across Charlton many times in the course of his subsequent life. 'A great man, a great man.'

Carlos Alberto remained a fixture in Feola's team all the way through to 1966. By then he had become the most expensive footballer in Brazilian history. Shortly after leading Fluminense to the Carioca championship in 1965, he was transferred to Santos for the then unheard-of sum of 200,000 cruzeiros.

His pride was soon to be dented. As Feola announced his 22-man squad for England, Carlos Alberto was overlooked in favour of the older, more experienced Djalma Santos.

To add insult to injury, Fidelis of Bangu was preferred as the reserve right-back. For all the glory he would go on to, Carlos Alberto still feels the rejection. 'There was no explanation. To this day I don't know why,' he says, shaking his head. In the aftermath of Goodison Park, however, he soon found himself taking centre stage.

Carlos Alberto has the charisma and the attentive, eager-to-please manner of the natural born politician. He stares you in the eye even when he is half-listening to a conversation elsewhere, squeezes your hand and wraps a fatherly arm around your shoulder when he wants to emphasize a point. His smile should be sponsored by Duracell. At the Clube Aeronautica his customers cannot get enough of it.

On top of all this he is also blessed with the sort of urbane, worldly-wise intelligence that used to shame British players when they travelled abroad. Like his old Cosmos friend 'Kaiser' Beckenbauer and Johann Cruyff, he has the air of the player-cum-international diplomat about him. He frequently flies to Europe to do work for Brazil's national airline Varig. It comes as no surprise to discover he spent time as a councillor in Rio. It is even easier to understand how the captaincy of Brazil came to rest on his angular shoulders.

Santos spotted his natural leadership qualities when the great Zito retired. 'I have always had that personality of talking in the game, calling the attention of my team-mates, giving advice,' he says. 'That is my spirit. Zito stopped playing in 1967 and I was selected captain of Santos.' As Brazil rebuilt in the aftermath of 1966, he seemed the most obvious candidate for the captaincy there too.

If there were politics involved in his acquisition of the black armband of Brazil he is politically savvy enough to have conveniently forgotten them. 'Since Santos was considered the best team in Brazil and the world at the time, maybe they thought there was nothing more fair than if I was the captain of the Brazilian team,' he says with a diplomatic shrug. Whatever the reasoning, Carlos Alberto quickly grew into the finest leader Brazil has ever possessed.

The first test of that leadership came in the chaotic aftermath of the Saldanha affair. Carlos Alberto had found little to fault under Saldanha's management, hardly surprising since he had built his early sides almost entirely around Santos players. At one stage in 1969 the captain led an all-Santos back five including goalkeeper Claudio, Djalma Dias, Joel and Hilton. With Pelé and Edu the Santos contingent reached seven. As Saldanha's confidence disintegrated, however, the captain could not condone his treatment of his friend and clubmate Pelé.

Since his arrival at Santos, his friendship with Pelé had been deep. 'We lived in the same building. I have always had good relations with him, we are still friends now,' he says. When Saldanha began suggesting that Pelé's eyesight was defective and he should be dropped, Carlos Alberto sensed that panic had overtaken the manager. 'I have never seen anyone who had anything against Pelé as a person,' he says simply.

Carlos Alberto's position is as unequivocal today as it was then. 'Pelé was the player in whom we trusted,' he says, still bemused to be asked whether the team could have prospered without him. 'If Pelé is with us, we are with God.' He does not know the whole truth, but suspects

Saldanha had simply become scared of the pressure. 'We knew that we had to win and the team had not settled. Maybe he feared losing the Cup?' he says, throwing his arms up. 'I don't know.'

Wherever the truth rests, Carlos Alberto's importance to the Brazilian cause only deepened in the weeks after their maverick manager's departure. On 26 March 1970, in the second of Zagalo's matches against Chile, he wielded his inspirational leadership on the field. By now the instability in the dressing room was affecting some players' performances. As Brazil once more failed to gel, Jairzinho and Roberto were ordered off following a mass brawl with Laube and Silva. The match was held up for twelve minutes as officials separated the players. It was Carlos Alberto who calmed the side's nerves, equalizing Castro's eighteenth-minute goal himself early in the second half.

In the weeks leading up to the departure for Mexico his influence was at its most profound off the pitch. After the frenetic Saldanha, Zagalo's reserved manner left the players frustrated and confused. Following a dismal 3–1 win over a local, 'Mineiro' selection in Belo Horizonte, Minas Gerais, and another goalless draw, this time at the Morumbi in São Paulo against World Cup finalists Bulgaria, there was an unmistakable whiff of mutiny in the air.

With Pelé and Gérson, Carlos Alberto formed the team's holy trinity. On the night of Tuesday, 28 April, in Pelé's room at the Hotel Paineiras in Rio, they held an hour-long meeting that effectively moulded the course of events over the next two months. The *cobras* gathered with the boos of the 70,000 Morumbi crowd still reverberating inside their heads. With Zagalo seemingly unwilling to share his thoughts on specific tactics, they chose the team and

51

the pattern they wanted to take on to the pitch for their final match before leaving Brazil, against Austria at the Maracanã the following night.

As the most directly affected, another three players, Tostão, Rivellino and Clodoaldo were later called into Pelé's quarters. Dario's failure against Bulgaria had proved once and for all that there was no place for an out-and-out centre-forward in games against tight European defences. Tostão agreed with the *cobras*' idea that he play at inside left with Pelé taking a position slightly forward of him in the middle. Rivellino would adapt to a dual role as a covering midfielder whilst attacking on both wings. The young Clodoaldo agreed to patrol the rear of the midfield.

Afterwards the trio had a meeting with Zagalo who, in turn consented to let them try their formation. He told them he would watch from the stands where he would reserve the right to change tactics via radio conversations with Mario Americo. Félix had been told of his reinstatement over Ado and Leao in goal the previous night. It was only in the dressing room on the following evening that the remainder of the team were made aware of the changes. Piazza, brought in for Joel, was told he would be playing as a fourth defender only minutes before he took the pitch. A fired-up Gérson gave the final pep talk.

Rivellino scored the winner in a 1–0 win. Far more importantly, however, the side rediscovered the shape and fluency it had lost since Saldanha's departure. Of the team that played that night, only Rogério, substituted for his great rival in the right wing position, Jairzinho, would not make it all the way to the finals in Mexico.

As far as Carlos Alberto was concerned, after that the key to Mexico lay with the stopwatches and slide-rules of

Coutinho and his Cooper Tests. 'Even if Zagalo had not taken over the team, even if we had Saldanha or any other coach, we had the team. We were not arrogant about it, but we were confident that if we were really well prepared physically we could win the World Cup.'

Carlos Alberto's natural political gifts found a perfect outlet in Mexico. Along with Pelé, he led a charm offensive that began the moment they set foot in Central America. It was not the hardest of sells. Carlos Alberto had seen the effect Pelé had on fans all over the world. 'Every place the club went Pelé and Santos were welcomed in an extraordinary way,' he says. Yet the Mexican section of their fan club was among the most devoted of all. 'Santos played in Mexico every season and the adoration they had for the players like me and Clodoaldo was something to see,' he says.

Preaching to the converted or not, Carlos Alberto charmed his way through press conferences and distributed autographs, pennants, paper hats and flags to children wherever the team travelled. More sophisticated minds may have seen the gesture as the 'beads for the natives' policy it undoubtedly was. It made little difference to the starstruck man on the street in Guadalajara. When Brazil played the Guadalajara team in front of a cheering 70,000 crowd, the whole city took the day off. The posters were on every street corner. *Hoy! No trabajamos porque vamos a ver Pelé*. No work today – we are off to see Pelé. 'It helped,' smiles Carlos Alberto.

Their success could not have presented a starker contrast to England's abject failure to win friends far from their Wembley home. The dour and occasionally paranoid Alf

Ramsey seemed to own as solid a grasp of public and international relations as he did of Einstein's theory of relativity. He had offended the sensitive Mexican press during what was supposed to have been a goodwill visit a year earlier. After a highly diplomatic 0–0 draw with the national team at the Azteca, Ramsey had been asked whether he had a message for the Mexican people. 'Yes,' he answered. 'There was a band playing outside our hotel till five o'clock this morning. We were promised a motor cycle escort to the stadium. It never arrived. When our players went out to inspect the pitch they were abused and jeered by the crowd.'

By the time Ramsey had backpedalled with the concession that 'we are delighted to be in Mexico and the Mexican people are a wonderful people' the damage was irretrievably done. He would return to Mexico as Public Enemy No. 1.

At the training camp in Brazil, Carlos Alberto's attitude had been characteristically Carioca. 'We would take our cars and would say: "I'm going out today, I'm going to make love with my wife, she's waiting for me at the hotel." We went and came back without problems,' he smiles. 'Of course, no one would stay out the whole night drinking, making love.'

Once in Mexico, however, he knew he had to set an example in terms of discipline. 'The most important thing was that we players were conscious that we needed to make that sacrifice.'

For all his good humour, no one was more acutely aware of the pressure his side would be under once the tournament began. Carlos Alberto knew anything less than a third Brazilian World Cup win was unacceptable. The gallows would be waiting at the airport. 'In Europe they celebrate being runners-up, winning vice-championships. Here in Brazil nobody accepts losing, even if it is in the last minute of the Final and it is offside. If you lose, you lose.'

Carlos Alberto's captaincy was from the Bobby Moore school – calming rather than confrontational. Pre-match speeches would be confined to simple prayers. 'Brazilian players do have the habit of praying. We pray that He will be good with us if He forgets the other team.' Beyond that *o capitão*'s words would be little more than a combination of encouragements and personal last-minute reminders. '"Let's go people", "Pelé take care of your back", things like that,' he says. 'We believed that we had been together a long time, four months of preparation, so we were more than united, there was no need for that thing before the game.'

Just before 4 p.m. on the afternoon of 3 June, as he had led a full-strength side out on to the Guadalajara pitch for their match against Czechoslovakia, *o capitão* knew better than anyone that it was time for his team to begin talking in deeds rather than words.

'Are you crazy?'
Brazil v. Czechoslovakia, 3 June 1970

As ever the Czechs had arrived at the finals on everyone's list of dark horses. After the draw in Mexico City, Pelé had ranked them with Brazil, England and Italy as the favourites for the tournament. The Rumanian coach Angelo Niculescu called his East European rivals the only team in the tournament capable of blending 'artistic football with good physical training'.

Their outspoken coach Joseph Marko was certain his side was capable of going all the way to their third appearance in a Final. 'If it plays according to tactical instructions and does not allow itself to be scared by the reputation of its adversaries it can happen,' he proclaimed. He was certainly not short of talent. In goalkeeper Ivo Viktor, defender Karol Dobias, midfielder Ladislav Kuna and the stylish Josef Adamec up front, he had four stars of the European constellation.

Marko's training regime verged on the Stalinist. Sex – for instance – had been banned back in Czechoslovakia. Yet his final preparations looked seriously flawed. He had kept his squad confined to Europe and an altitude camp at Font Romeu in the French Pyrenees. They had been the last of the fifteen overseas squads to arrive in Mexico and had then lost six days through jet lag before his players could train normally. When they eventually got going they could only manage two half-hour sessions per day. Their Pyrenees retreat had been at the same altitude as Guadalajara but the heat was another matter. Marko's players would have to drink water constantly and would collapse with exhaustion at the end of even the shortest run-out. Their cause was not helped by their Mexican bus driver's refusal to take them to two of their planned sessions because of Marko's unwillingness to pay him.

Yet after eleven nervous minutes inside the Jalisco stadium, it was Brazil who looked underprepared. Despite the fact he had been sent off in his one and only other international appearance, against Hungary, Marko had thrown in the blond, part-time locksmith, Ladislav Petras, as the spearhead of his attack. In what was effectively his side's first serious sortie into the opposition half, Petras unpicked the Brazilian defence with an ease that bordered on the embarrassing. After dispossessing Clodoaldo deep in the Brazilian half, Petras swept past Brito as if he was not there. Félix would come in for deserved criticism later but couldn't be blamed for failing to stop his drilled shot. As an overwhelmed Petras slid to his knees in prayer, the BBC commentary summed up the thoughts forming in several million minds around the world. As the global audience waited for its first glimpse of Brazil, the pre-match analysis had revolved around their lack of solidity at the back. 'All we had heard about them has come true,' crowed David Coleman.

For Carlos Alberto, it was clear the moment of truth had arrived. 'Of course you worry when you concede a goal in the first game of a World Cup. The first game is always important,' he says. 'So, of course, when we conceded that goal the team felt some shock.' With Gérson, Piazza and Pelé, he calmed the nerves of the younger members of the team. No one had looked livelier than Rivellino. He had already knocked Viktor back with a firecracker of a left-foot shot from the edge of the area. In the twenty-fourth minute a foul on Pelé gave Brazil a free kick in a similar position. Rivellino hammered a low, left-footed shot under Viktor's body. The relief was unmistakable.

As far as Carlos Alberto is concerned, there were few more significant passages in the entire tournament. 'It was at that moment that we got a big surge of momentum, that the team felt how powerful we were,' he says. Within minutes Tostão had brought another brilliant flying save out of Viktor.

No one embodied the renewed confidence more than Pelé. The final days before the kick-off had left him itching to prove his detractors wrong. After the disappointment of 1966 and his threat of retirement, there had been widespread doubt about his appetite for the battle. He had been wound up by Marko's dismissal of him as a 'spent force'. The Brazilian press had seized on a Mexican computer prediction that he would be injured in the first half and play no further part in the tournament. He was still stinging from Saldanha's accusations about his eyesight. His work rate alone in the first half silenced all his critics. Soon after Rivellino's goal, he proved he also had a trick or two up his sleeve still. Clodóaldo's tackling had by now begun to bite. A sliding interception in the centre of the field left Pelé in the centre circle alone and unmarked and with the ball at his feet. The following five seconds remain among the most famous in World Cup history.

Carlos Alberto had seen such imagination week in week out at Santos. 'Pelé was a player who, besides having a great technique – his acceleration, his heading – his great secret was improvisation,' he says. 'Those things he did were done in one moment. He had an extraordinary perception of the game.'

Even he had not seen anything quite so audacious, however. Pelé had spotted Viktor wandering far off his line while the ball was in the Brazilian half. As he let fly from 65 yards, his high, curving shot sent Viktor scrambling back towards his goal. The Czech had all but given up on the shot as it drifted inches wide of his left-hand post. The black-clad army officer patted the woodwork as if to thank it for saving his blushes. 'He was the only player that realized the goalkeeper had advanced,' says Carlos

Alberto. 'Everybody was astonished. Some of the players shouted "Are you crazy?" But when we saw the goalkeeper far from the goal and the ball almost going in . . .' His broad smile and exaggerated shrug of the shoulders says it all.

By half-time his team felt they were up to the challenge that lay ahead of them. 'It gave us the tranquillity we needed for the team to be conscious of how powerful it was,' says Carlos Alberto. 'From that moment on we started to prove we had everything to win the World Cup.'

The Czechs had their chances in the second half. After Pelé had nudged Brazil ahead with a masterpiece of control and finishing from an inch-perfect Gérson pass, substitute Kvasnak missed an open goal after another defensive mix-up from a corner. Marko knew the key to subduing Brazil was to keep their playmaking geniuses under pressure. Instead his defenders treated the game like a basketball session, backpedalling into their own penalty area whenever Brazil were on the ball. As the heat overcame them, Gérson found more and more space. The hours of training at Guanajuato paid off. Twice in the final quarter Jairzinho was unleashed for runs on goal. Twice the hurricane wreaked havoc.

Back at the Suites Caribes the effect was galvanic. 'We knew that technically we could beat anyone. Because we were the only team that really worked for three months, that stayed in Mexico for a month and a half getting used to the altitude, we also had good physical preparation,' Carlos Alberto says. By the time his side had seen off England, Carlos Alberto sensed another element was with them. 'The chances England had to score in that game, we felt that luck was following us,' he nods. He regarded the match as the key to the campaign. 'Besides the moral advantage there was the comfort advantage,' he says. 'The winner would stay in Guadalajara and the loser would go up in altitude to face Germany.'

Carlos Alberto's admiration for Moore and Charlton, Banks and Mullery ran deep. 'In my opinion that side, not the 1966 side, was England's best,' he says. Three decades on, the game is remembered as much for its sportsmanship as its sublime moments – Banks' save from Pelé, Moore's tackle on Jairzinho, Tostão's dribbling and Rivellino's shooting. Only Francis Lee seemed to be singing to a different hymn sheet. 'He was a little . . . excited,' Carlos Alberto says, choosing his words from behind a thin smile. Lee had begun the match with a series of stiff challenges on Everaldo and Félix. 'We agreed that the first player to come across Lee would give him a response. And it happened to be me.'

Whether it was meting out justice, or readjusting tactics, the chain of command operated easily. To Carlos Alberto, captaining the highly-paid troubadours of Santos was more difficult than leading a Brazilian squad committed to a common cause. 'Santos had more stars,' he says with a raised eyebrow. After months together, a unity had evolved in the national squad. 'When you have a well-blended team like we had, it's not necessary to keep saying a lot about strategy,' he explains.

In times of crisis on the pitch the inner circle of Gérson and Pelé, Piazza and Carlos Alberto made the necessary adjustments. 'We talked in an informal way, everyone was free. If we saw something was wrong we took the initiative and changed it,' he says. 'I think that has always been a factor in the success of Brazilian football – creativity and improvisation.'

As the tournament progressed, Carlos Alberto shook off

the nerves of the opening match and began to express himself. As he did so his attacking became a more prominent and menacing feature of the Brazilian game. Against England he set up Pelé's famous header, unleashing Jairzinho with a sublime pass off the outside of his foot past Cooper at left-back. He went one better and set up a goal for his team-mate against Rumania and proved a constant threat in the quarter-final against Peru. In the dour domains of the Joseph Marko and Alf Ramsey camps it would have been akin to heresy to admit such a thing, yet Carlos Alberto confesses that his overwhelming memory of Mexico is of the sheer enjoyment he got on the pitch.

'When you know that you are playing in a good team, it lifts you, you are in a paradise,' he says. 'We were confident that we were well prepared physically and technically so the atmosphere was one of joy.'

As the team progressed towards the Final, he recalls joining in the *batucada*, with the small but enthusiastic contingent of fans who had undertaken the expensive and arduous journey from Brazil to congregate outside the Suites Caribes. The exuberant, samba-driven support that would become synonymous with Brazil's World Cup campaigns in future years, was born on those warm Mexican evenings. 'We danced with the supporters. I think that crazy thing of the supporters following the Brazilian team to World Cups all over the world started there,' says Carlos Alberto.

Everywhere he goes, people remember his performance in the Final. His own memories of 21 June are a mixture of the vivid and the vague. There had been two team meetings, one on the Saturday night and another early on Sunday morning. At each Zagalo had reiterated his plan

61

to drag the Italian defence to the left side of the field, clearing a channel for Carlos Alberto to attack down the right. There were no inspirational speeches in the bowels of the Azteca. Brazil took the pitch after a prayer and a last-minute reminder of the game-plan.

Italy's arduous semi-final had taken place twenty-four hours after Brazil's triumph over Uruguay. Carlos Alberto's side had finished strongly in all five of their matches so far. More than ever, they knew the Final was a war of attrition. 'We played on the Wednesday and they played on the Thursday and had to go through over-time,' he explains. 'We were very rested, and we were confident we were going to win because they were worn out.'

The match lived up to their expectations, with Italy's challenge fading in the final quarter. Carlos Alberto's blind-side runs had paved a way for a goalscoring opportunity early in the second half. His low cross missed Pelé's toe by inches. By the eighty-sixth minute, however, he was ready for his moment of glory.

Clodoaldo and Rivellino had set the move running down the left-hand side of the pitch. Carlos Alberto had drifted into the right channel unnoticed. As Jairzinho passed it to Pelé he knew instinctively what to do. 'When it arrived at Pelé's feet I just believed the ball would come to me. I didn't have to shout. When we played at Santos we had a good understanding, I knew that if the ball was at his feet he would give it to me,' he recalls.

Carlos Alberto admits he was no Gérson or Rivellino in the shooting stakes. Pelés genius was such that he had even made an allowance for this in his calculations. 'He waited until the moment I arrived, I arrived just on time, that's why the shot was strong, because my shot was not strong,' he smiles. He knew it was a goal the moment he hit it. He can recall running around the pitch but little else of the high emotion that followed as he danced and hugged his team-mates. 'At that moment we just exploded, we shouted every bad word.'

At the final whistle he ran straight for the dressing room. The scenes there were as chaotic as those on the pitch. Many of the players had been stripped bare by the invading army of fans. 'There were lots of people almost without clothes. So we had to go back and get dressed again. There were lots of people inside the dressing room, journalists, lots of people. People went to have a shower with their clothes on. It was a very special moment.'

In the eye of the euphoria, Carlos Alberto recalls finding a moment of tranquillity and composing himself for the presentation to come. In the cool of the dressing room, his mind was alive with images of the parties that would be going on back in Vila da Penha and beyond. 'That's where everything comes to your mind. A World Cup for Brazilians is like winning a war, so we knew there would be the biggest party. We were conscious that Brazil was passing through a difficult moment, with the dictatorship. We knew that people would have forgotten the difficulties to celebrate. In Brazil people suffer and when we are in the World Cup we set ourselves free,' he smiles.

'The sleeping giant'
A night at the Maracanã

In the golden age of the 1950s and 1960s, tens of thousands of Brazilians would huddle round their radios to listen to the emotional commentaries of Waldir Amaral on the Globo radio station. At the end of the great occasions at the nation's home of football, Amaral would always sign off the same way. 'The giant of the Maracanã is deserted and sleeping,' he would proclaim in his trademark rumbling bass, as the crowds emptied and the lights dimmed inside the vast stadium. Three decades on from those glory days, on a balmy Saturday night, some of Brazil's brightest and best are playing under the floodlights at the world's most famous football ground. Once Flamengo against Botafogo drew 120,000 and more to the Maracanã. Tonight, even with one of the world's greatest players, Romario, restored to Flamengo's forward line and the destiny of the Rio Championship at stake, there are barely 10,000 on the banked, concrete terraces. Suddenly Waldir Amaral's famous phrase has never seemed so poignant.

As every football fan knows, the Maracanã was built for the 1950 World Cup, a monolithic metaphor for the scale of Brazil's ambition as well as its peerless passion for football. Europe has its great footballing meccas. Wembley, the San Siro, the Nou Camp, the Stadium of Light in Lisbon. Yet, even half a century later, nothing quite conjures up the magic of the Maracanã. Soon after parting company with Carlos Alberto, who has invited me back to share lunch at the Clube Aeronautica another day, I set off to see it.

The drive to the ground is dramatic, not least because the taxi driver sees himself as the reincarnation of Ayrton Senna. Nelson Piquet reckoned Rio was more dangerous than the Nürbergring. Even Jackie Stewart climbed out of a taxi ashen-faced. For a moment Christ on Corcovado is directly above us. Before I can formulate a prayer, however, He has disappeared and we are lost inside one of the tunnels that link the suburbs partitioned by Rio's peaks. The agony ends when we emerge unscathed in the Mangueira neighbourhood and within sight of the Maracanã itself.

The area is full of old, palm-fringed colonial homes. The lights of the Maracanã have turned the sky above them a lurid, light purple. As we roll up to the ground, cocky kids stalk the traffic, waving drivers towards parking spaces they have generously reserved for their customers.

'If you park and pay them, they'll protect the car,' I'm told.

'If you don't?' I wonder.

'Don't ask.'

The taxi dumps me and the Botafogo fans I am accompanying outside the main entrance to the ground. With five minutes to go before kick-off the place is a scene from an Arab souk, a pandemonium of T-shirt and banner vendors, stalls selling beer and *cachaça*. We grab the tickets, a bracing, bolted *cachaça* and race inside.

At first I know how overseas fans must feel when they finally see inside Wembley. Approaching its fiftieth birthday the Maracanã is a piece of faded futurism starved of money by the city's elders. (Politically there is more mileage in the opening of a new soccer school. Talk of a new national stadium surfaces and sinks as routinely as talk of a new Pelé.) Leviathan slabs of concrete cast long, menacing shadows. The concourses are dimly lit and devoid of life, the stink of stale urine and decay is everywhere. It is a reminder of pre-Premiership life back home.

My disillusionment does not last long. If the chaos outside the Maracanã is a scene from *Blade Runner*, the walk into the light-filled heart of the stadium is the climax of

Close Encounters. The Maracanã is a vast alien spaceship, a monumental rimmed bowl, glowing in the warm night. There is no seating as such, just layer after layer of broad concrete steps sweeping for what seems like forever into the distance. I take a position towards the back of the stand with the Botafogo fans. At the other end of the ground, the red and black Flamengo fans seem a Tube ride away.

To the purists the Maracanã was stripped of its soul when the vast, free-standing area underneath the stands, the *geral*, was closed down. Three people had been killed when part of the stand above collapsed on their heads. Today police cars drive around the barren perimeter of the ground. The *geraldjinos* were the Maracanã's Shakespearean groundlings, the fans with the least money and the most noise. Yet to the visiting eardrum, the place seems noisy and electric enough even without them.

Technically speaking the ground is holding five per cent of its full capacity. I have never seen a 95-per-cent empty stadium filled with such an atmosphere. The teams enter to a Chinese New Year worth of flares and fireworks; behind me the percussive poetry of the samba drums rolls like thunder through the night sky. The black-and-white-clad Botafogo fans greet their heroes with shouts of 'Foooooohhhhhh-gooooooooo'. Goodness knows what the noise is like at the Flamengo end. They outnumber the Fogo fans by at least two to one.

Rio's fearsome club rivalries go back to the turn of the century and the formation of the city's main teams. The grudge match is still Flamengo v. Fluminense, or Fla v. Flu, Brazil's equivalent to Rangers v. Celtic, Real Madrid v. Barcelona, Liverpool v. Everton. Flamengo's reputation as the 'people's club' is rooted in the racist 1930s when it led the way in fielding mixed-race sides in the Rio championship. Today it is loved and loathed all over Brazil with the sort of partisan zeal Manchester United evokes elsewhere. Apparently more than 30 million Brazilians count themselves as fans of the red and blacks.

In contrast Fluminense traditionally draws its support from more aristocratic, white stock. Flu's nickname, the 'rice powder' club, leads back to the day in 1916 when it secretly slipped a coloured player – also coincidentally called Carlos Alberto – into its whites-only side. A reporter caught the earlier Carlos Alberto covering his face in rice powder in the dressing room before taking the field. Flu fans responded to the taunts by christening the black-dominated Flamengo teams the 'coal dust' club. Even when both clubs gave way to the multi-racial tide, the difference between Fla and Flu remained as clear as black and white.

Botafogo's smaller fan base lies within the city's middle classes while the other major club, Vasco da Gama, traditionally draws its support from the Portuguese immigrants of the city. (In reality it was Vasco who led the way in fielding black players even before Flamengo.) With the two other major sides in Rio, América and Bangu, the big six lock horns each year to decide the city's premier side.

Even Stephen Hawking would be hard pushed to fathom the complexities of the Carioca championships. Suffice it to say that it is played in three phases with the winner of each phase carrying forward points into the next round of matches. So solid are the sands on which the competition is founded, that teams seem to spend more time in court injuncting each other than on the pitch. Tonight's match was, it appears, in the balance until the gavel came down

67

in a Rio courtroom the day before. What seems clear, however, is that a draw will all but guarantee Botafogo the title. Flamengo must win to keep their chances alive.

For all the problems it has in running its major competition, the real crisis facing football in Rio and Brazil as a whole is more fundamental. Drastically dwindling gates and a player drain that has taken 2,000 of its leading players over to Europe are driving the game at club level to the brink of anarchy. In 1996 Brazil's twenty-four leading clubs had debts totalling 100 million reals (around £60 million). In many cities the game is as good as bankrupt.

The problems are all too apparent at the Maracanã tonight. (Romario will soon be shipped back to Spain because Flamengo cannot afford to pay his European owners, Valencia, the fees they are due.) Yet to look at Brazil's greatest asset, the game should be in no difficulty at all.

For all its Murdoch millions, the Premiership would still struggle to serve up skills to compete with even an average Brazilian league match. From the kick-off, Flamengo v. Botafogo is neat and skilful, the passing and the movement rapier sharp. Flamengo start off on top with Romario at the hub of everything. The ultimate *favela* footballer darts around the pitch, quick, ruthless and sublimely streetwise. He is instrumental in the move from which Savio, on the fringe of the full Brazil team, scores with a lovely, low-flying volley half-way through the first half. It is difficult to take your eyes off him.

Savio's goal silences the Botafogo samba for a few, brief moments. The red and black hordes sing the '*hino di Flamengo*', the hymn of Flamengo. For a while afterwards it looks as if Savio and Romario will overwhelm Botafogo on their own. Only Gonçalvez, the Fogo No. 4 and a member of the Brazil squad, stands between them and a blow to their championship dreams. 'He'll be playing for Tottenham Hotspur next week,' winks one of the Fogo fans with whom I am standing.

The Fogo hordes are not silenced for long, fortunately. As Bentinho bundles a header across the Mengo line, an electronic scoreboard flashes '*MALUCO*' – 'crazy' in giant letters. Its operator has clearly been here before. It is half-time before the Fogo fans stop bouncing off the concrete.

Carlos Alberto had expressed surprise at the idea that I was going to the Maracanã. I might as well have said I was wandering into the heart of the *favela* Rocinha with a briefcase full of five-dollar bills. His expression said 'be careful'. In truth, in shorts and T-shirt, stripped of my watch and with only a few reals on me, I encountered no trouble at all. A lone *gringo* walking the terraces in his well-creased khakis drew far more attention. If there was violence it was no more shocking than anything I had seen at grounds around Britain in the 'Dark Ages' of the 1970s and 80s. At times it was almost touching in its half-hearted pathos.

At one point I am approached by a skinny, shirtless Fogo fan who points at my can of illicit Antarctica beer. (Illegal beer sellers run the gauntlet of the armed police throughout the match.) I assume he wants to celebrate what now looks like an inevitable draw with the dregs. But when I hand him the can he pours the remains on to the concrete, then stamps the empty cylinder with his trainers. Soon he is admiring the lethal, Kung Fu-style flying star weapon he has created. Soon after that it is winging its way towards the nearest enclave of Mengo fans. They are so far away the missile curves quietly on to a car-park-sized swathe of concrete. The whey-faced fan watches his star fall to the floor, shrugs his shoulders in resignation and returns to roaming the prairie-like spaces of the Maracanã in search of more discarded cans.

The second half remains goalless and Fogo get the draw they need. They have also held on to their unbeaten run in the championship which now looks as good as theirs, attorneys allowing. At the final whistle I see the shirtless kid among the Fogo fans who head for the exit chanting '*O Campeo*', 'The Champions'. We file out with them, eager to get away from the Maracanã district and head back into the smarter, safer bars of Leblon and Ipanema. In the vast concourse the black and white of the Fogo fans and the red and black of Mengo merge into one. One of the Fogo fans points at a posse of particularly ugly looking Flamengo fans and shouts '*O Campeo*'. As they surge towards us I am recommended to run for my life

Soon we are once more the prisoners of another Son-of-Senna taxi driver. As the yellow cab screeches away from the ground, I turn and watch the lights dim in the distance. Once more the giant of the Maracanã is deserted and sleeping. How much longer will Brazil allow it to remain in its slumber?

No sooner had Carlos Alberto brought the Cup back to Rio than the Jules Rimet trophy was stolen from its cabinet at the CBD buildings, never to be seen again. (When a copy was put up for sale in England in 1997, a Brazilian businessman, Marcio Leite, bid more than

£200,000 for the gilt-painted replica the English FA had commissioned during its four years in charge. It was not enough: an English tycoon topped him with a bid of £254,500.) As a piece of symbolism, not even the Maracanã's problems sum up the decline that followed the 1970 win so succinctly.

Carlos Alberto was injured and could not play a part in the defence in 1974. By 1978 he was at the New York Cosmos with Pelé, one of the team of frontiersmen hired to push the game through the last barrier of all. He played there for six seasons.

Behind him in his office there is a poster for a match between the Cosmos and Toronto to mark Carlos Alberto Day, the benefit organized near the end of his career in August 1980. He retired from the Cosmos at the age of thirty-eight in 1982, when he was lured back to Rio to the first of a string of coaching jobs at Flamengo. Over the next dozen years he coached two more of the city's big clubs, Fluminense and Botafogo. He also had a spell at Corinthians in São Paulo. He commentated on the 1994 World Cup in America, and the following year accepted the job of coach to the Nigerian national side, the so-called Super Eagles. He only stayed in Africa for a matter of months. Money seems to have been a stumbling block. 'They play good football, happy football. But their organization is very poor,' he says, silent for a moment as he mulls over what he has just said. 'In fact they have *no* organization,' he adds, baring his teeth for the biggest smile of the day.

Ask most Brazilians what makes their football superior to that of the rest of the world and they will offer little more than a look of divine bewilderment. It is almost tempting God to undo what He has done. It comes as no surprise to learn that one of the few to attempt a definitive answer has been João Saldanha. Asked the question in 1970 Saldanha came up with four, fundamental ingredients: Brazil's climate, its poverty, its ethnic mix and its peerless passion for *futebol*.

Over lunch at the Club Aeronautica, the much-travelled Carlos Alberto sees wisdom in each. 'In Europe you have many other sports – tennis, basketball, golf, swimming. Here we have only football,' he says. He agrees that in the same way that black Americans are genetically and culturally suited to basketball and the teak-tough South-Sea Islanders of Polynesia and New Zealand are somehow ready-made for rugby, Brazil may just breed better footballers too. 'Brazilians are not tall or strong, but we are suited to football. I think that is something to do with nature,' he says.

He would, however, add one other factor to Saldanha's equation – Brazil's sheer, gargantuan scale. 'I don't know how to explain the personality of Brazilian football. I think it is natural,' he says. 'But if you ask me why in Brazil there are so many great players I have an explanation – it is because of the size of the country.' Such is Brazil's sub-tropical vastness, you could almost certainly lose the other great footballing nations of the world in its rivers and rainforests, open plains and mountains.

With such God-given resources, Carlos Alberto believes, the production line will never cease: 'In Europe the countries are small, so they have cycles. Like in the Netherlands, for example, they had two cycles, the time of Cruyff and Neeskens, and the time of Gullit and Van Basten. Portugal has had one cycle, the time of Eusebio.

Italy, Paolo Rossi in the 1980s – France had good players then too. In Brazil we have players growing up every day.'

He remains an acute observer of football around the world. Despite his *muito poco Ingles* he still has a home in New York where he regularly spends time. He says he enjoyed 'everything, the whole six years' that he spent there. He despaired at the standard of play in the 1994 World Cup there. 'Boring,' he says. If FIFA had acted differently when it had its first opportunity to civilize the footballing world's last heathen frontier, matters might have been different, he believes.

He had been in America in 1982 when the decision was made to award the 1986 World Cup to Colombia. 'I followed it because I was there and the Americans were certain that they would be selected as hosts,' he says. Carlos Alberto was personally involved in plans being drawn up to attract all the world's leading players to a beefed-up version of the NASL – North American Soccer League – in which he, Cruyff, Beckenbauer and Pelé had played. He had been personally involved in lining up Maradona and Zico, Falcao and Rossi to move to the USA. 'They had the money to buy everybody, take the players and spread them all across the United States. That was the plan. I know because I made contact with the Brazilian players, players like Falcao,' he says.

When the tournament was withdrawn from a financially crippled and crime-riddled Colombia, FIFA, in the shape of its now omnipotent president, João Havelange, repeated the snub by opting for Mexico instead. American tycoons like Steve Ross, then head of Warner Brothers and the New York Cosmos, were incensed. 'Steve Ross said "I will not put in another dime, I'm out, it's the end of football for

73

me". Within one and a half years football in the USA was finished. In 1982 Cosmos had 60,000 people at each game; in 1984 there were a thousand people there. That's what shot down football in the USA; if the 1986 World Cup had been in the USA, the USA would today be the greatest power in the world, without any doubt. What they wanted to do, Italy did six years later. That's when everybody started saying their championship was the best in the world.'

The more time you spend with Carlos Alberto, the more you realize his natural political gifts. He must be the only person who has never quite understood why he entered the public arena. 'I was a coach at Corinthians and I earned about twenty times more than a town councillor. And suddenly I changed my profession. To this day I ask myself why?' he says with a bemused smile. During his four years as a public servant his duties included a spell in charge of the civic purse strings as First Secretary at the town hall. 'I signed all the cheques,' he explains. 'It was a good experience because I learned to deal with the process.'

Rather like his football, Carlos Alberto's politics seem to embrace the right wing. Driving back from Barra to Rio on the first evening I spent with him he shook his head in horror as we drove along the base of a hill and a gravity-defying *favela*. If he had his way, the slums would be pulled down and their population relocated to purpose-built suburbs. There, he suggested, they could get on with their crime in peace.

Yet he left Brazilian politics as he left Brazilian football, with the masses cheering for more. When the elections come, the governor of Rio calls him to his house and spends three hours trying to persuade Carlos Alberto to re-enter public life, he says. 'Every election they call me to go back,' he says. His answer is always the same. 'I don't want it,' he adds, shaking his head. 'My business now is sport.'

At this stage of its development, his football school is nearer to a charity than a business as far as he is concerned. 'I don't earn anything here, not a coin,' he says honestly. 'For five consecutive months I had to put in money from my own pocket.' If he has a long-term model in mind it is the school set up by another all-time great, Zico, in another corner of Barra where $5 million worth of Japanese sponsorship has created Brazil's most successful footballing academy.

It is impossible to travel around Rio without being reminded of the riches on offer to Brazilians possessed of the right stuff. On the drive along the Barra seafront, the balding, buck-toothed features of Ronaldo – known more affectionately as Ronaldinho here in Brazil – stare out from billboards advertising drinks and sports shoes. Carlos Alberto reckons 80 to 90 per cent of the boys at his school are driven by the dream of emulating Brazil's latest superstar. 'Yes, without doubt because of the commercial development that football has undergone. Today a lawyer does not earn as much as a football player,' he says. 'I think it is also a noble profession today.'

Whether or not his embryonic airfield school can take to the skies remains to be seen. He has been approached by a major Spanish sports company to prepare young players for its domestic league. It is far more likely he will return to the fray as a coach, he admits. In 1996 he came close to forming the first professional side within a Brazilian university, University Estacio de Sa in Rio. 'It is interesting, Mexico has the University of Guadalajara, Chile has the University of Chile, Catholic University,' he muses. 'But things didn't develop.'

In reality Carlos Alberto can spend the rest of his life talking about Mexico and 1970. Articulate and charismatic, *o capitão* has become, more than any other player, the personification of the third – and as far as most Brazilians are concerned – greatest of their World Cup triumphs. 'Here in Brazil, even if we want to, we are not able to forget it,' he says. 'Even today, everybody still talks about that team.' Certainly the subsequent World Cup win in 1994 does not excite the same emotions. 'They won but nobody talks about that team. It was not a team that was remarkable, it was not that real Brazilian football,' he says.

He clearly enjoys the simple pleasure his presence brings his fellow countrymen. I had seen the reaction the first time Carlos Alberto drove me into Rio. Faces would flicker into life at traffic lights, surprise turning to genuine joy at the recognition. As we climb into his car to return once more to downtown Rio, I see it once more as a group of workers from the airfield approach him.

'I cannot give you anything more, *o capitão*,' says one of them, as he extends his hands through the window of Carlos Alberto's car. 'You already have my heart.' The hero smiles, takes the man's hand and presses it in his own. As he eases his car away, he offers a final little wave. On the roadside, the man simply stands watching the car leaving. The broad, broken-toothed smile on his face is beatific.

Just as in the eighty-sixth minute of the Final, *o capitão* is still taking things perfectly in his stride.

CHAPTER III

Crazy As a Fox

---

*'Football reflects the nationality, it mirrors the nation.
Without football we Brazilians do not exist – just as one
would not conceive of Spain without the bullfight . . .'*
                                                    Betty Milan

---

'In England they say goalkeepers are crazy. In Brazil we
are crazy or queer.'

Even if he had not just introduced you to one of
his three daughters and regaled you with tales of the
female·lover he keeps hidden somewhere in Rio, you
would not dwell too long on which category Félix Mialli
Venerando falls into. For instance, he and his family think
it is hilarious they have a motor repair business called
Liar Special Cars.

'*Sim, mentiroso*,' laughs Félix, a pair of hod-carrier
shoulders shuddering as he squeezes in a fresh intake of

industrial-strength cigarette. 'Yes. In English it is a person who lies, isn't it?'

It is a blessed relief to find Félix is still as crazy as a fox. If ever there was a footballer to whom Tommy Docherty's most famous dictum truly applies – what was it, 'you don't have to be unhinged to play this game, but it helps'? – it was Félix Mialli Venerando. Without a touch of madness, and a sense of humour as wide as the Amazon Delta to go with it, he would never have emerged from the 1970 World Cup intact.

The small, slightly underfed-looking Félix was the butt of the vast majority of the jokes that flew through the rarefied, Mexican air in 1970. He was Félix the distinctly uncatlike keeper. He was the footballing version of the old Harry Truman joke that anybody could be President. Anybody could play in goal with Pelé, Tostão and co. in front of him. In the team of all the talents, Félix was the man with the gift for high farce. There were times when he looked as if he was auditioning for one of the Brian Rix knockabouts so popular on British television at the time. While Rix was forever floundering around on the floor looking for his trousers, Félix was on the grass grappling for a ball already nestling in the back of his net.

There was something heroic about his survival. He played in every match in the tournament, and even shone in one or two. Today, fast approaching his sixtieth birthday, it turns out life is little different. The most unintentionally comic goalkeeper in history is still laughing last and loudest.

Félix is one of three players I hope to find in São Paulo,

less than an hour south of Rio by air. Brazil's biggest – and the world's third most populous – city couldn't present a starker contrast to its flashy, ribald rival. If life in Rio is a Jackson Pollock painting, São Paulo is the endless background of the glummest L.S. Lowry. At first its nondescript, industrial greyness seems no different from any other overdeveloped city. It is only when you have been driving for an hour or so on the road from Guarulhos airport without a change of scenery that the truth dawns. All that happens when you eventually get into the centre is the endless factories change into endless skyscrapers. When Le Corbusier came here in the 1930s he mapped out a community with half a dozen towers. Six decades on there are more skyscrapers than there is sky. If the economist Schumacher was right and small is beautiful, then São Paulo is the third least beautiful city on earth. I do not ever want to see the first or second.

Félix runs the car repair shop at the business where he works with his daughter Ligia and son-in-law Angelo. (LIAR, it turns out, is an acronym of their initials and that of their son Rafael.) It stands in the heart of a vast, industrial no-man's land somewhere in the run-down Tatuape district.

São Paulo has 4.6 million cars – almost one for every two of its 9.8 million citizens. It is an impressive statistic until, that is, you realize no one actually gets anywhere by road. São Paulo also has the world's worst traffic jams. If you want a sound investment in São Paulo, try one of the city's booming helicopter taxi companies. In an attempt to ease the crisis, drivers are allocated alternate days when they can and cannot drive. In theory the police can spot wrong-doers by a letter on their licence plate. Needless to

79

say, the Paulistas have found a way around that one – a spare set of plates in the trunk.

The drive to Tatuape takes us through a seemingly endless wasteland of derelict dumps and scrapheaps. After half an hour or so crawling past the cutters' yards and crushing plants we realise that this is clearly a sacred section of the city, the place where all those cars come to die.

The Liar warehouse stands on the edge of a tower-block estate and a four-lane freeway on the Avenida Ver Abel Ferreira. Félix emerges from the back of the garage, greying, brilliantined but still recognizable from the old photographs. He looks like a less cranky version of Martin Landau's Bela Lugosi in the movie *Ed Wood*.

If he had not been something of a *mentiroso* himself, the young Félix might never have found his way into football. He was born on Christmas Eve 1937, in the Italian-dominated Mooca area of São Paulo, the second of five children. His father worked as an engineer in a nylon stocking factory called Mussolini but it was his mother who dictated affairs at home.

A stern, strict woman, she – like most of the team's mothers as it turns out – disapproved of Félix playing football. 'She was against it,' he says, shooting a plume of smoke skyward as we sit and talk in an office high above the workshop floor. 'My mother never wanted me to play football.' For Félix, however, there was no passion to compete with it. 'I think it is in the Brazilian blood, every boy sleeps with a football under his pillow.' It was while his son – and his wife – slept that Félix's father surreptitiously helped his son fulfil his dreams. He would leave home for work at 5.30 a.m. with his son's *chuteira*, football boots, hidden in his work bag. Félix would collect the boots from the Mussolini factory which was on his way to school. 'It was our secret,' he says with a conspiratorial smile.

Like every Brazilian boy – or at least, every sane, heterosexual one, if we believe Félix – he wanted to emulate Friedenreich and Leônidas, the great goalscoring heroes of the 1930s and 40s. 'I was a centre-forward,' he says. His courageousness – or perhaps emerging craziness – in throwing himself around on the streets soon marked him out as a promising goalkeeper, however. Any disappointment he might have had at discovering his best position was at the non-glory end was relatively short-lived.

'Here in Brazil if a player is no good playing in front, he'll be a goalkeeper. But not in my case. I started playing in goal because generally nobody wanted to play there and I was very courageous. We played on the streets and I would dive on the pavements,' he says, with an unsettling wink. 'I started to like it.'

His deception of his mother continued even after he found a place in a junior side at the Clube Atletico Juventus, at their ground on the Rua Javari. Félix had found a post as an office boy in the dispatch department of a large company, Maquinas Piratininga, and had convinced his mother he was on the road to a career in accountancy. As it turned out, double-entry book-keeping was his route to a career in professional goalkeeping.

By now Santos had expressed their interest in having him join as a *juvenil* goalkeeper and he had begun to leave work early to travel to their ground an hour or so away. The great Gilmar, like Félix a product of Juventus, was already at the famous Vila Belmiro stadium on the coast. The director whose permission Félix would seek to leave work early also happened to be a director of Portuguesa. 'He asked me: "Why am I setting you free to train for Santos? If you are good go to Portuguesa".' Félix showed the Portuguesa goalkeeping coach Valdinho de Morais what he could do. While Santos were away in Argentina, São Paulo's then leading club snapped him up instead.

Félix's role models were keepers like the star of São Paulo football, Oberlan Tacame of Palmeiras. 'He was a phenomenon, a legend,' he says. At Portuguesa he was groomed by Morais, who was one of the best goalkeeping coaches of his time. With his spindly legs and slight build, Félix hardly filled the goalmouth with a domineering presence. His nickname at Portuguesa was *papel*, paper. 'Because I was so thin.' Yet he refused his coach's advice to take up weight-training to bulk himself up. 'I would have become a robot,' he says. 'I was always against body-building, except maybe a little bit for the legs, for the power to propel.'

His rail-thin frame wrapped in the red and green hoops of Portuguesa, Félix cut one of the more colourful figures in São Paulo football. What he lacked in physical presence he more than made up for in bravery. At times his courage bordered on the reckless and he suffered a succession of injuries. He was also the most voluble goalkeeper in Brazil, often walking off the pitch hoarse from his efforts to be heard above the huge crowds at São Paulo's great stadia, Pacaembu and Morumbi.

One way and another, Félix could not fail to catch the eye and by 1965 Aimore Moreira had drafted him into his vast squad for England. Félix played in a Brazilian XI against Hungary at Pacaembu. After a faultless display in what would prove a false dawn, 5–0 win he was hopeful of a place in Moreira's final 22 for England.

When he relegated Félix to the *azulona* squad, 'the unlucky ones', Moreira may actually have been doing his career a favour. Both Gilmar and the second-string keeper, Manga, returned to Brazil in disgrace. Gilmar soon announced his retirement, Manga left for Nacional in Uruguay and Félix quickly emerged as the new No. 1 in a new-look Brazilian squad.

Félix was Saldanha's first choice in all the eliminators and he had, by common consent, done well enough, keeping clean sheets against Paraguay, Venezuela and Colombia in the away matches. But when the quixotic coach returned from Europe, obsessed with the idea that his team was about to suffer something akin to the Luftwaffe's assault on 1940s London, he dropped Félix for the bulkier, younger Leao of Palmeiras.

Félix fumbles for a new cigarette before he can bring himself to speak of Saldanha. 'Saldanha alleged that I was thin, that I had no strong body, that I could not bear the shock of those big guys,' he says, flicking fiercely at his lighter. 'I was always courageous, I would dive at people's feet. I had broken fingers, a broken jaw, I had fractured three or four ribs. If I was scared of crashing into these guys I would not have been in goal.' Félix extends his right hand. One of his fingers is crooked grotesquely, a permanent reminder of his willingness to take the heaviest hits.

To be fair, some of the coach's excuses did verge on the ludicrous. 'Saldanha said it was the rainy season in

Mexico and I would not know how to play with gloves,' he says, arching an eyebrow. Félix made a point of playing in the Final with gloves.

When Saldanha finally tilted at one windmill too many, no one, not even Pelé, was happier to see Zagalo taking up the reins. 'It was excellent for me,' chuckles Félix. Zagalo reversed Saldanha's decision, restoring Félix and dropping Leao from the squad. The younger keeper never forgave his replacement. On his final day with the squad, Leao threw a prima donna-ish tantrum effectively accusing Félix of being Zagalo's puppet. 'He left crying,' says Félix, seeming to suggest that Leao may be from the less barmy branch of the goalkeeping union.

Félix still recalls the moment when Leao was later called back to the squad and to camp Guanajuato. 'Zagalo asked my opinion and I said: "Call that boy". The place was a castle, the door creaked and Leao came in. I said: "Congratulations". He said: "Justice has been done!".' Félix shrugs. 'I'm not the kind of person to keep rancour; I think he is.'

In the run up to the first match, a poll of Brazilian football fans gave Félix a resounding vote of confidence by naming him their number one No. 1. He put the fact that 92 per cent thought all three of the squad's options inferior to Gilmar to the back of his mind.

At the age of thirty-three, Félix was comfortably the senior member of the squad. 'I was the ancient one,' he says with evident pride. He roomed with the youngest player, the teenage Marco Antonio, his team-mate at Fluminense, where he had moved by now. With the squad's other senior professionals, Gérson, Piazza, Brito and Carlos Alberto, Félix served on a five-man players' committee that would represent the squad's cause in meetings with Havelange, Zagalo and the men of the CBD. The quintet kept the younger players in line. Their message was clear: 'You may have another chance but we may not.' 'We were a little bit older, we knew we would not play in the next World Cup,' he says. 'We said to each other. "Let's see if we can finish our career in a good way".'

If he was a father figure, he was also – with Brito – one of the squad's two jesters-in-chief. Félix's off-beam humour was no respecter of reputations. Everyone had to have a nickname. Brito was *cavalo*, the horse, Rivellino *orelha*, big ears. Piazza was *PePe*, Clodoaldo, *corro*, his nickname at Santos. Jairzinho, J. J. or *furacão*. Carlos Alberto was simply *capitão*. Pelé was far happier being called *criola* or *negrão*, neither of which needs translation, than he was being called, as Brito sometimes did, *o rei*, the king. 'He was a simple man and he didn't like that,' says Félix.

Tostão arrived at Guanajuato, sensitive, nervous and insular, after a major eye operation. His parents had even followed him to Mexico, worried at his state of mind. Félix's idea of a welcome was to provide him with his freshly minted, Mexican monicker. He took one look at Tostão, still badly marked from his surgery, and knew instantly what to say. 'Cheer up egg-face,' he laughs. He shoots me another one of his looks. 'I thought it might brighten his mood a little.'

The intellectual Tostão may have found it hard to appreciate, but there was method in Félix's peculiar brand of madness. The more positive and optimistic the atmosphere inside their fortress, the less the squad would worry about the ugly mood of pessimism swilling around back in Rio, São Paulo and the rest of Brazil.

Brazil claims much that is unique in its football. The extraordinary fickleness of its fans and its press in particular is one of its unsung traits, however. The vast majority of the Brazilian media was convinced its squad was too weak in defence to mount a serious assault on the Europeans – England, Italy, Germany and Czechoslovakia in particular. 'It is easier to find a giraffe than an optimist,' mused the poet and football fanatic Nelson Rodriguez at the time. No one took more flak than Félix. 'I was the most criticized player in the team,' he says defiantly. 'It was unfair but I'm the kind of guy who can swallow it.'

Predictably his greatest detractor was João Saldanha, by now restored to his natural habitat at the typewriter and in the radio booth. Petras' soft goal in the opening match only provided him with more bullets to fire. With England on the horizon, he was unequivocal: Félix Must Go. As it turned out the defending world champions inspired him. That Félix himself is a little fuzzy in his recollection of his – and the tournament's – most accomplished game is largely down to Francis Lee.

'A team of thieves and drunks'
Brazil v. England, Guadalajara, 7 June 1970.

By the summer of 1970, against almost impossible odds, Alf Ramsey had succeeded in lowering his stock even further in the eyes of the Mexican masses. By now, even the most trivial of the England manager's movements were driving the hosts crazy.

Ramsey's squad had taken a leaf from the Brazilian book by planning their day-to-day life in meticulous detail. Carefully measured intakes of sodium tablets had proved a major success as a means of lessening the dehydrating effects of the baking Mexican heat. To avoid outbreaks of Montezuma's Revenge, Ramsey had also insisted his players drink the squad's own supplies of imported orange juice rather than the local produce. Gallons of English juice was flown in to their camp at the Hilton Hotel. To the Mexicans, producers of some of the world's better oranges, it was another slap in the face from the arrogant colonialists.

Even more insulting was the news that Ramsey had shipped a British-made bus over in advance of his party. The new British Leyland coach boasted air-conditioning, a galley with a fridge, tea and coffee machines, a stereo system and – most important of all for travelling footballers – three card tables. The team driver Sid Brown had picked the bus up in New Orleans where it had been shipped from Southampton. 'Do you think we have not yet discovered the wheel or the internal combustion engine?' ran one headline.

By the time Bobby Moore had been falsely arrested for 'jewel theft' in Bogotá en route to Mexico, and the aerophobic Jeff Astle had climbed off a plane in an extremely 'tired and emotional' condition, the die had been cast. 'A team of thieves and drunks', one newspaper called them. England entered the tournament as the team Mexico loved to loathe. The Union Jack was roundly booed as it entered the Azteca during the opening ceremony.

The English had done little to improve their image during their first match against Rumania at Guadalajara.

Their football was hardly the stuff of world champions. There were positives. Geoff Hurst picked up where he had left off at Wembley in 1966 with a sharply taken, left-foot goal in the second half. Terry Cooper, the attacking Leeds left-back, added a new menace to the supremely cool defence of Moore and Banks. In general though England looked uninspiring. Even the world's favourite English footballer, Bobby Charlton, suffering more than most in the heat, couldn't engineer opportunities to let fly in the rarefied air.

As they watched the evening slide shows at the Suites Caribes, few in the Brazilian camp believed they had seen the real England. Félix knew the threat would come from Charlton and Alan Ball in midfield, Geoff Hurst and Martin Peters up front. If all four were familiar from television highlights of Wembley four years earlier, England's other star attacker, Manchester City's Francis Lee, was a new face. He would not remain a stranger for long.

On Sunday 7 June, Bobby Moore led his men on the field trying to look unintimidated by the furnace fierce heat and the rabidly anti-English crowd in the Jalisco. (Many of the 70,000 had spent the previous night camped outside England's hotel chanting 'Brasil, Brasil' so loudly some of the players had to move rooms.) As the sun reached its apex in the midday sky he issued final reminders of Ramsey's game plan. Mullery – as he had done success-fully at the Maracanã the previous year – would stick like glue to Pelé. If his batteries failed him in the heat, Nobby Stiles would take his teeth out and bite at the great man's heels for the remainder of the match. Both full-backs, Terry Cooper and Tommy Wright, would be encouraged to take on the Brazilian flanks. Lee and Charlton were under instruction to shoot on sight. Above all, Félix was to be put under an aerial bombardment.

For the first ten minutes or so all went worryingly to plan for the English. Lee warmed Félix's gloveless hands with a wicked cross-cum-shot from the right flank. In their first serious attack, however, Pelé and all Brazil thought they had scored. With a superb pass off the outside of his foot, Carlos Alberto set Jairzinho off on a run to the dead-ball line. His cross eluded Cooper and climbed its way towards Pelé at the far post. Pelé's ability in the air had been one of the wonders of the footballing world for fifteen years. In all that time he had rarely met a header so cleanly. He was shouting '*gol*' as it arrowed in towards the right-hand post of Banks' goal. Somehow, however, Banks had made up the ground from the near post and had launched himself downwards. In mid-air he was able to claw at the bouncing ball and deflect it around the post. The implacable Stoke City keeper picked himself up as if he had performed nothing more than a routine save. The expressions on the faces of the Brazilian players – Pelé admitted later he simply stood there swearing – and the fraternal smile on Bobby Moore's face as he ruffled his keeper's hair, told a rather different story. 'I clapped, it was the best save I have ever seen,' says Félix, shaking his head at the memory.

All too soon it was his turn to be tested, and once more it was Lee who was at the heart of Brazil's troubles. The industrious Mullery released Tommy Wright for a run on the right flank. The Everton full-back's cross drifted over the Brazilian defence to find Lee unmarked less than ten yards out. Félix brilliantly parried the Manchester City man's flying header but then fumbled the ball as he hit the floor. In the split second that the ball was free, Lee flicked out a right-foot kick that caught the keeper full in his face.

Félix's arms are outstretched. 'It was one of the greatest saves I made in the World Cup,' he says. 'I let the ball loose, but not that much. Lee kicked me and it was a knockout.' As he lay on the floor, Brito, Carlos Alberto and Rivellino surrounded the stocky Englishman. Despite his claims that it had been a legitimate 50–50 ball, Lee was booked for the foul by the Israeli referee Abraham Klein. Félix says he was oblivious not only to the mêlée and the booking, but to the remainder of the first half. 'I spent the first half not knowing where I was, doing everything automatically. It was the same as a boxer who has been knocked out but keeps standing.' Luckily for Félix, England's assault on his goal abated for the remainder of the half.

As usual at half-time Félix and his friend Gérson were greeted in the tunnel by an assistant with two lit cigarettes. He swears it was the cigarette that revived him for the second half. Félix has watched the tape of the match time and time again. He is still of the same opinion as he was twenty-seven years ago. 'It was a wicked move,' he says, staring at the floor and shaking his head for a moment.

As they let England roast under the sun before beginning the second half, Félix had time for another cigarette and a pep-talk from Zagalo. Some of the Little Ant's famous luck rubbed off. Félix won't deny he led a charmed life in a second half which fulfilled all the predictions of those who had called the match the tournament's Final in all but name.

The deep and abiding respect the two managers held for each other was mirrored in Ramsey and Zagalo's preparations for the match. Both sides played with a level of tactical sophistication that elevated the match to the footballing equivalent of Spassky v. Fischer. 'Even we were impressed,' Bobby Charlton said after watching a recording of the game at the England hotel later. 'You could take that film and use it for coaching.'

After fourteen minutes of finessing, however, Brazil took the lead with a piece of inspiration from Tostão. The diminutive No. 9 embarrassed Bobby Moore with a nutmeg, found Pelé with a magnificent, blind pass then watched as his striking partner drew England defenders towards him before feeding the onrushing Jairzinho. From five yards even Banks couldn't keep the ball out.

In an unforgettable final half hour, Ramsey took off Charlton and sent the lanky Jeff Astle of West Brom on to lead a new heavyweight assault on the Brazilian goal. Manchester City's Colin Bell replaced Félix's tiring nemesis Lee. Inspired by Moore who made amends for his error against Tostão with the most beautifully timed tackle anyone had ever seen on Jairzinho, England took charge. A sustained spell of pressure culminated in Ball hitting the top of the crossbar with an angled shot and Astle blazing wide after Everaldo had swung at thin air in the heart of the penalty area.

For Astle it would remain the most painful memory of his career, a bad dream exacerbated by the fact it has recurred a million times since on television. If it is any consolation, Félix is convinced he played his own part in forcing the most infamous miss of the tournament. 'I didn't think he would score because when I saw Everaldo miss it, I moved to close him down. He tried to place the ball away from me and shot it out of play.' When I suggest he should still have been beaten with ease, Félix smiles and nods. 'Perhaps I was lucky?'

Félix doesn't offer any dissent from what is, by now, the common view that England were by far the best side Brazil were to face. Given that they were the only side he kept a clean sheet against and that his performance forced a major reappraisal of the Brazilians' so-called weak link, he would have been truly unhinged to say otherwise.

The day before the match, Félix had been angered by a column Saldanha had written in the Mexican paper, *Esto*. 'He said Brazil must change the goalkeeper. He is thin, he can't take the crashing that will be the English tactics,' he says, still riled. Of all his performances in Mexico it is the one of which he is most proud, not least because it forced Saldanha to eat his words.

Few moments in the campaign brought a broader smile to Félix's face than his sudden elevation from zero to hero at a press conference on the Monday after the England match. His face is beaming again now. 'The following day, the English journalists said: "We were betrayed by the Brazilian Peronistas!" He was nothing like we were told.'

Within days, however, Félix had reverted to his former erratic self, conceding two soft goals against the Rumanians. Of the two more he conceded in the 4–2 win over Peru in the quarter-final, only the first, from Gallardo, was realistically stoppable. He had picked the ball up wide on the left and looked as if he was going to cross. The power of the Peruvian's shot left Félix once more looking sheepish. 'I went with my hands to palm it away, but it was so strong it took my hands backwards,' Félix admits.

He saved his most schizophrenic performance for the semi-final against Uruguay. In the seventeenth minute of an already nervous match, Brito's poor clearance presented Morales with the chance to free the muscular Cubilla out wide on the right. As Piazza closed in on him, the Uruguayan was still struggling to bring the bobbling ball under control. The lame shot he hit off his shin was borne of desperation rather than hope. No one was more amazed at the outcome than Cubilla himself. Félix had somehow positioned himself on the near post and found himself hopelessly wrong-footed. He could only watch in horror as the ball drifted across the face of his goal then kicked off the pitch into the net at the opposite post. As Brito and Piazza stood over him, he simply sat on the pitch in despair. As a piece of goalkeeping it belonged to a hungover Sunday morning on Hackney Marshes rather than a World Cup semi-final.

Félix was never braver than when he held his hands up afterwards and admitted his crime. Today he is no less honest. 'I made a mistake,' he says simply. He offers an explanation – of sorts. He says something about the Guadalajara pitch having been remarked for the game and two goal lines being visible. Momentarily confused by where he was, he compounded the error by tying his feet in knots. He simply wishes Cubilla had connected cleanly and hit a more powerful shot at him. 'It is much easier for a goalkeeper to suffer a goal from a mishit,' he grimaces.

Yet before the match had ended, Félix had redeemed himself with a crucial save to deny Cubilla a second when Brazil were clinging to a 2–1 lead. He ranks the save, a reflex leap to clear a close-range header, with his stop from Lee as the best of his World Cup. 'I didn't know how I could fly the way I flew,' he smiles. 'We had about seven minutes left and we were leading 2–1. Besides being an excellent save it came at a difficult moment. If it had been 2–2 we would have had extra time. If I'm not wrong we scored our third goal straight afterwards.'

After the torrential thunderstorms of the previous three nights, Félix took the pitch for the Final in gloves. 'To show Saldanha I could,' he snarls. Seven minutes into the game Luigi Riva let rip from 30 yards. Félix saw the ball all the way and deflected it over the crossbar with an air of calming confidence. He is flattered when I recall the save as a good one. 'It was important psychologically. A goal seven minutes into the game changes a lot,' he nods.

The blame for the Italians' goal in the first half lay primarily with Clodoaldo, whose extravagant backheel to Brito misfired leaving Boninsegna with a clear run in on goal. But Félix did little to help matters with his Banzai charge off his line and out of the penalty area. He collided with Brito and left Boninsegna arguing with Riva about who would put the ball in the empty net.

His second half was not without its fraught moments. Twice he miscalculated as crosses came in, but twice he was saved by his defenders. As Gérson took a grip on the game, however, he was – with the rest of the world – content to watch the mesmerizing football unfolding in front of him. At the final whistle Félix ran to jump on Gérson's back. 'I cried, laughed, jumped, everything. I didn't know what else to do.'

Two moments in the aftermath of the Final will always live with him. Among the pressmen offering handshakes and hugs in the dressing room afterwards had been a Rio journalist, Jacinto Vitoti, whose columns in the *Diario* newspaper had been among the most cruel and critical of Félix.

'He came to me when I was under the shower,' Félix recalls. 'He said: "Hey, Félix, sorry I was the one who criticized you the most. But I didn't think you were in good enough condition." I told him, "Hey, Jacinto, it doesn't matter, now it is only happiness". He gave me his hand, he was wearing a jacket and tie, and as he did so I pulled him under the shower with me.' As Félix drowned the *Diario* man, he started singing, '*Vale tudo hoje*, anything goes today.'

The second came later in the press centre within the Azteca complex. Brazilian radio interviewers had arranged a live, telephone link-up with Félix's family back home. 'I didn't know about this. They told me my eldest daughter Ligia wanted to speak with me,' he explains. 'She was seven years old at the time. She said: "Hey, Papa, they said so many bad things about you, but you are a champion of the world". I started crying and that was the end of the interview.'

Félix will defend the contribution he, Carlos Alberto, Brito, Piazza and Everaldo made to the campaign to his last, nicotine-filled breath. 'It was a great unfairness,' he says of the criticism they received before, during – and even after – Mexico. 'A great unfairness.' His sense of injustice would only deepen with the years and the shabby treatment that followed.

Félix remained at Fluminense but was eased out of the

Brazilian squad for the 1974 World Cup. Leao finally got his revenge for 1970 by taking the No. 1 shirt in West Germany and again in Argentina four years later. Félix retired as a player in 1977, just short of his fortieth birthday. For the next three years he remained as goalkeeping coach in Rio.

The final insult came in 1980 when he was coaching Fluminense's junior side. He had travelled to São Paulo from Rio in advance of his side to organize facilities for a cup match. 'I had come ahead of the junior team to arrange accommodation. When the team arrived they came with a new trainer.'

Félix, furious, refused to go quietly and sued. 'I was very aggrieved by the way I was fired,' he says. 'It was another injustice.' Fluminense succeeded in dragging the case through the courts for eleven painful years. Félix paid his legal fees by selling electronic equipment at the Ponto Frio department store and coaching at a second division club Madureira. Eventually he won a settlement of around $30,000. Fluminense were also obliged to reinstate him, although he found it impossible to remain at the club that had given him such happy years.

Instead Félix coached smaller clubs in Rio. He returned to his roots and Portuguesa where he worked as a junior coach before leaving the game for good. When his son-in-law offered him a post in the repair shop at Liar Special Cars, Félix accepted.

He had run his own business buying and selling cars while still playing for Fluminense. He called his agency, on São Paulo's 24 de Maio, *Gato* Félix, Félix The Cat. 'People came to see me more than to buy cars,' he says, shooting me another sardonic smile. 'But in the end they bought cars.'

Today he lives nearby in Tatuape, the neighbourhood that produced Britain's best-loved Brazilian import, Juninho. If he has not gone on to make the millions of Pelé and Carlos Alberto, he is happy to have a job and a family and to have escaped the penury and the scandal that players like Garrincha suffered. 'In my time I had examples of well-known players that died in poverty. I am not poor, I'm not in a bad situation, thank God.'

To a generation of Brazilians, Félix's association with the 1970 triumph is now nothing but a happy one. The old jibes may still pinch, but the adulation more than makes up for it. I had seen it myself when the taxi driver heard we were travelling to see him. 'Félix, how is the old rascal?' he had laughed. As Felix had introduced himself at the warehouse, the driver had been there in the queue for a handshake. An unmetered, discount ride to the airport was fixed on the back of the experience, the highlight of his week, he said.

'Money, you know, today we have it, tomorrow we don't,' says Felix, taking one final pull on another cigarette, then stubbing it on the floor, as he prepares to head back down to the shop floor. 'What you really earn is the recognition, and, after I was discredited, I fought for that.'

That recognition comes wherever he is in Brazil, he says. 'Sometimes I'm with my wife or my daughter and a guy passes by and shouts "Hey Félix" as if he has known me for twenty years. I answer with the same enthusiasm and my wife or my daughter asks me "Who's that?".'

He leans forward, and offers one last, maniacal arch of his eyebrows. 'I say: "I don't know, but they know me".'

The room lights up with laughter. Once more though, it is Félix who laughs longest and loudest.

CHAPTER IV

Ipanema Icons

With the possible exception of Alf Ramsey's PR person, the least enviable job in Mexico in 1970 was marking the man designated Brazil's *ponta direita*, or right winger. In all six matches, the magnificent, muscular menace of Jairzinho was as great – and at times greater – than even Pelé himself.

No defender in the world, not even Bobby Moore, succeeded in taming him for an entire match. Jairzinho scored famously in every match of the finals, but even that statistic failed to do justice to the brilliance of his play as provider as well as predator. It is perhaps then, hardly surprising that almost thirty years on he is proving the most elusive member of the beautiful team once more.

Even before I arrived in Brazil, approaches to him at his Rio office had been met with a firm refusal to meet unless money exchanged hands. Explanations that his colleagues were all contributing their time for nothing, seemed to make no impression on him. During my stay in Rio, his words had been as direct as his running was in Mexico. 'It is a professional matter,' ran his response. 'I expect to be paid like a professional.' As I move on to São Paulo there is talk of intervention from senior figures at his old club Botafogo. Breath is not being held, however. 'Jairzinho is very difficult,' seems to be the consensus in footballing circles.

In my dealings with Gérson and Carlos Alberto it had already become obvious that a core of the team have remained close. Pelé has stayed friendly with his two fellow *cobras*. The trio are inevitably pressed into punditry duties together when World Cups come around. Rivellino and Tostão are also enlisted by the big stations. Jairzinho, by contrast, seems to have slipped from the limelight. The more I learn about him, the more a pattern emerges. As in 1970, he remains something of an outsider.

Jair Ventura Filha was born in the northern Rio suburb of Duque de Caxias on Christmas Day in 1944. His prodigious speed and strength on the ball was quickly spotted by the coaches at Botafogo where he signed as an amateur in 1961 at the age of sixteen. He turned professional shortly after winning a gold medal for Brazil in the 1963 Pan-American Games. It was at Botafogo that he had been first called Jairzinho, 'little Jair'. The name distinguished him from the then more famous international Jair da Rosa Pinto of Portuguesa. It was on the terraces of the Maracanã that he won his distinctive nickname *furacão*, the hurricane.

With Gérson, Tostão and Brito, Jairzinho had been one of the new generation to witness the humiliation of Goodison Park at first hand. He played in all three matches but offered little or no evidence of the greatness that was to come.

By 1970, however, his star was in the ascendant. He had

scored freely in the eliminators and had developed a good understanding with Gérson and Pelé in particular. Only Rogério offered a serious threat to his position on the right wing. By the final warm-up in Rio against Austria, his rival's indifferent form and injury problems had effectively ended his challenge.

Jairzinho arrived in Mexico determined to make amends for 1966. He was one of the players to benefit most from the Cooper Tests and Captain Coutinho's disciplinarian training regime. Photographs of a shirtless Jairzinho at the training camps reveal a heavily muscled upper body and a powerfully built all-round athlete. In the sprinting tests he was comfortably the quickest of the 22-man squad over 50 metres.

From the opening match against the Czechs, the quiet man of the squad did his talking on the pitch. Jairzinho scored twice, first collecting a Gérson probe, flicking the ball over Viktor's head before volleying extravagantly home, then crowning an irresistible, barnstorming run down the right with a perfectly placed shot inside the right-hand post. From then on he could not lose the goalscoring habit.

He scored again against England and Rumania in the group matches and Peru in the quarter-final. In Gérson's absence, Rivellino and Paulo Cézar had taken over the role of provider. Both provided passes that gave him the half-a-yard headstart he required to skin defences alive. Only Bobby Moore, with the most perfectly timed tackle of the tournament, worked out a way of curbing him.

Yet there was much more to Jairzinho's game than mere bullish power and pace. No one suffered more from the

Uruguayan tackling in the semi-final. It was a measure of the restraint Zagalo had instilled in him that he failed to react once. Instead he replied in the best manner possible, latching on to an impeccable through ball from Tostão to outrun Mujica and score what would prove the decisive goal in the match.

His contribution to the Final illustrated his abilities without the ball too. Against Italy Jairzinho's most effective work was done in drawing his man-marker Facchetti out of position in the middle of the pitch. Carlos Alberto wreaked carnage in his wake.

The reward for his selflessness came in the seventieth minute. As he forced Pelé's knock-down over the line, Jairzinho's place in history was assured. No player before or since has matched the flying *furacão*'s record of scoring in every match of a World Cup finals stage. In the cat-and-mouse climate of modern World Cups, it is hard to see how anyone ever will.

In the years immediately after Mexico, Jairzinho remained in Rio and at Botafogo. He suffered a badly broken leg in 1971 and was sidelined for most of the following season. For a while he became something of an Ipanema icon, one of the faces featured whenever European camera crews came to capture the spirit of Brazil and its beach-loving football playboys. By the time it came to defend Brazil's world champion status, however, Jairzinho – with Valdomiro of Internacional and Leivinha of Palmeiras – became the spearhead of a new-look attack.

Starved of the ball, space and the genius he had been surrounded by four years earlier, he became an increasingly isolated figure. He scored against Zaire and Argentina, but was helpless as the campaign fell apart in the second stage of the competition against Cruyff and Holland.

Back in Brazil his frustration was obvious. In 1975 he was banned for punching a referee while playing for Botafogo. Soon he had left Brazil for a brief and largely unrewarding spell at Olympique Marseilles. He retired from the game shortly afterwards, 102 international caps and 42 goals for Brazil the lasting statistical legacy of his greatness.

Jairzinho moved into a career as an agent rather than a manager. Here, at least, he rediscovered a little of the inspiration of the past. His most spectacular discovery was the buck-toothed son of a telephone company worker called Nelia Nazario Lima. He spotted the boy playing for one of the city's smaller indoor football sides, the Ramos Social Club. The Limas called their little boy Dadado because of his inability to pronounce his name properly. Everyone else simply called him by his Christian name, Ronaldo.

When, three years ago, Ronaldo moved to Europe and PSV Eindhoven, Jairzinho's ten per cent apparently ran into six figures. The telephone numbers that ended up in Ronaldo's pocket allowed his father to quit his old job and set up a pizzeria on the Copacabana. According to sports reporters at the *Jornal do Brasil* I spoke to, Jairzinho's contract with Ronaldo qualified him for a share of his next transfer move as well. In 1995, the player's move to Barcelona brought another bumper payday.

It had been during my time in Rio that the first rumours of Ronaldo's world-record move to Inter Milan began circulating. By the time the mind-bending deal was clinched, it emerged that the Italians were giving Ronaldo a nine-year contract worth £3.7 million a year, Barcelona a further £18 million and three agents a total of £8.8 million. Jairzinho was not, apparently, a member of the fortunate trio.

'He is not a very happy man,' one of the *Journal* sports reporters said. The *furacão's* taciturn behaviour was perhaps not so surprising after all.

In the heady days that followed the 1970 triumph, Jairzinho's most regular partner on the beach volleyball games on Ipanema and Copacabana had been the lantern-jawed Paulo Cézar. A day or so after I leave Rio, resigned to missing out on the team's No. 7, my researcher Pedro spotted its unofficial No. 12 in a social kick-around at a smart sports club at the foot of the mountains near the Lagoa area.

Today Paulo Cézar is regarded as something of a lost soul – a slightly bitter figure now on the fringes of the game he learned to play amidst abject poverty in Botafogo in Rio, near the São João Batista Cemetery. His football education had come on the streets. 'I played barefoot, with a ball made from my mother's socks. I took the socks and filled them with newspaper,' he explained.

As he had begun to play more organized football, his precocious abilities were spotted by Marinho Rodrigues de Oliveira, one of Botafogo's most famous coaches in the 1950s and 60s. Such was Oliveira's affection for the boy, he seems to have adopted Paulo Cézar and his brother and taken them with him as he accepted a series of coaching posts all over South America. Paulo Cézar spent his childhood in Honduras, Peru and Colombia.

It was in Colombia that he made his mark, as a fourteen-year-old prodigy. By the time he was sixteen he was on the books at Flamengo back in Rio. His talent had been marshalled by Mario Zagalo. When Zagalo took over from Saldanha, few were surprised when Paulo Cézar's stock within the squad began to rise.

His explosive temper and playboy reputation made him a controversial figure within Brazil. Extravagant though his talents were, there were those fans who wondered about his willingness to adapt to Zagalo's 'two-shirted' philosophy. Unlike his rival Rivellino, covering back when possession was lost was not an aspect of the game in which Paulo Cézar had shown much interest.

He is honest enough to admit that for the younger, more highly charged members of the squad like him, the discipline of the *concentração* was hard to bear. He admits he, Edu and Marco Antonio fell foul of the team's adjutant-in-chief, Admiral Jeronimo Batsos. The players had been allowed out on one evening a week. Cézar, who had celebrated his twenty-first birthday during the tournament, had been caught with a group of local girls at the rear gate to the camp. The Admiral's ultimatum to the players was simple. 'If I see you behind there one more time you'll be dropped.'

'We were scared,' Paulo Cézar confesses.

If Paulo Cézar understood the choice before him, however, the flamboyant, good-looking Marco Antonio seemingly did not. According to Paulo Cézar, Marco Antonio's misbehaviour cost him a place in the first-choice side in Mexico and a place in football's immortals to go with it.

'It was not that he was irresponsible, but he was just a teenager and he lost his mind, he was flying,' Paulo Cézar explained. The *cobras* were at the heart of the decision-making process that promoted the more dependable, mature Everaldo to the first team. 'The guys had a meeting. It was better for everybody.' (I would hear the story confirmed elsewhere. 'He wanted to joke around, he did not accept the rules. The players themselves decided against him,' the respected *Jornal do Brasil* columnist, Oldemario Touguinho told me.)

While Marco Antonio would have to wait until the quarter-final for his one and only run out in Mexico, Paulo Cézar found himself in the thick of things immediately. With the odds on Gérson making it through the entire tournament slim to non-existent, he had already been briefed on how to shadow the *papagaio*. 'I was already prepared. There was no need to say anything,' he says now.

As Gérson was nursed through the tournament, Paulo Cézar became the team's twelfth man. He had come on for Gérson near the end of the win against the Czechs. Against England, however, he played the whole match.

He becomes animated at the mere memory of Moore, Labone, Mullery and company. '*Foda*,' he called them at one point, 'fuckers'. 'They had that arrogant way, they were looking at us from top to bottom. Those guys looked at us like we were shit. I almost told them "fuck yourselves".'

His dislike of the English attitude clearly played its part in the immaculate performance he turned in. While Jairzinho made Terry Cooper's life difficult, Paulo Cézar gave Wright on the other flank an uncomfortable afternoon too. Alf Ramsey had warned Wright beforehand: 'He can beat you.' Paulo Cézar duly did just that, repeatedly.

He had come close to breaking the deadlock with a vicious dipping and swerving right-footed shot that Banks did well to push round a post early in the second half. He admits he felt his 'heart in his hands' when he saw the giant figure of Jeff Astle lumbering on for the final assault on Félix.

Any suggestion that Brazil may have been fortunate to come away with a win draws an instant response, however. 'No fucking way,' he snaps. 'Brazil played better, we were much more superior.' Clearly the win represented the highlight of his personal World Cup. 'We knew that the team that won that game would be champion of the world,' he says.

Against Rumania, with Rivellino and Gérson sidelined, Paulo Cézar's talents began to enjoy an even freer rein.

'*Street fighting men*'
Brazil v. Rumania, Guadalajara, 10 June 1970

Under Angelo Niculescu, Rumania's first appearance in the finals since 1938 had exceeded expectations. After pushing England hard in the opening match they had surprised many by beating Marko's Czechs 2–1 on 6 June. Niculescu's side blended hard-nosed defence with genuine flair in attack. In the flamboyant Florea Dumitrache, a handful for England and scorer of the winner against the Czechs, they had a genuine world-class striker.

Brazil needed the win to guarantee topping the group and remaining in Guadalajara. The city had, by now, become a little corner of a foreign land destined to remain forever Brazil. With Peru or Bulgaria the likely opponent, and a semi-final also set for the Jalisco after that, Zagalo's side could remain at the Suites Caribes until the Final itself with a little luck.

Yet Rumania were far from finished in the tournament themselves. Provided the result of the England v. Czechoslovakia match went the right way, Niculescu's men still had a shot at progressing themselves. Against what looked like a weakened Brazil they rather fancied their chances. Rivellino had also been sidelined after the exertions of the England match. Piazza had been returned to his natural position in midfield and Fontana drafted into the defence.

Rumania had clearly learned from England's tight-marking performance the previous Sunday. The acres of space donated by the Czechs were closed up and the tackling was the fiercest the Brazilians had yet seen. Yet it was Brazil who took the lead when Pelé, in charge of free kicks in Rivellino's absence, blasted past the Rumanian's unconvincing keeper, Adamache.

Pelé's durability was by now beyond doubt. The free kick had been given after he had been brought down for the umpteenth time by the thuggish Mocanu. Pelé wondered in the post-match press conference whether the Rumanian had 'confused tackling with street fighting!' Yet unlike 1966, it was now becoming plain that he was not going to be kicked out of the tournament.

No one played better than Paulo Cézar. Two minutes after Pelé's goal, he made a dancing run down the left side of the penalty area. His precise pull-back from the dead-ball line fell perfectly into the path of Jairzinho. Brazil had scored two goals in two minutes and appeared to be coasting to the quarter-finals.

Carlos Alberto had remembered the excellence of Paulo Cézar's performance in the Rumania match. 'It was an exhibition,' he had told me. 'Very nice.' Indeed, the skipper could think of no better a team performance overall. 'Despite the scoreboard at the end, it was an extraordinary display, the best the team played in my opinion. The quality was ten out of ten.'

Paulo Cézar came close to scoring himself on two occasions only to be denied by a combination of woodwork and bad luck. Against England he had remained shackled in a tactical straitjacket. Against Rumania, his undoubted genius began to emerge. 'I had acquired self-confidence, I felt that I was a first-team player,' he says of his performance.

The sheer quality of their opening induced a bad attack of complacency, however. When, late in the first half, Dumitrache picked up Dimitru's speculative ball into the penalty box, Brito, Carlos Alberto and Fontana were around him. A swivel of his snake-like hips and the Rumanian was free. His shot was low yet eminently saveable. Félix let it slip underneath him.

Even when Pelé scored again after the break, sliding in when the Rumanians messed up a Carlos Alberto cross, the Europeans refused to lie down. Again Félix was at fault, opting for a flamboyant interception when a floated cross came in from the right. As he grabbed thin air the ball found the head of Emeric Dembrowski. He placed it into the empty net.

By the end, however, Brazil had regained complete control of the game and could have scored a hatful more.

Paulo Cézar came off the pitch convinced he had played himself into Zagalo's plans for the remainder of the tournament. Yet he did not start another match in Mexico.

His bitterness at being dropped once more to make way for Rivellino and Gérson in the quarter-final against Peru is palpable. 'I played the two most beautiful games. Zagalo told me I would play more but I was unfairly dropped,' he says angrily.

If it had not been for Clodoaldo's unexpected intervention against Uruguay, he believes he may have played in the semi-final. He will never know how history may have unfolded from there. Gérson's fitness had once more been in question as Brazil struggled to break down the tough Uruguayan defence. 'I was warming up, Gérson was going to leave,' Paulo Cézar says. 'I was crazy to play.

'Then Clodoaldo, who never attacked in his life, never scored a goal, scored.' It was the moment Paulo Cézar's World Cup came to an end. 'The game was equalized and Zagalo told me to stay on the bench.' After a brief pause for thought he swears again. 'Damn shit.'

His contribution to the Final was limited to acquiring the match ball. The ball had been intended for a church, Nossa Senhora da Aparecida. 'I was responsible for getting it,' he says. When the final whistle went Domenghini of Italy had picked the ball up. 'I slapped it from his hands, then I ran,' he laughs. According to Paulo Cézar, Domenghini wanted to step outside at the post-match banquet: 'He wanted to fight me.' Paulo Cézar claims the ball eventually ended up in the hands of a businessman instead. Although rumours abound in Rio, no one seems to know for sure how this happened.

Grudgingly, by the end of the campaign even the loosest canon was willing to live by the Platonic principles at work within the squad: 'The Brazilian team was fabulous, and so was the spirit. There was no envy, no way of becoming angry.' Today Paulo Cézar has come to terms too with his relegation to a supporting role in the golden age of Brazilian football. 'It was the best team of all time, and I was in the team,' he says simply.

He went on to enjoy his own moment in the sun. As the older generation left the stage, Paulo Cézar was promoted to the role of chief playmaker in Brazil's new-look side under Zagalo. He remained an enigmatic and occasionally infuriating figure within Brazil, however.

His regular run-ins with the law won him few friends in the game. The most extraordinary incident came while he was at Palmeiras in 1972. Paulo Cézar was sidelined by an injury and had been outside the ground listening to the match on a radio. He had become so angry at the commentator's claims that the referee was biased against Palmeiras, that he ran into the ground then on to the pitch where he attacked the official, a certain Mr Braga. He was banned for seven months.

His habit of shooting from the hip in interviews did little to endear him to the CBD either. When he attacked them again in 1972 he was dropped from the Brazil squad for the Independence Cup.

Paulo Cézar made it into the team for the defence of the trophy in Germany but, as Pelé discovered, he travelled to the Brazilian camp in Frankfurt with his mind elsewhere in Europe. Pelé recalled later how he had dropped in to see the squad on the night before their opening match against Yugoslavia. To Pelé's disgust, all Paulo Cézar could talk about was whether he should demand more money from the French club he had been offered a contract with. 'You've got a World Cup game tomorrow and all you're doing is thinking about this job offer,' Pelé raged. 'You are out of your mind.'

Cézar eventually went to France where he worked as assistant manager at Strasbourg. Soon, however, he was back in Brazil, a peripheral figure in the game. His failure to grasp the greatness that could have been his is, of course, an old and all-too-familiar footballing story. Whenever Paulo Cézar's name came up in conversation during my subsequent travels in Brazil, people would either smile or shake their head ruefully. I always recognized the expression. It's the one most of us use when we talk about George Best.

Much like the fallen idol of British football, Paulo Cézar today drifts around Rio seemingly happy to live off his former glories. He plays occasionally on the veteran 'Masters' circuit with his old friend Marco Antonio and turns out in the kick-arounds of what Cariocas call 'football society', a social circuit where the post-match drink is every bit as important as the game itself. 'I cannot live without football,' he admits. Football, it seems, has long since learned to live without him.

Talk of business ideas drifts in and out of his conversation. At one point he says he is planning to open a football shop, called 'Peladeiro'. His most pressing priority, however, is to maintain the lifestyle that has sustained him so far. 'Cariocas don't like to work,' he says, summing up his philosophy. 'They like to sleep a lot.' Few can take such unfulfilled dreams to bed with them . . .

CHAPTER V

A Brooklin Tale

'The Englishman considers a player that dribbles three times successively a nuisance; the Brazilian considers him a virtuoso.'

Tomas Mazzoni, *World Sports*, 1950

Nicolino Rivellino's hair may be albino white and his skin as lined as sun-dried leather but, at the age of seventy-nine, he is still the proud and protective head of his family. To them he will always be their *pai coruja*, father owl.

On a sweltering afternoon in the São Paulo suburb of Brooklin Paulistana, Nicolino is sitting in the shade, surveying a scene he never tires of. In front of him three astroturfed football pitches are filled with hyperactive schoolboys and girls. On one Nicolino can see his youngest son gesticulating and shouting instructions. Outside another he watches his grandson, deep in conversation with one of his coaching staff.

Above him a giant metallic revolving sign is casting a long, late-afternoon shadow over the pitches. Nicolino, of all people, would not argue with the legend glinting in the sun. 'Rivellino Sports Center: *Muito mais que uma escola de futebol.*' Rivellino Sports Center: Much more than a football school.

According to the Brazilian joke, God made São Paulo ugly so that its people would go to work each morning. In reality it was the Italians who built Brazil's equivalent of Chicago, South America's 'city of big shoulders'. In the early decades of the century, they braved the waters of the southern Atlantic, bound for another version of *l'America* and *la terra promessa*, the promised land.

Nicolino Rivellino's father, Biagio, had been among those who left the old country and the rugged poverty of the Abruzzi region. Biagio was a son of Campobasso, a town famous all over Italy for its cutlery makers and its Sagra dei Mistrei procession. As a boy each June, Biagio watched hundreds of elaborately costumed pilgrims walk Campobasso's cobbled, medieval streets dressed as devils, angels and saints. In the New World his family would be visited by all three.

Biagio began life in Brazil as a *carpir*, a labourer clearing land for the owners of coffee plantations in São Paulo. As ambitious as he was hard-working, he was soon putting a grander plan into action. Through a blend of common sense, business acumen and sheer graft he acquired a large area of *mato*, undeveloped land, in the suburb of Brooklin Paulistana. With the help of his five sons he established three brickworks and nine acres of fertile farmland. By the time his son Nicolino had reached manhood, his father was one of the most respected figures in his community. In honour of all that Biagio had achieved, the Italian-dominated neighbourhood was named the Piazza Rivellino.

When Biagio died, unfortunately, the family's life changed for the worst. Nicolino and his four brothers couldn't pay the huge income tax bills he left behind and, piece by piece, were forced to sell everything their father had worked so hard to build. The Piazza Rivellino became the property of outsiders. Today it does not officially exist any more. Within the family, the loss remains a matter of sadness and unspoken shame to this day. 'It is sad,' says Nicolino quietly. 'But we don't have to regret the past any more, thank God.'

Legally his father's land remains the property of faceless, city landlords, absentees. Thanks to the youngest of Nicolino's three children, however, the Rivellino name is once more among the most revered – and visible – in Brooklin Paulistana. On the deeds to the Rivellino Sports Center it states its address as the Piazza Rivellino.

As he walks towards his father, a bandit smile is breaking across the face of the son who has made the Rivellino name famous far beyond the tenement blocks of Brooklin Paulistana. 'My father is full of shit,' he shouts, oblivious to another, smaller sign that reads '*Evite Falar Palavrões Obrigado*,' Please Refrain From Swearing. 'The next thing he will tell you is that he was a good footballer. He was just a kicker. They called him Nicolino Cavalo, Nicolino the Horse.'

'That is not fair,' Nicolino protests. 'They called me *cavalo* because I could jump to compete at the same height as everyone else. I was fantastic.' His son shakes his head and laughs even louder. He ruffles his father's hair and takes a seat alongside him in the shade.

The girth may be wider, the shock of gypsy curls thinner, but Roberto Rivellino is still the footballer most suited to a career in spaghetti westerns. I had come here to Brooklin to meet him. I got Nicolino as part of the bargain.

Rivellino's school has been open for a year or so and was three years in the planning before that. A grid of green and blue steel bullpens, astroturf pitches and jungle netting, it is a state-of-the-art playing area. Overlooking it all is the clubhouse – a shop and changing room downstairs, a bar and restaurant upstairs. The bar is Philippe Stark meets the All England Club, modernistic furniture and tasteful striped awnings. The place drips success.

If it was paid for by the riches Roberto Rivellino earned indulging his love for football it is a monument to an even deeper devotion, *la famiglia*. Roberto's wife, Maisa, a leading Paulista architect, came up with the concept and designed the school. Roberto's youngest son, twenty-four-year-old Marcio, is one of the centre's managers. The *pai coruja* keeps a constant, vigilant eye.

Roberto Rivellino himself is as visible a figure as his time allows. He is a popular pundit on Bandeirantes television and still plays on the lucrative 'Masters' veterans circuit. The day after I meet him he is off to the Czech Republic for an exhibition match. He makes half a dozen such trips a year, he says. He will keep playing as long as his famous left foot allows.

The game has seen few weapons more potent than Rivellino's left foot. Gérson's was perhaps more precise,

Puskas' maybe more feared. Neither were more spectacular, however. It was in Mexico that it announced itself to the world. It was here in Brooklin Paulistana that the son of Nicolino the Horse first demonstrated he owned a kick like a mule.

Rivellino was born in the nearby suburb of Aclimação on New Year's Day, 1946 and grew up in Brooklin Paulistana. In the 1950s, São Paulo was still a city of open spaces. As a kid Rivellino played his *pelada* at Ponte do Morumbi, an open area of full-sized pitches on the site of what is today Brazil's second-biggest stadium, the vast, bowled, 150,000 capacity Morumbi stadium. 'Those fields do not exist any more. Today I have this school because there is no space,' he frowns.

It was at Ponte do Morumbi and on the pitches of the nearby Clube Atletico Indiano that Rivellino realized the ferocious power he could generate with his shooting. 'I was born with that ability. I always hit the ball very strongly, it was something that God gave me,' he says. One day one of his thunderbolts hit a school friend. 'He was a kid who didn't like to play that much,' he recalls. The shot was so powerful it knocked the boy out. 'He was unconscious for three days. My friends tortured me: "You have killed the guy", "You will be arrested". I cried,' he admits.

He would not keep the habit for long, but Rivellino said prayers for his first footballing victim. He admits his devotion to the Catholic Church, where he was a *coroinha*, an altar boy, had less to do with faith than the free cinema tickets his priests used to bribe boys like him with.

117

'If you went to Mass you won a ticket to see the serial the following Sunday. It was a beautiful childhood, I was a child of the streets in a good sense.'

It was away from the streets, within the confines of the five-a-side-style *futebol de salão* courts that Rivellino's talent was spotted. When overseas coaches come to Brazil in search of the source of its natural born footballing skills, *futebol de salão* is invariably at the heart of the thesis they return home with. Played, usually indoors, on a hard pitch the size of a basketball court and with a ball that is smaller and heavier than normal, the game polishes the skills learned in the *peladas*. Players learn to think and act faster in the tight spaces. Control and technique are improved by the fact that the ball rarely leaves the floor. By the time the good *salão* player graduates to the full-size version, he should have a clear advantage.

Rivellino played for a city bank, BANESPA, where he quickly became a star of São Paulo's *futebol de salao* league. As a boy with Italian blood in his family he was inevitably a Palmeirense, a supporter of the green and whites of Palmeiras, the club founded by Italian immigrants in the early decades of the century. When he shone against his boyhood favourites, in the final of a tournament, he could barely believe that the club's coach, Mario Cavalini, invited him to join his training sessions. 'We won and I played very well. I was fifteen,' he says.

Cavalini was not the only one whose interests were aroused that fateful afternoon. Until then Nicolino had been a rare spectator at his son's games. In his day football was a third-class profession. 'I was beaten for playing,' he says. 'I was invited several times to go to a

Day of destiny – Brazil line up for the final against Italy.
Left to right. Carlos Alberto, Brito, Gérson, Piazza, Everaldo, Tostão,
Clodoaldo, Rivellino, Pelé, Jairzinho, Félix. (© Popperfoto)

Third time winner: Pelé is raised aloft on the Azteca pitch. (© Popperfoto)

Gérson, in his beloved Niteroi (© Garry Jenkins)

'a little excited' – Carlos Alberto locks horns with England's fractious Francis Lee.

(© Mirror Syndication International)

Gérson *centre,* helps
Brito deal with Italy's
Mazzola in the Final.
(© Popperfoto)

Twin passion. Carlos Alberto, *left,* with his brother Carlos Roberto at
their new football school in Barra. (© Garry Jenkins)

History Man. Jairzinho scores – and then celebrates becoming the only player ever to score in every World Cup Finals match. (Top and bottom © Popperfoto)

Still Crazy After All These Years. A smiling Félix in his workshop in São Paulo.
(© Garry Jenkins)

Gato Félix. Denying England and Geoff Hurst.
(© Allsport/MSI)

Angel face. Clodoaldo today.
(© Garry Jenkins)

Piazza at his office in Belo Horizonte.
(© Garry Jenkins)

Breaking into a sweat at last. Piazza, *second from left,* deals with the menace of Lee, Ball and Charlton against England in Guadalajara. Brito and Carlos Alberto look s on.
(© Mirror Syndication International)

Roberto Rivellino and his father Nicolino at the family-run sports
centre in Brooklin, São Paulo. (© Garry Jenkins)

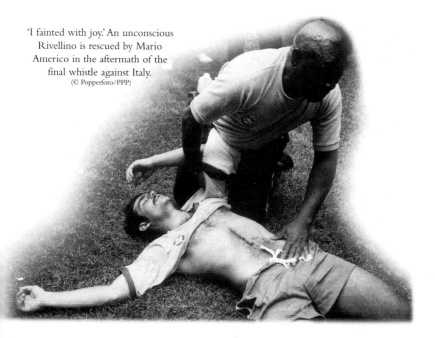

'I fainted with joy.' An unconscious
Rivellino is rescued by Mario
Americo in the aftermath of the
final whistle against Italy.
(© Popperfoto/PPP)

Almost a person again.
Tostão in his penthouse
above the Rua Curitiba in
Belo Horizonte.

(© Garry Jenkins)

Denying God himself. Tostão looks on in disbelief
as Banks defies gravity and Pelé. (© Hulton Getty)

big club, but my salary at the telephone company where I worked was higher.' When he heard Roberto was a keen player he intervened.

Nicolino ran the Rivellino house with iron discipline. As a boy the talkative Roberto had the nickname *curio*, the name of a particularly loud songbird. On the streets Nicolino was happy to let him fly free. 'A boy must be a *moleque*, he must play football in the streets, he must break windows,' he smiles. But at home his word was absolute. 'I cut his wings a lot,' says Nicolino. 'He was beaten a lot with a belt, as was his brother. I wanted their understanding, I wanted them to be good people, to see what life is like.'

When he saw the gifts his son had developed – and the money now available in the game – he became his son's first unofficial manager. Roberto was happy to have his father take the reins. 'He saw a lot of qualities in me so he motivated me very much,' he says.

Word of Rivellino's talent had spread to Palmeiras' greatest rivals in São Paulo, Corinthians Paulista. When they made a more lucrative offer, Nicolino recommended Roberto follow his head rather than his heart. Roberto went on to wear the white and black of Corinthians Paulista for more than a decade.

Rivellino's heroes were Didi, Chineisinho, the star of the Palmeiras side, and Jair da Rosa Pinto, a reserve in the Brazil squad of 1962 and a master of the dead ball situation at Portuguesa. Rivellino would spend hour after hour trying to replicate Jair's lethal armoury of *bater falta*, free kicks.

His rise through the game in São Paulo was rapid. He was far from a one-trick pony. As well as his shooting skills he possessed a flair for Garrincha-like dribbling. Like the Joy of the People he revelled in handing out the humiliations his sleight of foot could inflict on defenders. Like his grandfather and father, he was also a fighter. His high-octane style soon made him a darling of the Corinthian crowds.

By 1965 he had been drafted into one of Feola's squads preparing for England. He sat on the bench during the 5–0 thrashing of Hungary by a predominantly Paulista team at Morumbi. He would have to wait until after the disaster of Goodison to win the first of his record 121 caps, however.

If there were winners and losers in the aftermath of the Saldanha affair, Rivellino was the man who hit the rollover jackpot.

Saldanha had seen him as little more than what he calls a *reserve de luxe*, a supersub. With the manager committed to playing two wingers in Edu and Jairzinho, Rivellino had been forced to sit out the matches away in Colombia, Venezuela and Paraguay. When he came on for Gérson in the second half of the game against Colombia back at the Maracanã, he wisely seized his opportunity in style. Within moments he shook the crossbar with a stupendous shot then, with only four minutes left, he scored Brazil's sixth and final goal. His flamboyant performance instantly endeared him to the Carioca press. 'The next day the newspapers were asking: "Who was the best – Tostão or Rivellino?"' he smiles. More importantly, the Maracanã masses installed him as their instant new favourite.

Four days later, with the final game against Paraguay

deadlocked, Rivellino heard the great cathedral of Brazilian football filled with the sound of his name. 'I still get goosebumps at the thought,' he says. 'There were 190,000 people shouting "Ri, Ri". I was a boy, I trembled.' He shone once more as Brazil won 1–0. From that moment on, he admits, the considerable force that was Brazilian public opinion was with him, particularly when Zagalo took over.

At first Zagalo's appointment seemed like bad news. 'I didn't think Zagalo would think about me as a left wing,' says Rivellino. But as the new coach mulled over the type of game he would want his team to play in Mexico, Rivellino – by now enjoying mass support in the press – emerged as a cornerstone of his plans. In footballing terms, his selection became Zagalo's masterstroke.

Zagalo feared that using Edu and Jairzinho as out-and-out left and right wingers respectively was simply too much of a luxury. Even with the industrious Clodoaldo, his 4–2–4 formation would leave him too open against the hard-working European sides. Jairzinho's goalscoring in the *eliminatorias* had edged him ahead of Edu. Rivellino assumed Pelé's Santos team-mate would be replaced by Paulo Cézar Lima, whom Zagalo had worked with at Botafogo. For all his extravagant gifts, however, Paulo Cézar was deeply unpopular. 'Even if he was playing well, even if he was scoring goals, everybody booed Paulo. They started saying Rivellino must play, there should be space for him. There was pressure,' he explains.

Today it is his name that is known around the footballing world. Immortality could just as easily have been Edu's or Paulo Cézar's. 'Both played beautiful football. But unfortunately I was the one who became part of a team that went on to be considered the best of all time.' The shrug and the skyward look he completes the sentence with says it all. Fate smiled on him and not them.

Rivellino admits he found life within the *concentração* difficult. 'Who likes it?' he says. In his case, the frustrations were understandable. He had become engaged to a beautiful young architect, Maisa Gazola just before leaving São Paulo.

Along with Félix and Brito, he attempted to lighten the mood by indulging his penchant for practical jokes. He recalls pulling stunts on Mario Americo and assistant trainer Nocaute Jacks while still at the camp at the Retiro dos Patos in Rio. 'We would put them inside the bags that held the balls, hold them down on a table and throw balls at their head. They suffered,' he smiles. Americo's habit of summoning players with a giant, bosun's bell drew an inevitable response. 'Brito left a bucket of water on the top of the door. When Mario Americo came in calling he got a shower.'

Rivellino's most outrageous practical joke only added to the agitation he felt locked up at Guanajuato, however. 'Pelé was scared of two things, knives and snakes. If you hold a knife near him he jumps, he is like a cat,' Rivellino reveals. One day a particularly restless Rivellino decided he would find a local wood snake and slip it into Pelé's room for a joke. 'I put one under his sheet and left the room.' He was soon consumed with panic. He returned to his own room where he confessed his crime to his cellmate, Edu. 'Can you imagine if something happens? I will not be able to go back to Brazil.' Before he could remove the snake he heard screams coming from Pelé's room.

'Suddenly I heard him going *Aaaaaaaah*! He beat the snake with his guitar. The next day he came to me and said: "You son of a bitch".' Rivellino was simply relieved Pelé was still around to vent his anger. 'Thank God, nothing happened. I almost killed the *negrão*.'

No one would have missed Pelé's influence more. 'I learned a lot from Pelé, he was an example, he always was an example,' he says, massaging his moustache as he does when he becomes emotional. Pelé used his experiences in Chile and England in particular as case studies in the importance of fitness. 'He knew that even the greatest player in the world had to be fit when he took the field. If he was not fit physically he did not play, he did not do what his head imagined he was able to do,' says Rivellino.

At Corinthians, Rivellino had a reputation for playing in bursts and for burning himself out by the later stages of matches. In Mexico he pushed himself to fitness levels he may have imagined beyond him. 'I knew that I was a player that would be marked, so I tried to be physically better prepared than everybody else,' he says. His was among the performances that had lifted the team's morale when the results of the final Cooper Tests were announced.

Saldanha had originally thought they should have spent two months in Mexico. Zagalo's suggestion that twenty-one days would be sufficient to adapt to the high altitude was greeted with relief by the team's coaches. 'If we had stayed two months in that castle we would have gone mad,' one of them, Cirol, admitted in Mexico. Zagalo's decision looked even wiser when the squad acclimatized quicker than anticipated. In the first test of endurance in

Brazil the players had run 2,750 metres in an average of twelve minutes. In Mexico they were running 2,950 metres in an average of nine minutes. Another of the coaches Carlos Alberto Parreira compared their progress to lowering the world 100 metre record from eleven seconds to ten seconds. If it was not quite that impressive, it was encouraging nevertheless.

No training could prepare them for the overwhelming Mexican heat. Brazil were happy to create the impression that the conditions were nothing new to them, but in reality the searing Mexican sun was as hard for them to bear as anyone else. 'When we played at midday it was unbearably hot. Even for us. And at that time no one took even a cup of water on to the field,' says Rivellino. As in the USA in 1994, the welfare of the players took a back seat to the welfare of FIFA and the television paymasters of the game, he believes. 'An absurdity, a crime,' he calls it.

If Rivellino's state of high anxiety had remained hidden amid the secrecy of Guanajuato, his relief when he opened his team's goal account against the Czechs at the Jalisco was laid bare for the whole world to see.

He and Pelé had stood over the ball with Jairzinho at the left edge of the Czech wall. If Pelé's prowess from free kicks was well known, Rivellino's was then less so. He introduced himself by trusting in the power he had learned in the playground rather than the placement he had polished at Guanajuato. The moment he hit his low, swerving shot, Rivellino knew Viktor had no chance of stopping it. 'He went one way then tried to come back. The ball was so strong he was not able to get a hand to it.'

Even within a team of demonstrative individuals, Rivellino's celebrations were masterpieces of high-combustion madness. He would rant and rave at himself, his thick-set arms thumping an imaginary punchbag. 'I always did it that way, I don't know why, maybe because a goal is the ultimate in football. When you score a goal you let loose everything which is inside of you,' he says. Pelé once compared scoring a goal to an orgasm. At those moments can scoring a goal seem better than sex, I wondered? 'It depends on the goal, but yes it can,' he grins.

There would be more spectacular goals in Rivellino's canon of cannonballs. (His personal favourites are the free kick he threaded over a ducking Jairzinho and through the East German wall in the 1974 finals, 'incredible precision'; a goal he scored from the half-way line, direct from the kick-off against his old club Corinthians – 'it was three or four seconds, the fastest goal in history'; and best of all, a dribble past Franz Beckenbauer and a shot that left the great Lev Yashin shaking his head in wonder in a 1968 Rest of the World v. Brazil match – 'it was disallowed because Natal was offside but it was still a great goal'.) He can think of none that matched his first in the World Cup finals for sheer intensity, however. 'It was just an unforgettable moment,' he says, words failing him for a moment. Like Carlos Alberto, he counts the moment as one of the most significant in the campaign. 'When we conceded that first goal to Petras, we just carried on playing. We knew how powerful we were.'

In Brazil, Rivellino simply confirmed what the Corinthian

crowds had known for years. To the foreign press, however, his performance against the Czechs marked him out as the first great discovery of the tournament. Days earlier the name Rivellino had been on no one's lips. When Pelé was asked at a post-match press conference whether he believed his team-mate could become a world star, he leant into the banks of microphones and shrugged: 'Rivellino already *is* a world star.' (No one thought to check the spelling of the new sensation's surname. In Brazil and beyond ever since, it has been spelt wrongly – with one 'l' rather than two.)

With Gérson impersonating a chimney stack in the stands, Rivellino reverted to a more central role against England. The match proved the ultimate test of his all-round game. Rivellino was in the thick of the action at both ends, squaring up to Francis Lee one moment, testing Banks with a firecracker shot the next. 'Lee was terrible,' he smiles. 'And very dangerous, a great player.'

Years later he was reunited with Banks at a Masters tournament. 'He told me: "That shot burned my hands".' Rivellino still shakes his head in disbelief at the most famous of Banks' stops in that match. 'That save he made when the *criolo* headed the ball. Perfect.'

'That game could have been the Final,' he adds. The game took its toll. He left the Jalisco limping from a twisted ankle. Against Rumania, Piazza and Paulo Cézar filled the midfield with Fontana at the back.

*   *   *

3-D
Brazil v. Peru, Guadalajara, 14 June 1970

Even in a squad of superstitious players, Rivellino was a one-man religion of ritual in the pre-match dressing room. His famous moustache was a product of his conviction that Brazil would not lose while he refused to shave. (Luckily when he returned to Maisa looking like an extra from *Viva Zapata!* she approved. 'She said: "You look good, keep it". I have kept it ever since.')

In the final moments before matches, two routines in particular were observed with what one might call meticulous regularity. As the dressing room cleared Rivellino would – along with one or two others – relieve himself in the toilet. 'We would say: "Let's throw away the fear".' After that he would observe one last piece of ceremonial. 'I always enter the field with the right foot, never with the left,' he says. He sees my raised eyebrow and consoles me. 'Don't worry, it's a Brazilian thing.'

If he and his team-mates were looking for bad omens, the quarter-final against Peru provided plenty. Plotting to derail them from their third World Cup was the man whose tactical genius had contributed so much to their first two, Rivellino's boyhood hero Didi.

For the man born Waldir Pareira, the match was everything he had dreamed of and dreaded. Didi had prospered as coach of Sporting Cristal Club Lima. In 1968 he had become the first foreigner to coach the Peruvian national side. Their qualification ahead of Argentina in 1969 had turned him into a national hero. He used his popularity and power to introduce the indisciplined Peruvians to the sort of rigid regime that had served his great Brazilian sides so well.

'They had a series of complexes – after all Peru had never been in a World Cup since 1930,' he said of his squad after guiding them to Mexico. 'The Peruvian player has a tendency to overrate himself before a match and underrate himself during the match. I have to re-educate their minds, give them confidence.'

He had kept his players 'confined to barracks' at the Leoncio Prado Military School in Lima since 13 January. He had also drawn up a programme to prepare for the Mexican altitude at Puno, 3,900 metres above sea level. Life in the *concentração* was too much for some of his stars. His extrovert attacker Perico Leon would frequently climb over the wire for a night on the town.

A highly strung chain-smoker, Didi cut an emaciated – and occasionally eccentric – figure in Mexico. At one point he told the press he believed his players would have no altitude problems 'because they eat a lot of onions'! The Peruvian authorities began vetting Didi's interviews after he argued that the Mafia had infiltrated the competition and Morocco would be tougher than the Germans. By guiding his side to the quarter-finals, however, he had guaranteed himself a million soles ($22,000) bonus on top of his $1,000-a-month salary.

His disciplinary regime had paid off in their group matches. The opening match against Bulgaria – with Peru the most obvious candidate as runner-up to West Germany in a group in which Morocco were expected to be the whipping boys – had always looked like the key to Peru's campaign. At 2–0 down after forty-nine minutes, to goals from Dermendjiev and Bonev, their chances of progressing in the tournament looked lost.

Within a minute, however, Peru had begun what – until

Seeler, Beckenbauer and Muller broke English hearts a week later, at least – was to be the best comeback of the competition. First Gallardo hit a scorching right-foot shot past Simeonov in the Bulgarian goal. Within six minutes Hector Chumpitaz hit a free kick through the Bulgarian wall to make it 2–2. Teofilio Cubillas scored a third and two more goals were disallowed for offside. In the end, in an echo of Brazil's strong finishing performances in Guadalajara, Peru overwhelmed their European rivals.

After a rampant Cubillas, with two, and Challe saw Morocco off in a 3–0 win, their own 0–3 defeat by a Gerd Muller-inspired West Germany mattered little. In his heart, Didi had already realized it was his destiny to confront Brazil in the quarter-finals.

To many Brazilians Didi's adoption of Peru amounted to treachery. His reputation had sunk even lower with his less than complimentary comments about the quality of the present Brazilian team. To Didi the 1970 side was inferior to the 1958 vintage. 'Pelé, Vava, Amarildo, Zito, Zagalo, Djalma and Gilmar just happened to get together by one of those lucky twists of fate that happen in football,' he said. 'I don't feel Brazil have those players today.' He damned Pelé with faint praise, predicting he would be once more kicked out of the tournament. 'Pelé will again suffer from close tackling and rough play as he suffered in 1962 and 1966,' he said. 'And he is – although a more seasoned player – almost thirty years old.'

His old team-mate Zagalo reverted to his first-choice midfield and attack to deal with him. Rivellino returned along with Gérson. With Zagalo still vacillating over who was his best left-back, the squad's youngest member, Marco Antonio was given a run-out in place of the injured Everaldo.

129

The baptism of fire he would be given by Gallardo and Cubillas would make it his first and last game.

As an exhibition of football at its most fluid, the tournament provided nothing finer. 'Peru were excellent. They had movement, speed and quality. Didi created a team and it was a very difficult game for us,' says Rivellino.

The game was eleven minutes old when Rivellino opened the scoring with another gem from his repertoire of rocketry. It was Tostão who provided the lay-off, setting up Rivellino on the left corner of the Peruvian penalty area when a Pelé cross rebounded to him off a defender. Rivellino seems to have a name for each of his shots and each of his dribbles. He describes the low, scudding shot he unleashed as his '3-D'. I assume he is referring to the way the ball moved through all three dimensions as it bucked and bent its way along the surface of the grass before going in off the inside of the post. Even at full-stretch Peru's keeper Rubinos couldn't cope with its wilful refusal to obey the laws of footballing physics.

Rivellino was in the thick of the action five minutes later. He and Tostão worked a short corner move that ended with a subtle but deadly through ball for the No. 9 to run on to. Tostão, until now an embodiment of the Biblical belief that it is better to give than receive, scored his first goal of the tournament with a sly shot inside Rubino's unguarded near post. With the match now moving with all the grace of a ballet, Gallardo dragged Peru and Didi back into the reckoning. His near-post shot was a facsimile of Tostão's. Once more Félix's fallibilities were exposed.

In the second half Tostão stretched Brazil's lead further when he latched on to a Pelé pass. Cubillas came back with another fine goal, a resounding volley when the ball broke loose to him in a chaotic penalty area. Jairzinho finished the game off with his customary goal.

To many observers the Peruvian game may well have represented Brazil at the very peak of their artistic powers. 'If we had stayed there a whole year there would have been no team to beat us. There is no such thing as an unbeatable team, but Brazil at that time was the closest to it,' Rivellino says, a rare attack of Gérson-like hyperbole suddenly overcoming him.

With himself, Jairzinho, Gérson, Tostão and Pelé firing on all cylinders, there was an extraordinary poetry to the performances they were now beginning to string together. Yet to dismiss him and his team as a mere force of nature is to insult the quality of the organization and preparation they had gone through, not to mention the acute tactical awareness they applied. To Rivellino, Jairzinho's second goal against Peru was a perfect case in point.

As Gérson's shadow in the squad, Rivellino had familiarized himself with many of the moves the master had perfected with Pelé and Jairzinho. He mimicked the *papagaio* perfectly in sending the *furacão* on his way. 'Jair made a movement towards his marker then said "go". I played the ball over the defender's head and he dribbled and scored from there. It was just like we rehearsed.

'There was freedom, Zagalo gave us that, but if you analyse it we played 4–4–2,' he says. 'If we lost the ball Pelé and I would drop back a little and fill up the space with Clodoaldo and Gérson. Jairzinho would remain the point of escape. We worked hard in Guanajuato; it was a sacrifice but we were rewarded.'

*   *   *

Rivellino scored again in the semi-final against Uruguay. His celebration there outdid even the hysterics of the Czech match.

In the chess matches leading up to the Final, Rivellino had been Zagalo's most effective piece. He proved no less useful against Italy. The manager was almost certain Italy would play a man-to-man marking system, at least on his attackers. So as to be sure, Rivellino and Jairzinho were given instructions to switch wings straight from the kick-off. If the rock of Italy's defence, Facchetti, followed Jairzinho, phase two would be implemented. 'He followed,' smiles Rivellino.

As the game developed, Jairzinho began to drift further and further inside from his normal position on the right. As Facchetti followed like a love-sick puppy, Carlos Alberto began to exploit the three-lane motorway open to him.

Rivellino had spent much of the night before the game dreaming of scoring. '*Then* I would have gone crazy,' he laughs. Yet as he found himself slipping and sliding all over the thick, greasy Azteca pitch, his early contributions were a mixture of mis-hit corners and free kicks that ended up in the third tier of the stadium. Of his twelve shots only one was on target. 'We used rubber soles not studs. Because of the rain the grass was wet and it was long. And because of the altitude in Mexico the ball tends to go up. It was terrible.'

As he adjusted to the conditions, however, his contribution was telling. In the thirtieth minute he picked up the ball from a Tostão throw-in. Rivellino's clashes with Bertini had already taken on an abrasive edge. As the Italian clattered towards him he improvized a volleyed cross into the penalty box. No sooner had he dispatched the ball than he was jumping out of his opponent's firing line. 'If I hadn't jumped up into the air I would have broken my leg,' he says.

Rivellino's instincts told him that either Jairzinho or Pelé would be under the ball somewhere. 'Gérson was not a player that would arrive there,' he says. 'In my mind there were only two players that could be there.' As he lay on the pitch he looked across to see his hunch pay off. With Burgnich the central defender hopelessly wrong-footed, Pelé was hovering in the air. 'The *gringo*'s head is in his belly,' laughs Rivellino. 'Pelé was up there waiting. It was an incredible thing.'

When Gérson scored Rivellino found himself crying along with his mentor. At the final whistle the emotion simply overwhelmed him. 'I fainted,' he says sheepishly. 'I fainted with joy.' He discovered later that Mario Americo had carried him back to the dressing room through the crowds. 'I don't remember anything. All I remember is being in the dressing room.'

Before leaving for Mexico Rivellino had proposed to Maisa and they had chosen their wedding day. A week after the Final, on 30 June 1970, they offered Brooklin Paulistana an excuse to continue the celebrations. Rivellino smiles at the memory: 'It is a foolish thing, but I had true confidence in our potential.'

Rivellino interrupts our conversation to head back down to begin a new class commencing on one of the pitches. Down on the astroturf he shows off two of his dribbles: the snake and the *elastica*. We remember his dribbles but we remember the left foot more. 'I used to take bets that I could hit a post or a crossbar from 30 or 40 yards,' he says, rolling a ball under the sole of his left foot. 'I would bet money or beer.' A five-a-side goalpost stands unguarded around 30 yards away. 'Go on then,' I suggest.

Rivellino takes his hands off his hips, steps off and away from the ball and swings. He connects with all the nonchalance of a pro golfer blowing the cobwebs off on the practice range. Automatic pilot, a swing executed a million times. I watch the ball fly in a perfect parabola, bending and dipping as it arcs its way toward the target. It misses the crossbar of the five-a-side goal by the thickness of his moustache. Roberto shrugs and smiles, then apologizes that he must get back to his class. No money or beer is exchanged. There had been no formal bet. Why does the wink he gives me suggest things would have been different if there had?

Nearby, Nicolino is still watching over the school as the floodlights come on for the evening. 'I'm proud of having a *trabalhador*, a worker son, a son who has never been humiliated at any club he has joined,' he says, nodding at Roberto. For the father owl of the family, watching his son play was often an ordeal. The Final against Italy had been beyond him, he admits. 'I went walking through the streets alone,' he says. 'Whenever I heard fireworks I went home and asked "Who scored?" Then I left again.'

The following week, when Rivellino arrived back at São Paulo, Nicolino did not even attempt to meet his son at the airport or join in the parade through the city. Instead he waited at home, with the rest of Brooklin Paulistana as their favourite son toured the nearby neighbourhoods of Ibirapuera and Santo Amaro. It could have been a scene from the Imperial Italy of his ancient forefathers. Rivellino was welcomed like a Caesar, home in triumph from Gaul. 'From the road to Santo Amaro to the entrance of my house there was a carpet of rose petals. It was about one metre wide and forty metres long,' Nicollino recalls.

When his son eventually picked his way through the throng, Nicolino was there waiting. 'It was very touching. I embraced him until we reached the entrance to my house,' he recalls.

By the time the next World Cup arrived, Pelé, Gérson and Tostão had left the game, their legends intact. Rivellino remained to witness the decline that followed at first hand.

While tougher zonal marking reduced Jairzinho to a shadow of his enthralling Mexico self, a darker, more menacing Rivellino became the team's heart and soul in West Germany. It is a toss-up whether his free kicks or his fighting spirit was the more valuable commodity as they won through a difficult opening group containing Scotland, Zaire and Yugoslavia. On the wall of the restaurant there is a photograph of him squaring up to Scotland's Billy Bremner during their ill-tempered 0–0 draw. As Rivellino bears down on him, Bremner looks like he is ready to do battle standing on tip-toes. 'What else could I do?' Rivellino smiles when I ask him about it. 'He wouldn't stop kicking me.'

In the end Brazil lost the third-place play-off to Poland before watching the Dutch robbed of glory by Beckenbauer's West Germans in the Final. 'We did not play great football. But if you analyse our problems, fourth place was wonderful,' he says. In the Polish team of Lato and Deyna, the West Germany of Breitner and Muller, and, most of all, the Holland of Cruyff and Neeskens, he believes he saw three of the best sides ever to take the field. In the best of them, Cruyff and co., Rivellino saw the natural heirs to the geniuses of Brazil and 1970. 'Their football caused a revolution, it was totally different,' he says, nodding his head as he speaks. 'We made that exit so that the men behind could enter.'

His own World Cup farewell lacked the same dignity. At the age of thirty-two, he travelled to Argentina in 1978 and struggled to find form, fitness and a place in the side under the controversial Claudio Coutinho. The tournament was overshadowed by his public rows with Coutinho and the stench of corruption that fixed itself to Argentina's belief-beggaring 6–0 win over Peru – which nudged the hosts above Brazil in the second group stages and therefore into the Final. Brazil finished third, but might as well have finished nowhere for all its people cared after the Argentines had cheated them of a place in the Final.

After the glory of Mexico, the ignominies of Germany and Argentina were somehow easier to swallow for Rivellino. 'I don't play to lose. On the contrary, I hate losing. But you must recognize that it happens. Can you imagine if it didn't? The world would make no sense.' In the twilight of his career Rivellino spent time in Saudi Arabia at the Al Halil Club. He retired from the game having scored 43 times in 120 appearances for Brazil.

As a coach he worked in Japan after the 1994 World Cup. Now, though, he says he is back in Brazil for good. Since establishing his school he has passed on a player or two to Corinthians and São Paulo. He is not in business to produce a new Rivellino, however. 'I am very exacting,' he says of his training methods here. Besides, within the confines of a more heavily coached game, he suspects his job is that of a diamond cutter rather than a diamond miner. 'You cannot teach football. Nobody taught me how to play. It's bullshit. If somebody said: "I taught Rivellino" it would be a lie. My philosophy is not making stars, my philosophy is to make competitive boys.'

He will never get used to the fact that some of those boys arrive at his school to announce their parents have christened them Roberto Rivellino. 'It's crazy, it is something you cannot explain.' He heard once of a boy in Russia who has taken his name.

All that he has, has come from the game. 'Football is everything for me; it was everything and it still is today,' he says, running fingers through his moustache once more. 'I started playing when I was a boy, I stopped when I was thirty-seven. Everything I have learned about the moves of life has come from football. I don't see me out of football. I don't know how to do anything else.' He will never need to.

Today the third-generation Rivellino lives a lifestyle far beyond the imagination of his immigrant forefathers. Apart from Pelé, he is probably the most wealthy and successful of the surviving members of the 1970 side. His family is close to Gérson's, with whom he appears on television as a pundit. They spend time together in Niteroi or on Rivellino's farm outside São Paulo. 'I cook pizza on the farm,' Rivellino smiles. 'I like to enjoy myself.'

Like his friend he is a deeply religious, devoutly Catholic man. His footballing career was a mission he believes he fulfilled with honour. 'It was what I was supposed to do,' he says, leaning forward. 'I think I was able to leave my mark, and I think it was a positive mark, that's the important side of this thing.'

For a moment he is silent as he surveys what was once the Piazza Rivellino. 'I built the building God gave me to build,' he says, nodding to himself. To judge by the intensity of his faraway expression, he is talking about much more than a football school.

CHAPTER VI

The Altar Boy

'If in your childhood or adolescence you didn't have a very good life, I think it makes you fight for your goals with more determination than a person who has been born in a golden cradle.'

If they were being delivered upstairs in the corporate conference suites of São Paulo's Hotel Melia, Clodoaldo Tavares Santana's words might sound like another slice of self-help psychobabble, a glib one-liner from the latest motivational management manual. Whispered like a liturgy downstairs in the lobby of one of the city's most opulent buildings, however, they carry a simplicity and sincerity it is impossible to find uninspiring.

On the surface, at least, Clodoaldo exudes the same look of well-pressed well-being as the American and Japanese businessmen milling around the hotel's entrance. Dressed in an immaculate Italian shirt and slacks, a chunky Rolex on his wrist, he seems as natural a part of his surroundings as the polished marble and the crystal chandeliers. Beside him sits his mobile phone and his personal organizer. The cards in his wallet are probably platinum.

Yet in truth Clodoaldo's roots could not lie further from this golden cradle of modern Brazil. The extraordinary story of his childhood and adolescence explains why he regards every day as a fight for his life.

Appearances have always been deceptive where Clodoaldo is concerned. Back in 1970, for instance, he looked like an altar boy and played like an assassin. The twenty-year-old was the team's energetic enforcer, its midfield fetcher and carrier, willing to run himself into the Mexican ground for the Brazilian cause. It was only in the dying minutes of the Final, as he began the unforgettable move that set up Carlos Alberto's goal, that we glimpsed the angelic skills he had subdued for the greater good of what he still calls 'the motherland'. Clodoaldo's mazy dribble past four Italian defenders was an unscripted blend of football, samba and sheer humiliation. It was as if Nobby Stiles had suddenly turned himself into George Best.

Clodoaldo had proved no less evasive during my stay in São Paulo. Attempts to contact him through various office numbers had come to nought. In the end it took Rivellino's help to track him down to a meeting of senior footballing figures from Rio and São Paulo being held at the Hotel Melia.

Scour the endless sprawl of São Paulo as hard as you like and you will find no monuments to the memory of Charles Miller Esquire, formerly of Banister Court School, Hampshire.

It is hardly surprising: Brazil is not a country much interested in dwelling on its past. One of the most hurtful put-downs is to be labelled *ja era*, part of what has already been. Like Americans, Brazilians have a horror of growing old that probably stems from their nation's youth.

Yet the moment Miller picked his way down the gangplank and disembarked a steamer from Southampton in 1894 may just be the most significant in Brazilian sporting history. The son of colonialist parents, Miller had completed his education back in England. He arrived at São Paulo docks with an extra rucksack filled with regulation leather balls and boots. As he arrived in Brazil so too did organized Association Football. During the next twenty years Miller went on to become the founding father of the game. If anyone deserves a statue in Brazil, he does.

Of course, Miller's footballs were not the first to be kicked on Brazilian soil. According to some, the first *peladas* were played by British or maybe Dutch sailors on the beaches of Rio twenty years earlier. According to others they were played between workers on the Leopoldina Railway in 1875. The game's organizer had been a mysterious Scot known as Mr John. What is indisputable, however, is that Miller organized the first official match – between teams drawn from the São Paulo Gas Company, the London and Brazilian Bank and the São Paulo Railway Company at the Varzeo do Carmo in 1895 – and that the game caught on instantly. What is also indisputable is that all this happened at a fulcral moment in Brazil's history.

In 1888, as the Football Association was being formed in London, Queen Isabella of Brazil had finalized the legislation that would abolish slavery in her country. Tens of millions of African negroes, forced into labour by the colonial powers of Spain, Portugal and Britain, found themselves free to live as they pleased. The human palette that was Brazil's already multi-ethnic mix of Europeans and indigenous Indians became even more colourful as a result.

At first organized football had remained the private pursuit of the élite European classes. Members of Fluminense in Rio, founded by the aristocratic Englishman Oscar Cox, travelled to matches with dinner jackets and toasted King Edward VII after the final whistle. In the early years of the new century, however, *futebol* had become the game of choice for the coloured workers at the coffee factories, docks and railway yards of São Paulo, Rio and beyond. Along with samba dancing and *capoeira*, a highly choreographed combination of dance and hand-to-hand combat, it fulfilled much the same role for the negroes and mulattos as jazz did for the blacks of the United States. The game unburdened them, it allowed them to express themselves and their natural, physical gifts without repression. In 1914, the chairman of Exeter City, on tour in Brazil, expressed his astonishment at the skills he saw in a kick-around on a Rio dockside. Even more amazing to him, apparently, was the fact that these gifted players were 'all niggers, as black as your hat, and most of them playing in bare feet'.

The sporting emancipation did not become complete until 1923 when the newly promoted Vasco da Gama ran away with the Carioca first division championship by fielding a team of mixed race players. (The club was ostracized by the rest of the city's élite afterwards but within a decade Flamengo had followed suit, laying the foundations for its 'people's club' reputation in the process.) By the 1930s, as full-time professionalism arrived, black players like Leônidas da Silva and Domingos da Guia, had become

Brazil's first great, national sporting idols. It is one of the most crashingly obvious coincidences in football history that the coloured players' arrival on the world stage also heralded Brazil's emergence as a footballing force.

In the first World Cups of 1930 and 1934 the Brazilian team made little impression and were eliminated in the last sixteen and in the first round respectively. In 1938, with Leônidas in full flight in their attack and Domingos da Guia in outstanding form at full-back they reached the semi-finals. (Incredibly the manager Adhemar Pimenta 'rested' Leônidas – scorer of four goals against Poland – for the game against Italy and lost 2–1 as a result.)

Brains the size of the Maracanã itself have been employed to explain why Brazilian football became the sublime thing it is. I heard plenty of theories while I was there. None came close to this one in terms of plausibility – or more importantly, poetry. While in the British Empire the game was an extension of the barracks square, a form of well-drilled discipline with its own rigid rules and tactics; in Brazil it quickly emerged as something rather more profound. The world is full of countries in which football is enmeshed in passion, power and politics. Nowhere else, it is nice to think, is it so inextricably linked to the concept of freedom.

A hundred years on from its beginnings, Brazilian football now dominates the international stage. Domestically, however, it is once more in crisis. In the city of Brazilian football's birth, it turns out Clodoaldo is at the forefront of the fight to drag the game into the next century.

The drive to the hotel is – even by São Paulo standards –

a nerve-jangling one. We are told Clodoaldo is due to leave early in the afternoon. After more than an hour and a half stuck in traffic it is approaching 2 p.m. before we get to the Hotel Melia.

Homogenized, hermetically sealed, a gleaming monument of steel and plate-glass built in the early 1990s complete with its own conference centre, shopping mall, helicopter pad and Japanese restaurant, the hotel is about as Brazilian as sushi. If it is exactly the environment in which American and Japanese executives feel comfortable doing business, it also seems to appeal to the egos of the power-brokers of Brazilian football.

We discover the meeting is taking place in one of the conference suites on the third floor of the hotel. We walk in to discover a collection of leading figures from the game in Rio and São Paulo sitting around a suitably presidential, polished, white-wooded table eating their lunch. The presidents look much like football club presidents the world over, a mixture of fatcat enthusiasts and dodgy-looking politicians. Apart, that is, from the greying, angel-faced representative from Santos FC.

Clodoaldo's lean, ludicrously healthy looks belie his status as a forty-seven-year-old grandfather. He is eating a salad and drinking mineral water. He says later that he doesn't drink or smoke and still runs and plays football when he can. 'I try to be an exemplary athlete,' he smiles. To my relief Clodoaldo says he has no further appointments after the meeting is over. He is happy to talk in the lobby downstairs. We leave him to his salad and wait.

Like his friend Pelé, Clodoaldo lends Santos the sort of clean, unimpeachable image that Bobby Charlton lent Manchester United. It is, he says an hour or so later in the lobby, the least he can do. 'I feel very proud to be part of one of the most famous clubs in the world. Santos has been a mother, a father, a family, it is everything to me,' he says. A few minutes into his remarkable life story, and I soon start to see what he means.

Clodoaldo was born on 25 September 1949 in the town of Aracaju in the state of Sergipano in the north-east of Brazil, the youngest of ten children, four brothers and six sisters.

The north-east, or *Nordeste* is the poorest, most chaotic part of the country and that with the closest links to its African past. It was here that the vast bulk of the slaves were put to work in the darkest days of the colonialist nineteenth century. To many it is the soul of the country. 'The core of our nationality, the bedrock of our race,' the writer Euclides da Cunha called it. With his limpid, childlike eyes and utterly unaffected air, Clodoaldo has the sort of simple serenity that his big city countrymen make fun of but which comes as close as you can get to the essence of Brazil – if this vast, infinitely varied nation can be said to have such a thing at all.

There is much that is remarkable about Clodoaldo. That this tranquillity survived the tragic events of his early life is perhaps the most remarkable quality of all. Clodoaldo was just six years old when his life was altered for ever. 'My parents were killed in a car accident,' he explains, matter-of-factly. Understandably, Clodoaldo does not like to dwell on the details. It seems his father was a transport worker. Apparently the accident happened on a danger-ous stretch of road outside Aracaju.

What is clear is that the loss so devastated the family that Clodoaldo and some of his brothers and sisters could no longer bear to live in Aracaju. With what little money they had, they made the long journey south, ending up in the town of Praia Grande on the southern seaboard, near São Paulo. From there they moved on to the bustling port of Santos.

For his brothers and sisters, life in the south was no less forgiving than that they had left behind. Eventually they returned to the *Nordeste*. For Clodoaldo, however, there was no turning back. 'I decided to stay and confront life alone,' he says.

His fate was, of course, far from unique. Thousands of orphaned young boys lived a similar existence in the *favelas* of Rio and São Paulo. There they learned to live by their wits, or perish. According to the colourful, conventional wisdom, the roots of the Brazilian footballing phenomenon lies on the streets of these shanty towns. It is here that boys learned to play football with rolled up socks and oranges. It is here they schooled themselves in the methods of the Malandro, a folklore figure popularized in the songs of the 1920s and 1930s. The Malandro was a workshy, bohemian rascal, a ducker and diver able to use his guile to move in all circles of life without being pinned down to responsibility by anyone. Football was an extension of the Malandro's arts, a game to be played with spontaneity and the wisdom of the street. It was the philosophy of Garrincha. It may never have been better personified than in the streetsmart genius of Romario.

Clodoaldo lived on a *morro*, or hillside slum, on the edge of a small Chinatown in one of the poorest parts of Santos. Whatever means he used to survive, however, he was no Malandro in the traditional sense. To begin with, he was willing to work for a living and did so from the age of nine. With the consent of the local courts, to whom he was answerable as a minor, he was hired at one of Santos' vast coffee warehouses.

He was too slight for the back-breaking routine of loading and unloading the coffee sacks at the docks. 'I could not bear the weight,' he says. Instead he spent long hours sweeping the floors and keeping the stores in order. What little time he had left was spent sleeping or playing *pelada* on the streets.

What he lacked in physicality he more than made up for in fighting spirit. By 1965 he had graduated to a small local club, Barreiro, from where he later moved on to the junior side of Santos. As his talent blossomed at the club's famous Vila Belmiro ground, Santos' coaches encouraged Clodoaldo to skip work to concentrate on his training. When his bosses at the coffee warehouse detected his waning interest they sacked him.

As an amateur Clodoaldo earned nothing from his football. 'Not enough for a sandwich,' he says, shaking his head. Once more forced to live off his wits, he turned first to the Catholic Church for salvation. The Church had offered some semblance of sense when his world had been turned upside down. He had, from the age of six to ten or so, spent part of most days performing his duties as an altar boy. With his future uncertain, he persuaded the priests at a Santos seminary to take him in. A quiet, contemplative boy, Clodoaldo briefly considered a life of the cloth. To their eternal credit, however, his temporary landlords encouraged him to follow another path. 'They saw I had another vocation,' he says with a gentle smile.

When Clodoaldo explained his predicament to his coaches at Santos, they came up with an alternative solution. For the next two years of his life, the Vila Belmiro stadium became Clodoaldo's orphanage instead.

As Catholicism's most serious rival as a religion, it was perhaps fitting that football was second only to the Church in providing futures for the poor boys of Brazil. As Clodoaldo discovered, even for those boys who did not go on to become *titulars* or first team players, the benefits of being taken on the books of a major club like Santos were immense.

Boys could be taken on as young as ten or eleven, when they would become members of the *mirim* squad. Between the ages of twelve and fourteen they would graduate to the *infantil* team, then the *juvenil* between the ages of fifteen and seventeen. The clubs treated their investments like young princes. As well as providing players with a monthly allowance, boys could expect to have all their medical, dental and nutritional needs looked after. When Pelé joined Santos, for instance, he had been put on an intense high-protein diet and a calisthenics programme to build up his slight-framed body. The clubs also contributed to improving their boys' education by putting them in the better big city schools. If their careers as footballers did not work out, they had higher education or white-collar work to fall back on.

For many boys from the rural areas of Brazil the intensity of the training and the big city left them feeling homesick. Pelé tried to run away from Santos after five days there. For Clodoaldo, however, life inside the Vila Belmiro offered security he had never dreamed of before. 'I had lost my job and had no means to support myself. I had no salary but at least there at Vila Belmiro I had somewhere to sleep and somewhere to eat.' For the next two years of his life, the Santos ground became his life. It has remained central to his very existence ever since.

As a boy in his *favela*, Clodoaldo was given the nickname *Corro* (pronounced Co-ho). 'I was very small and there is a bird, in the North, called *corro*.' By his seventeenth birthday, Corro was ready to fly.

In the mid-1960s, the step into the dressing room of the Santos first team was an intimidating one for any player. The all-whites of the Vila Belmiro were by now the most famous – not to mention the hardest working – team in not just Brazil and South America but the world. Their first team included three double World Cup winners – Gilmar, Zito and Pelé, two more 1966 squad members – Orlando and Edu, and two more new Brazilian national stars – Joel and Carlos Alberto.

Since winning the World Club Championship in 1961 and 1962, the all-star eleven had superseded Real Madrid as the glamour club of the international scene. The lucrative, whirlwind tours of the world that had come with the status had already earned them uncharitable comparisons with basketball's Harlem Globetrotters.

A 'lightning tour' in the summer of 1969 summed up the treadmill-like existence that Clodoaldo suddenly found himself facing. In just over two weeks, Santos squeezed in seven matches in four countries, criss-crossing Europe to fulfil lucrative contracts in Yugoslavia and Spain, England and Italy. Even by the standards of the day, their travel arrangements were arduous. The final leg of their tour involved leaving Sarajevo at 5 a.m. for Manchester, arriving at 11.45 p.m. that night, travelling for a match at Stoke the following evening, then on to London and a 3 a.m. flight to Genoa that night. The miracle of their tour was that they returned unbeaten.

Pelé was the unquestioned star attraction, filling stadia wherever he travelled. Clodoaldo shakes his head quietly at the memories. 'Some people wanted to touch him, some people wanted to kiss him. In some countries they kissed the ground he walked on,' he says. 'I thought it was beautiful, beautiful.'

Yet, just as on the streets of São Paulo, Clodoaldo refused to be intimidated by the exalted company he was now keeping. Once more he soaked up everything he saw and heard. And once more he fought every day of his working life. Sharing a dressing room with Pelé was, he admits, an inspirational experience. 'I would have been a fool if I hadn't profited by learning something from the greatest player of all time,' he says, laughing quietly at himself. 'I learned lessons every day.'

Pelé taught his resilient young colleague to use his eyes as well as his heart. 'Pelé was always ahead of everyone in reasoning, speed and physical condition. One of his main virtues was that he observed *everything* – the supporters, the terraces, the goalkeeper, the work of the referee. If Pelé was without the ball he was observing. I learned very much about this aspect with Pelé.'

On the training pitch, Clodoaldo saw the extent of Pelé's vision. He would regularly embarrass his team-mates by exposing their weaknesses. 'When you were marking Pelé in training, he knew when he controlled the ball which was your worst side and that was the side which he should go to,' Clodoaldo says. 'He was always, always in front of everybody.'

Yet if Clodoaldo had a hero at Santos, it was the man who wore the club's No. 5 rather than its No. 10 shirt. Zito – with Didi – had been Brazil's midfield lynchpin in both Sweden and Chile. With his pencil moustache and brilliantined hairdo, Zito looked more like an Argentine tango crooner than a footballer. For a generation he had been the sheet anchor of both the Santos and Brazilian sides. Though perfectly capable of breaking forward and scoring – as he proved in the 1962 World Cup Final when he scored Brazil's second and decisive goal – Zito's genius lay in his tireless tackling and simple yet destructive distribution. He was the closest the Brazilian national side had to a conventional, English-style right half. 'As a man, as a leader, he has always been a person that I have modelled myself on. He was a world champion and great example,' says Clodoaldo of the mentor to whom he still talks on an almost daily basis.

Under Zito's watchful eye, Clodoaldo had eased his way into the Santos first team by his seventeenth birthday. Soon the São Paulo press had earmarked the teenager as the great man's heir apparent. By 1967, the torch had been passed on in a suitably symbolic scene. 'Zito was the absolute owner of the No. 5 shirt,' says Clodoaldo, recalling the most powerful and evocative moment of his young career. 'It was a game against Portuguesa de Desportos and we were in the dressing room. Zito called me and the coach over and he said "Today, the No. 5 shirt belongs to Clodoaldo". That day he played with the No. 8.' His eyes well up with tears as he recalls the moment. 'Every time that I remember that I become emotional,' he says, his voice faltering.

Within a year, he had replaced Zito as a cornerstone of

the Brazilian national side too. Clodoaldo had forced his way into Zagalo's first team with a string of iron-lunged performances in the run up to Mexico in 1970. 'Clodoaldo has seven winds,' the Flamengo coach Yustrich said of him. He offered the perfect supplement to the passing skills of Gérson and the power of Rivellino. He was their willing workhorse, filling the space behind them as they moved forward into the opponents' half. 'I was the more defensive player, it became a position called the *cabeça de alho*, the clove of garlic,' he says, his interlocked hands illustrating his point.

Level-headed and dedicated, quick to learn and slow to argue, Clodoaldo offered Zagalo a welcome contrast to some of the more temperamental youngsters in the squad. Clodoaldo admits he was happy to subordinate himself to the greater good of Brazil. 'I was young and I was serving the motherland,' he says simply. Whatever political overtones the removal of Saldanha and the presence of Coutinho and the other military men may have had, Clodoaldo remained oblivious to them. Instead he once more listened and learned.

At Guanajuato, Gérson became a guiding spirit. To Clodoaldo, he was one of the greatest players of any period in Brazil's glorious history. 'I had always been a fan of Gérson's even before I was a professional,' he says. 'They talk about the great players, Didi, Jair da Rosa, but I think he was the most precise of all.' His room-mate Carlos Alberto offered another grounding influence whenever his feet left the ground.

Even today Clodoaldo can catch himself daydreaming of the events of twenty-seven summers ago. 'I have everything recorded in here,' he smiles, tapping his temple.

'Every detail, from the music, to the goals, how they were scored. I have a tape inside my head.' More often than not, he dwells on the three most dramatic matches, against England, Uruguay and, naturally, Italy.

His memory of the first of them is dominated by the weight he lost chasing Ball, Charlton and Peters around the Jalisco that Sunday afternoon. 'I lost about four or five kilogrammes,' he says. 'I was not able to eat properly afterwards. I could only eat water melon and soup. It was not until the next day that I was able to eat.' He is one of those who concedes the result should have been different: 'England had better opportunities to score than Brazil.'

Yet the most vivid of his mental home movies are of the games that, in very different ways, guaranteed his Brazilian side immortality. It was during the final two matches that Clodoaldo's importance to the Beautiful Team shone through.

'The end of a war'
Brazil v. Uruguay, Guadalajara, 17 June 1970

To Clodoaldo, the quintet of Pelé and Tostão, Gérson, Rivellino and Jairzinho were 'the fantastic five'. 'With the five best players in the world in the team everything was possible,' he says. In the early afternoon of 17 June in Guadalajara, however, it fell to the five's young midfield minder to free them from the nightmare that was their semi-final against Uruguay.

For twenty minutes after the Peru match, none of the team had changed or showered as they sat in the dressing room listening to a radio commentary on the Russia v.

Uruguay match that would decide their semi-final opponent. When Victor Esparrago of Nacional and Uruguay scored a controversial goal close to the end of extra-time, there had been barely a word exchanged. When the final whistle confirmed the Uruguayans' place in the semis, the players trooped off to the showers deep in thought. 'We all smiled grimly,' Pelé remembered.

For many back in Brazil, the match they now faced was a Final in itself. With Germany and Italy playing off in the other semi-final at the Azteca, the game at the Jalisco was effectively the championship of South America. Far more importantly, it was Brazil's opportunity to lay the ghost that had haunted its football for twenty pain-riddled years.

For a generation Brazil's neighbour to the south had cast a shadow utterly out of proportion to her geographical size, economic strength and – in reality – footballing ability. Since the afternoon of 16 July 1950, it had been Brazil, the continent's giants, who had harboured an illogical yet deep-seated inferiority complex.

Pelé and Gérson had been ten-year-olds, Clodoaldo a mere baby when the blue-shirted Uruguayans beat Brazil 2–1 in the final match of the 1950 World Cup at the new Maracanã. The finals had been played in two groups rather than on a knockout basis. Thumping 7–1 and 6–1 wins over Sweden and Spain in the second group phase had taken Brazil to the verge of their first World Cup win. With 200,000 squeezed into the new cathedral of Brazilian football, Jules Rimet himself was there to present the trophy at the end of the final pool match in which Brazil needed only to draw. All went to plan as Brazil took the lead through Friaça early in the second half. As Schiaffino and then Ghiggia turned the match around, however, what was meant to have been a consecration transformed itself into a wake. Jules Rimet presented Uruguay's captain Varela with the trophy with an apologetic handshake on the pitch in an all but empty stadium.

No loss in the history of football has been taken so badly. Brazil did not play as an international team again for almost two years afterwards. It was four years before they could bring themselves to return to the Maracanã. The white shirts worn that day would never be worn again by a Brazilian side. Describing his feelings as a ten-year-old boy once, Pelé described 'a sadness so great, so profound that it seemed like the end of a war, with Brazil the loser and many people dead'.

The Brazilian press had begun building the psychological significance of the match as soon as Uruguay booked their place in Guadalajara. Much as elder statesmen like Gérson dismissed the hype as 'bullshit', the extra relevance of the match was unmistakable. 'It did have some weight, there was fear,' says Clodoaldo, nodding his head. As they began to analyse television footage of the Uruguayan performances in Mexico, the iron-fisted professionalism they saw only seemed to make the task look even tougher.

As a striker at Penarol, the Uruguayan manager Juan Eduardo Hohnberg had revelled in breaking the reputations of defenders. The terraces called him 'the hangman'. In Mexico the poacher had turned gamekeeper. His team was built around by far the strongest defence in South America. In the 25-year-old Ladislao Mazurkiewicz of Penarol, Hohnberg had comfortably the continent's best goalkeeper. Spectacular and safe at the same time, he was protected by a solid back line marshalled by his club centre-back Roberto Matosas and Atilio Ancheta of Nacional.

Hohnberg's pre-tournament promise that he would not tolerate rough play had turned out to be the weasel words everyone feared they would be. In their Group Two matches in Toluca and Puebla they had been as tough and uncompromising as ever. The Brazilians had winced at the tackling meted out by Ubinas, Ancheta, Matosas and Mujica. Uruguay had begun with a clinical 2–0 win over Israel. Ildo Maneiro and Juan Mujica had put them clear soon after half-time. Israel could have played for days and not got back into the contest as the Uruguayans closed the game down from then on.

A 0–0 draw against Italy had surprised no one, particularly as it all but guaranteed both sides' place in the next stages. By the time Uruguay came to play Sweden, the least adventurous group in the competition had been all but ruined as a contest. Even a last-minute goal by Ove Grahan could not take the smiles off Hohnberg's face at the final whistle. Goal difference had seen his side through as runners-up.

In the quarter-final at the Azteca, the Russians had every reason to be angry at the way the Uruguayans beat them. The game had remained goalless for the first ninety minutes and all but a minute of the half-hour of extra-time. As Uruguay launched a final assault, the ball seemed to have gone over the dead-ball line before Cubilla scooped it back for Esparrago to win the game. For the superstitious Brazilians, the omens looked bleak.

As Zagalo's men walked on to the pitch on the afternoon of 17 June, Rivellino took special care to enter with the right foot first. For most of the first half, however, he, Clodoaldo and the rest of the side performed a passable imitation of a group of rabbits caught in the headlights. Clodoaldo concedes they played most of the first half terrified of putting a foot wrong. 'We were holding them, respecting them, but also remembering the tragedy, thinking "What is going to happen?".'

Uruguay had the better of the opening exchanges, raining down four shots to Brazil's one in the opening quarter of an hour. When Félix and Piazza conspired to help Cubilla's mis-hit shot spin over the line in the eighteenth minute, all Brazil's fears were confirmed – the game was *catimbado*, cursed.

For a few moments Félix lay on the floor holding his head and even Gérson looked stunned. As the Uruguayan fans chanted 'We repeat Maracanã, you are still frightened', Brazil stared into the abyss. It would be Clodoaldo who drew them back from oblivion.

Hohnberg had studied Brazil enough to know Gérson held their strongest tactical cards. Towards the end of the first half the *generalissimo* had realized he was not going to shake off the shackles of his man-marker Montero and began encouraging Clodoaldo to venture forward in his place. 'He started telling me to leave my position more,' he says. Referee Mendibil of Spain had allowed almost a minute of injury time when Gérson pulled his marker to the right, allowing Clodoaldo space to break forward in the left channel. After passing to Tostão, he broke into space in the Uruguayan penalty area. Tostão, working on the left flank and spotting Clodoaldo's run, delivered a perfectly weighted, inch-accurate pass inside the retreating Uruguayan defenders. Clodoaldo's instant right-foot volley left the immaculate Mazurkiewicz power-less for once.

When he returned to the dressing room, Clodoaldo found himself swamped. 'Everybody came and embraced me,' he recalls. As he remembers it, it was the extraordinary spectacle of Mario Zagalo crying that brought the celebrations to an abrupt ending.

Zagalo had remained his usual, ice-cool self throughout the tournament. The sight of his team's limp capitulation proved too much for him to bear, however. 'He was very emotional, he was crying,' says Clodoaldo. Zagalo went on to make the most impassioned speech of the campaign. 'He told us: "You cannot continue playing this way". He spoke to us of the love of our motherland and of the Brazilian shirt.' By the end of his oration, Zagalo's were not the only tears on the dressing-room floor. Brazil returned to the pitch with his battle cry still reverberating in their ears.

Once more Pelé personified the new spirit of the side. Watching and rewatching film of the Uruguayans, he had spotted that after making saves Mazurkiewicz almost habitually kicked a short, punted pass out to his midfield. Early in the second half he chose his moment. Turning suddenly as he trotted back to half-way, Pelé slipped past a defender, ran on to Mazurkiewicz's flat kick and volleyed a waist-high piledriver straight back at him from 40 yards. To his frustration Mazurkiewicz reacted just in time, wrapping himself around the ball as it hit him with all the force of a body punch.

As the half wore on, only Mazurkiewicz seemed to be standing between Brazil and a comfortable win. It took half an hour before Jairzinho finally found the space to attack the Uruguayan defence. His speed and strength took him into the penalty box and his low shot finally ended the keeper's one-man resistance movement.

Jairzinho's sixth goal in five games was the cue for Uruguay to finally climb out of their shell and for a succession of Brazilian counter-attacks. After Félix had made his best save of the tournament to deny Cubilla's header, Pelé ran deep into their half before stroking a simple, inviting ball to the inrushing Rivellino. He buried the shot low inside Mazurkiewicz' left-hand post.

Pelé still had one final trick up his sleeve. With barely a minute left, Tostão split the defence with a killer ball and he was suddenly one on one with Mazurkiewicz. It was only after Pelé had veered off to the right that the keeper realized the great man did not have the ball at his feet. By then it had passed him by on his left and Pelé was around him and gathering the ball to shoot. Again he was denied his dream of the ultimate goal by the thickness of the post.

Clodoaldo is sure that Zagalo's rousing speech made the difference. 'He really changed things. In the first half we played with the handbrake pulled on. It was the worst forty-five minutes in the World Cup for Brazil,' he says. 'In the second half we were more aggressive, braver, more self-confident. It really was an important moment. We really were looking into an abyss.'

Clodoaldo's air of quiet self-assurance had been a beacon on the pitch. 'I'm very calm in any situation. I've always been like that, I think it's because of the way I grew up, the lessons of life I received,' he says. Yet inside his emotions were, by now, boiling away. In their bedroom, Carlos Alberto had constantly reassured his young friend and Santos team-mate that the Cup would be theirs. 'Carlos Alberto always passed on a lot of confidence to me. He was always telling me: "We'll be the champions".' After the Uruguayans had been put to the sword, he finally believed him. Clodoaldo would have to survive a Jekyll and Hyde performance in the Final first, however.

His role had been to watch Italy's most potent playmaker, Sandro Mazzola. With Brazil cruising towards a 1–0 lead at half-time he seemed comfortably in control. For reasons still unknown to him, he chose to commit *hari kiri* in front of 103,000 people. Picking the ball up in his own half seven minutes before the interval, Clodoaldo decided to back heel the ball to Brito. His mistimed piece of flashiness presented Boninsegna with a run on goal. By the time Félix and Brito had compounded the error by crashing into each other on the edge of the penalty box, Boninsegna had a twenty-yard tap in. 'It was a risky move, a move for effect,' he says, shaking his head at the memory. In the aftermath only Brito offered words of consolation. He apologized for having put him in the situation in the first place. For the remainder of the first half, Clodoaldo admits his morale was dented. 'I felt responsible; it allowed Italy to go into the second half much stronger.'

The half-time scene could not have presented a starker contrast to the Uruguay game. 'Zagalo pulled my ears in the dressing room,' he smiles. For Zagalo there were none of the histrionics of the semi-final. A few soothing words of support, and Clodoaldo's confidence was restored. He re-emerged to play with more authority than ever. By the eighty-sixth minute, like a butterfly emerging from its

160

chrysalis, Clodoaldo offered a tantalizing cameo of the player he could become.

His dribble through a Praetorian Guard of Italians was one of the most gloriously expressive moments of the Brazilians' entire campaign. Clodoaldo admits it was borne of desperation as much as inspiration. 'I noticed there were two of them on me, then two more. It was a risky move again but I was suffocated by them. I had no alternative,' he smiles. He executed his escape in the most thrilling way imaginable, weaving his way out of trouble to begin the move that culminated in Carlos Alberto's goal.

At the final whistle he ran for the dressing room, where with Gérson he said a prayer of thanks. His memories of the following moments are simply ones of pride. 'I was proud of winning, proud of knowing every Brazilian was feeling what we were passing through at that moment,' he says.

Beyond that, the quietest member of the Beautiful Team says he cannot find the words. 'I think it's something that only the ones who lived through it can describe,' he says with an apologetic shrug of his shoulders.

In 1974 Clodoaldo married Clery da Costa Santana, with whom he now has two daughters, Claudine and Simone. With great pride, he tells me he is already the grandfather of an eight-month-old boy. In the years following Mexico, as adversity returned to his life, it was his surrogate family who once more saved him, however.

He had returned home as one of the triumvirate of young players on whom Brazil's future now seemed to rest. With Rivellino and Jairzinho, Clodoaldo was expected to form the foundation for the defence of the world championship in Germany four years later. He continued to shine for Santos and Brazil. He utterly dominated the side in 1972 when Brazil won an international tournament at the Maracanã. 'I was then considered the greatest player in Brazil,' he says. As the 1974 World Cup loomed, however, his fearless tackling finally took its toll. He suffered a severe ankle sprain and was forced to drop out of the Brazilian squad. 'It was the biggest disappointment of my career. I was at the top of my career, I was twenty-four,' he says. He travelled to West Germany with the squad but could only watch their failure from the touchline. 'It was very hard to watch. I really felt our disqualification against Holland.'

If the early part of his career had been blessed with good fortune, the second half began to be blighted by cruel bad luck. By the time the next World Cup came round Clodoaldo's playing career was all but over, cut short by a recurrence of his old ankle injury.

Once more he turned to Santos for salvation. Clodoaldo worked for a while as one of the club's coaches but found himself unable to handle the overpowering passion he had for the club. He has had to walk out of the Vila Belmiro midway through games overcome with nerves. 'I suffered much more than as a player. I still do, sometimes I have to leave the ground,' he says. Today, however, he has learned to live with the pain. With Pelé, Clodoaldo is fighting to restore the club to its former glories.

As Santos' twin vice-presidents, Clodoaldo and Pelé divide the work. Clodoaldo handles domestic affairs, his former hero the overseas aspects of the club's business.

In truth, those international affairs are far more likely to revolve around the latest multi-million transfer of one of its players to Europe than one of the cash-in-hand paydays that used to be a way of life in the 1960s.

On his way back to Brazil from Europe Pelé was famously stopped at Heathrow once. A non-football fan failed to recognize him and demanded to know why he was carrying a briefcase brimful of dollars. Today both he and Clodoaldo are facing the reality of a new footballing age. 'Football inside Rio, Brasília or Minas Gerais today is practically bankrupted. The teams today do not have resources, that's the truth,' says Clodoaldo.

In the face of Europe's financial muscle, Santos can no longer hang on to the sort of internationals that graced the legendary sides of the past. Despite efforts from Minister Sergio Motta to block the transfer, Pelé and Clodoaldo have recently reluctantly agreed to sell Giovanni to Barcelona for more than $15 million. If the rot is to be stopped and his club is to return to its position alongside the Barcelonas, Manchester Uniteds and Juventuses of the world, Clodoaldo is convinced it must be involved in the kind of deal he is discussing today at the Hotel Melia.

The meeting had been called to finalize a new tournament being organized with Brazil's fourth channel, SBT Television. Clodoaldo describes it as a South American version of Europe's Champions League. It is an exercise in Rupert Murdoch-style sports marketing. Big money, big-name clubs, big profits all round. Being Brazil, however, there are big problems too. Demand for places among the Brazilian clubs will far outstrip supply. The presidents had come here to debate who the lucky clubs will be.

It was the 1970 side that first showed the potential of the

163

marriage between television and football in Brazil. Esso, Gillette and the cigarette company da Souza Cruz, made fortunes after persuading President Medici to allow them to sponsor the broadcasts of games live at 3 p.m. and 7 p.m. on Brazilian television. 'I think television discovered football as a product there,' says Clodoaldo.

Today, Brazil's ruling powers know they cannot live without its deep-pocket patronage. Otherwise its stadiums will remain empty and the player drain to Europe and Japan will only worsen.

Clodoaldo believes Brazil must turn the tide back in its favour by delivering a product comparable with the Premier League, the Spanish League and Serie A. 'In England and in Spain, Barcelona, for example, why do they have stadiums full of people even if the game is being broadcast? Because they give their supporters great quality,' he says. 'We are still producing the sort of footballers for which Brazil is famous – the difference is that they are playing overseas, Brazilian people cannot go to see them play, they have to watch them on television. If Ronaldo, Juninho, Leonardo, Rai, Roberto Carlos, Giovanni were playing here, of course it would change. They would bring quality.'

It should not be beyond them. Brazil is the leader of a dynamic, new South America; a member, with China and Russia among others, of the Big Five emerging nations of the world and the second most important market in the world if we are to believe recent US studies. American companies like AT&T and European giants like Fiat, Renault and Volkswagen are pouring resources in. The money is there.

One thing is certain. Clodoaldo, like his partner Pelé, has too much of an emotional investment to allow the sleeping giant of the Vila Belmiro to slip away in its slumbers. 'I have always been a person that has fought, and there is a very big sentimental involvement for me,' he says. 'Santos took care of me when I was young, gave me a home and food and an opportunity to be what I am today. That is why we are working today, so Santos can be great again.' No club could wish for a better, more committed man fighting its corner.

After two hours or so in the lobby, Clodoaldo says he has regretfully got to make a start on the long journey back to Santos. His wife and daughters are expecting him, he says. At various times during the afternoon he has looked close to tears. The emotion is there at the end as well. 'I want to thank you for doing this,' he tells me. 'I think it is history, I wish you every success,' he adds with a sincere smile.

As I take a few photographs in the lobby and outside, I ask him where he keeps the No. 5 shirt from Mexico. I am not in the least surprised to learn he gave it to a church at Aparecida do Norte, one of Brazil's holiest Catholic shrines. Clodoaldo has carried his faith with him throughout his life. In return, he believes, it has played an important part in his eventful journey from Aracaju.

'We have talked here of many good things that happened to me. But I also had obstacles in my life, it is not all glory. My faith is very big,' he says.

As he prepares to leave, his mind returns once more to the 1970 Final against Italy, and the moments of madness, misfortune and ultimate glory he still dwells on most days at some point. In many ways Clodoaldo believes they were a metaphor for his life.

'A friend of mine told me: "You've always been a person who knew how to get out of adverse situations in your life and you knew how to get out of an adverse moment in the Final in 1970. It could have been your moment of glory or misfortune". It was exactly that,' he says. 'I think it was all related to my past and the path of my life.'

Throughout our afternoon together he had talked of the *trajetoria*, the path he has followed. It is difficult not to be moved by the simple certainty he has that someone else was responsible for ensuring that journey led to the Azteca on the afternoon of 21 July 1970.

'There is a saying here in Brazil that God is a Brazilian. I believe that nothing in life happens by chance,' he says, his voice once more near a whisper. 'When I was nine years old, alone in the streets and I needed work, I'm sure that the hand of Jesus led me. My story, my life, my childhood, the road I had to follow, something guided me. I'm sure it was the hand of Jesus. Today I think that more than ever.'

CHAPTER VII

Waiting for G-O-D

Malcolm Allison: *'How do you spell Pelé'*
Pat Crerand: *'Easy, G-O-D.'*

ITV, World Cup Panel, 1970

President Fernando Henrique Cardoso's Special Minister for Sport looks tired of the far from beautiful game that is politics. 'I don't belong to a political party, I am independent. I am not here to play politics,' he says, standing at his desk, a portrait of his President and a large, lifeless, Brazilian flag behind him. 'That way I can get out of here quickly.'

In the midst of the most extraordinary period since he took office, few would blame him if he bolted for the door right now. It will not happen, however. Once more, too many of his countrymen are depending on Edson Arantes do Nascimento.

* * *

Brazilian mystics believe the vast, verdant plains on which their most remarkable city was built from scratch in two and a half years at the end of the 1950s is a source of supernatural power. To them Brasília is ley-line central, the point where the continent's ancient energies and spiritual slipstreams converge. It is why the city still has the nation's highest concentration of sects and pseudo-religious movements.

To others Brasília is a paradise lost. What was conceived as a Utopia has become another crime-ridden, debt-crippled metropolis. As the customized capital struggles with middle age, even its stunning, modernistic architecture is wearing badly. If there is any magic left it resides inside one of the pale green, Lego-like buildings overlooking the *Praça dos Três Poderes*, the Plaza of the Three Powers. Even the least mystically minded Brazilian believes in Pelé.

After weeks of negotiation and re-negotiation, I had come to Brasília still unsure whether I would be granted an interview or even an audience with the capital's most famous citizen. 'Unfortunately you couldn't have picked a worst day if you had tried,' one of his assistants, Tania Ramos, told me in her impeccable English when I arrived at the third-floor complex of offices that is the nerve centre of his Ministry. 'It has been quite a week.' She is not kidding.

Pelé took office shortly after Brazil regained the World Cup in the USA in 1994 and the charismatic Cardoso swept into power. Three years on, it is clear that the honeymoon is over. For all his pleas to be left out of the party political arena, Pelé is being shown as many favours as he was on the football pitch. How he must wish he could retaliate in the same straightforward way he used to there!

His week from hell began with a piece of political circus unworthy of even the silliest Banana Republic. As if the most revered sportsman in history did not have enough silverware, the city council of Brasília had announced its intention of making him an honorary citizen. At the meeting to confirm the honour, however, a workers' party activist, Lucia Carvalho, made an impassioned speech opposing him. Amongst other things, she accused him of racism, citing Pelé's unwillingness to admit he was the father of an illegitimate white child in a high-profile paternity suit. At the end of her tirade the move was vetoed and the honour withdrawn.

Brasília's slur so outraged the rest of Brazil that virtually every other major conurbation in the vast nation immediately decided to confer its freedom-of-the-city award instead. My first piece of bad luck is that the day I arrive for my pre-arranged audience with Pelé, is the day on which delegations from the Amazon, the Mato Grosso, Bahia in the north-east and Rio Grand De Sul in the South have travelled to Brasília in a show of solidarity. Each has been promised a chance to personally present Pelé with the large, framed certificates and assorted honours they have brought with them. Each of them, naturally, is ahead of me in the queue.

It is the latest scandal surrounding Brazilian football that has thrown Pelé's office into the most severe spin, however. I had been in Rio when Brazil's major television station TV Globo broke the story. It led its evening news with a tape-recording of the head of the CBF's referees committee, Ivens Mendes, offering a helping hand to Mario Celso Petragalia, the president of a leading club, Atletico Paranaense. The tape seemed to show that, in return for money, Mendes would find a 'friendly' referee for Atletico's impending Copa Brasil match against Vasco da Gama.

Globo's belief in the authenticity of the tape had been deepened by the knowledge that when the game was held, Vasco's most dangerous player, Edmundo, had been sent off in deeply dubious circumstances. As the story took on a life of its own, Globo ran an interview with a leading referee who had fallen foul of Mendes. Valter Senra claimed to have been dropped from the CBF list after refusing Mendes' instructions to keep a minor team, Remo, from reaching the élite first division of the Brazilian game in 1993.

Even the most minor footballing scandal tends to monopolize the Brazilian media for days. When the Korean War broke out in 1950 it took a back seat to a front-page report on the World Cup. (Why not? To Brazilians that was equally life and death.) The invasion of Washington by aliens may have struggled to displace the referee scandal on the front pages and at the top of the evening news.

In Rio I had seen Pelé hijacked by microphones on the television news as he left his Ministry. For all the new tricks he will have learned in Brasília, Pelé is not a man to mask his inner feelings. He looked ashen and genuinely shaken by the implications of the story – both for him and the game.

Over the following days, Tania Ramos explains, his Ministry has been in overdrive. Pelé and his ministerial advisers had been at work on a revolutionary plan to restructure the entire Brazilian soccer system. *Lai Pelé*, or Pelé's Law, is his answer to FDR's New Deal, a wide-ranging reform that proposes turning the privately run, and therefore highly corruptible, club system over to public ownership and reducing drastically the power of the CBF. It has its opponents – unsurprisingly many of them within the Rio corridors of the CBF – who are already trying to scupper it. The CBF had successfully rebuffed a similar move by Zico when he had been given the lesser title of the nation's Sports Secretary in 1990. Zico had resigned as a result. FIFA's aging demagogue, the eighty-two-year-old João Havelange, whose son-in-law Ricardo Teixeira inherited his role as President of the CBF, is already threatening to have Brazil kicked out of France 1998 if Pelé's Law is passed. (On what grounds, no one is quite sure.)

For Pelé, however, it is time to clean the Brazilian game up or wash his hands of it for good. In the wake of the scandal, he had brought forward the presentation of his new plan. On the morning of my visit, in the full glare of the media, he had outlined his reforms to Cardoso at the Presidential Palace. This is the second reason why I couldn't have picked a worst day if I had tried. As Tania Ramos says with a mock matronly shake of her head: 'You can't say no to the President.'

My first glimpse of the world's most famous piece of town planning is from the air. Brasília's creators, Oscar Niemeyer and Lucio Costa, envisaged the city as two intersecting axes, 'crossing at a right angle, like the sign of the cross'. Emerging through clouds from 10,000 feet it is difficult to see the original shape of the city that has now spread outwards and upwards from its origins. Instead

Brasília looks like a giant eagle, its wings extending out to Lake Paranoá. Even from here, though, it is unlike any other city on earth.

It was President Juscelino Kubitschek who commissioned the building of the capital and then moved the machinery of Brazil's government here from Rio in 1960. As I travel in on the empty freeway from the airport, it is as if Whitehall and its mandarins had been decanted into a concrete 1960s new town and set down in a particularly faceless part of the Norfolk countryside.

To be fair, the weather was not doing its famous architecture any favours. In sunshine, showpiece buildings like the Foreign Ministry and the Presidential Planalto Palace apparently glint like jewels in the sun. On a chilly, windy day they can only reflect the slabs of sludge-grey cumulus hanging overhead. The colours conjure up echoes of an aging Eastern Europe, an Orwellia of totalitarian tower blocks and utilitarian homes. The vast majority of Brasília's population live in its endless 'superblocks' – self-contained six-storey villages, complete with kindergartens and supermarkets.

The strangeness of the place is summed up at the heart of the city's main shopping centre, at the point where the original axes meet. In theory this is the focal point of the nation, the geographical hub of Brazil itself. At this nexus is a giant C&A store, the scene for a nearly-new sale of woollens. Maybe Brasília was having a bad day, maybe there was some astral disturbance going on. Either way there was something deeply unsettling about the place.

* * *

Like much of Brasília, Pelé's cabinet office has a vaguely
stale, 1960s feel to it. The furniture is chunky, cubic
and mustard. A few photographs of Pelé with champion
Brazilian sportsmen line the wall. One side of the room
is dominated by a model of one of the new multi-purpose
sports stadia Pelé is trying to build in major Brazilian
cities. I am told there is a chance he can fit in my appointment during his lunch break. As the ante-chamber fills up
with the first of the out-of-town delegations, it is soon
obvious I have about as much chance of this as I have of
winning the football lottery tonight. Even if I had bought
a ticket.

In the cabinet office protocol dictates the Minister is
referred to by the name he was christened with: Edson
Arantes do Nascimento. It is the name on his livery, on
the brass plate of his door. It is the name he is referred
to whenever he addresses the Brazilian Congress, less
than 200 yards away. Life can be mind-numbingly dull in
Brasília. (Watch the crush to get on board a plane bound
for Rio on a Friday evening.) The assembled deputies and
mayors cannot conceal their excitement at the prospect
of an encounter with the nearest Brazil has produced to
a Living God.

By three o'clock pockets of politicians are gathered in
the hope they will be next to be summoned into Pelé's
inner sanctum. By half-past I have seen a greater variety
of political animal than there are insects in the Amazon.
A hood-eyed smoothie from Rio is constantly whispering
into his mobile phone. It turns out he is closing the deal
on a work of art. 'I have a physiological need to own this
painting,' he pleads at one point. In another corner an
older man in a crumpled suit, a member of one of the

delegations from the interior, is assuring his friends that he once played football with Pelé. 'He will remember, I'm sure he will,' he is telling his disbelieving colleagues.

One by one, they are led to a large wooden door which is opened by a baby-faced security guard. It is amazing to witness the effect the brief audiences have on the politicians' faces. When they re-emerge, ten minutes or so later, even the most pompous and po-faced of them (and being politicians there are plenty of those) is glowing like a kid on Christmas morning. No one has a grin, as gargantuan as the man in the crumpled suit who emerges with his story seemingly confirmed. He will not stop dining out on it this side of the millennium.

Occasionally a photographer leaves the inner chamber with the delegations, returning soon afterwards with what look like fresh supplies of film. I am told most visitors expect a photo of themselves with Pelé. (I know I did.) The *realpolitik* of all this becomes clearer with an outburst from a particularly heavy-looking politician in a shiny *Goodfellas* suit, who has been repeatedly told he cannot get in to see the Minister.

'How do you expect me to get re-elected if I cannot get my picture taken with Pelé?' he says, not a trace of shame on his face. One or two people smile, assuming, I think, it is a joke. The rest of the room stares at their loafers. (All Brazilian politicians wear loafers, I have learned by now.) I decide to bury myself in the small mountain of books and articles that have been written on the man behind Brasília's busiest door.

*   *   *

Politics and football have always seemed like variations on the same game to Pelé. In some ways he had become a political football before he truly became a star.

Of course if it had been up to his mother, Dona Celeste, her first-born son would have remained known as Dico, the first nickname given him by his family. As the wife of a failed footballer, Dico's mother rated her son's greatest passion somewhere beneath 'bank robbery and the seven deadly sins'. Pelé was a name he picked up playing football and she didn't want the stupid game ruining her son's as well as her husband's life.

Dona Celeste had given birth to Edson on 23 October 1940, in the town of Três Corações (Three Hearts) in Minas Gerais. He was the first of the five children she would go on to have with her husband João Ramos de Nascimento.

On the streets of Três Corações everyone knew João as Dondinho, the undoubted star of the town's football team. Dondinho clung to the Micawberish belief that he only needed a stroke of luck to lift his family from poverty and into a life of luxury at one of the big city clubs in Rio, São Paulo or Belo Horizonte. His big break duly arrived when he was spotted by a scout for Atletico Mineiro, in Belo Horizonte. But during his first match for the club, against Sao Cristavão in Rio, he collided with the giant Augusto, later to captain Brazil in the 1950 World Cup. Dondinho fell so awkwardly and violently he was left with severely torn knee ligaments. The team doctors told him he would never play properly again. Atletico Mineiro paid for his return ticket to Três Corações and his dream was over.

Dondinho continued to play football in Três Corações, packing his knee with ice between games to avoid being permanently crippled. As his son said later, 'It was the only way he knew of making money'. It was only when he was offered a place with FC Bauru in the state of São Paulo – and a public service job to go with it – that Dona Celeste finally stopped moaning that he should forget the insanity that was football. The extra money he would earn from his proper job would finally allow the family a decent home.

If Dona Celeste had hoped for better for her son, she was sorely disappointed during his early childhood. Edson failed to shine at school in Bauru, a railway town, where the family settled on the Rua Rubes Arruda. Rather than doing homework he would earn money as a shoeshine boy or selling the discarded peanuts he picked up from passing trains. On the fields of the Noroeste Club at the end of the Rua Rubes Arruda he also discovered his ability to play football.

On the football pitch his father's influence was obvious. His father in turn thought Pelé had inherited the spirit of his uncle, one of Dondinho's brothers who had died young. In years to come, however, it would be obvious that Edson's genius owed as much to his mother's gifts. As well as Dona Celeste's small, slight build and her beguiling smile, he had also inherited her fearsome, inner strength. 'Anyone who made a judgement about Dona Celeste based either on her lovely smile or her petite figure was in for a surprise,' he would say later in life. Like mother like son. Even at the age of ten he possessed a strength of mind, body and spirit everyone thought extraordinary.

By then those who did not call him Dico were calling him by the name he would turn into the most famous four-letter word in sport. Pelé has no idea where his name came from, despite his own efforts to retrace its history. It may have come from his mispronunciation of the name of one of Minas Gerais' most famous players at the time, Bele. It may have been a half-Portuguese, half-Turkish concoction dreamed up by one of the many Turks who watched him play. All he recalls for certain is that as a nine-year-old he hated it so much he would get into fights with those who called him it. 'I must have lost most of them because the name stuck,' he is fond of saying.

By the age of ten he was playing with much older children in a neighbourhood team, named September 7. It was there he was spotted by the former Brazilian international, Valdemar de Brito. Edson was thirteen when Brito invited him to play for the junior team at the town's other club, AC Bauru.

As an attacking midfielder with the Syrio Libanes club in São Paulo, de Brito had played in the 1934 World Cup side under Luiz Vinhais. Even by Brazil's voluble standards he was a loud and opinionated coach, 'a shouter' according to Pelé. He had been told to keep away from the town's older players because of his boorishness. He seems to have introduced discipline into Pelé's game, however. 'He kept on to us continually about our mistakes, and was very good for me and four or five of my friends,' Pelé recalled. As it turned out, Pelé was to be very good for Valdemar de Brito too.

De Brito had been posted to a civil service job in Bauru but was tired of life away from the more vibrant political centre of São Paulo. He had been working on a way of persuading São Paulo's Governor Janio Quadros to bring him back to the cauldron of the capital. As he watched Pelé develop he saw his train ticket back to São Paulo.

De Brito approached a friend, Athie Jorge Couri, a member of the state legislature who also happened to be president of Santos – a club with ambitions to break the stranglehold the upper-class clubs like Corinthians, São Paulo FC and Palmeiras had placed on the São Paulo regional championship and the Brazilian National Championship, the Silver Cup. He was soon restored to the thick of the action with a civil service job in the state government offices. He also benefited from an agent's fee from his friend Couri.

Dona Celeste had been against Pelé's move to Santos. She had seen his father sacrifice everything for football and emerge penniless. 'To me you are still a little boy, but everyone else seems to think you're grown up,' she complained. Ultimately, however, she saw that football offered his only realistic chance of an escape from life in Bauru. 'You were never a good student, and I don't want you sewing boots for the rest of your life,' she told him.

Pelé found the transformation frightening. On the training pitch he stood out immediately. He was put on a special high-fibre diet and told to build himself up in the *juvenil* and *amadores* sides. By day the encouragement of elder statesmen like Zito and Jair kept him going. As one of the club's unofficial errand boys he was also given a new nickname, Gasolina. ('Get me a coffee kid, and don't spare the gasolina.') But by night, alone in a room with two cots, Pelé cried himself to sleep. After five days at Santos' he rose one morning at 5 a.m., packed his belongings and began creeping his way out of the Vila Belmiro. If the Santos odd-job man, Big Sabu, had not spotted him with his suitcase as he left the ground for the local market, Pelé's career as a professional might have ended there and then. Perhaps they should put a bust of Big Sabu next to the monument to Charlie Miller?

Pelé made an immediate impact for Santos' *juvenil* and

amadores sides, scoring the crucial goals that gave them the state championship. Yet, despite the special diet and training he was given, he remained too small and slight to make his mark at senior level. A piece of the luck his father had waited for all his life changed everything, however. Pelé had been in the stands when Santos' main striker, the stylish Vasconcelos, suffered a gruesome broken leg in a match against São Paulo. Pelé stepped into the No. 10 shirt at the age of sixteen. He scored his first goal against Corinthians of Santo Andre on 7 September 1956 and scored sixteen more in his next ten appearances. He never stopped rewriting the history of football from then on.

As every eternal schoolboy knows, Pelé announced himself at the 1958 World Cup in Sweden. Brazil's infamous psychologist had counselled against giving him a game against Russia in the second round. As Pelé himself admits, Brazilians usually do the opposite of what they are advised. Feola duly put him in and Pelé scored the winner.

By the time he had scored the only goal again against Wales in the quarter-final, a hat trick against France in the semi-final and two more in the Final against Sweden, football had its first, five-star phenomenon on its hands. Even after he limped out of the 1962 triumph in Chile, his legend simply grew and grew.

As a footballer he had no peer. Pelé combined the power and speed of a sprinter with the explosiveness of a gymnast, an extraordinary imagination and vision on the field with the mental and physical toughness of a boxer.

179

He could outjump taller defenders with ease, outsprint entire defences. Against Benfica in Santos' second World Club Championship win in 1963, according to watching journalists, he scored one goal by 'throwing himself into a long jump of at least seven metres' to connect with a cross from his team-mate Pepe. To score another he made a run that left Benfica's toughest defenders literally bouncing off him as they tried to bring him down.

A year earlier, Lula, the famous coach at Santos, had already declared, 'Pelé can no longer be compared to anyone else.' Later he would expand: 'He is fast on the ground and in the air, he has the physique, the kick, the ball control, the ability to dictate play, a feeling for the manoeuvre, he is unselfish, good-natured and modest.' Lula had seen some extraordinary players in his time, but no one with skill levels to compare. Pelé, he said, 'is the only forward in the world who always aims the ball at a precise point in the opposition's net at the moment of shooting for goal.'

It is impossible to overstate the power of the fame that came Pelé's way. Within Brazilian life his importance rose way above football and his achievements in the World Cup. In a vast, multi-cultural country, struggling to integrate its people, he was a unifying force, a smiling symbol of hope. Everyone loved him.

His lack of militancy, his willingness to play within the system endeared him to the government. (He served briefly in the army.) On the streets Pelé used his infectious smile and easy-going personality to work crowds in a way no Brazilian personality had ever done before. 'Player No. 12' he called his fans. Streets, brands of coffee, candy bars and – naturally – thousands of babies were named after him.

Overseas he gave his countrymen and women a sense of pride. People who didn't even know where Brazil was on the map would want to talk about Pelé. In the process he became the most globally recognizable face in Brazilian history. He was the first black man to appear on the cover of America's *Life* magazine. Even his marriage to a white woman, Rosemeri Cholby, was held up as an example of Brazil's new enlightenment on the subject of racial integration.

In 1960, when the Italians came in with offers of a then staggering $1 million to take him to Europe, the Brazilian Congress went into emergency session. The Italians were told to wave their lire elsewhere and Pelé was declared a 'non-exportable national treasure'.

By then Pelé's earnings were a national treasure in themselves. When he signed a new contract with Santos that year he was paid a $27,000 signing on fee, a $150,000-a-year salary – whether he played or not – a $10,000 home for Dona Celeste and Dondinho and a new Volkswagen. By 1963 he was generally acknowledged to be the world's highest-paid sportsman. He repaid Santos by remaining loyal throughout his career and turning them into the most famous and glamorous club in the world. Santos' world tours were built around Pelé's ground-packing presence. Most exhibition match contracts stipulated that he played for sixty-five of the ninety minutes.

All over the world he generated a magic way beyond even the most charismatic politician or member of official royalty. In São Paulo in 1964, there had been genuine concern over the correct protocol when Pelé met the visiting Duke of Edinburgh before a game. Who should be introduced to whom? The King or the Duke? In the end the Duke came to Pelé. In Paris he was greeted by a French minister at Orly and swept into Paris in a motorcade like a visiting president. During a civil war in Nigeria, a ceasefire was arranged so that soldiers could take time off to watch Pelé play.

The Brazilian writer Jorge Amado gave the world magical realism. In Pelé, Brazil also provided the first magical realist footballer.

His surreal effect on the game was never better summed up than by an incident in Bogotá in 1969. In a brutal match, Santos' Colombian opponents had attempted to kick and bait Pelé and his black co-strikers, Edu and Lima, out of the game with racist insults. Pelé, never one to back out of a confrontation, had launched into the referee after Edu had retaliated. He had been sent off for his dissent.

Pelé was in the dressing room taking off his boots when another match official ran in demanding he come back on to the pitch immediately. A bemused Pelé emerged from the tunnel to discover play suspended, the stadium filled with acrid smoke and the perimeter of the pitch lined with armed police. The sending off had so enraged the Colombian crowd they had begun chanting obscenities and threats at the referee and rained down a stream of flaming cushions on to the pitch. Fearing a full-scale riot, the police had ordered that Pelé be brought back on to the pitch and that the official be escorted out of the stadium. Public opinion had demanded that it was the referee, not Pelé, who should be sent off.

If he was a God on the pitch, he was all too human off it. Somehow his frailty only added to his appeal. For all the

millions he had earned, Pelé was twice driven to the brink
of bankruptcy. When he was twenty-five he had been
forced to walk into the Santos boardroom cap in hand
after discovering his property business, Sanitaria Santista,
was on the verge of collapse. In return for bailing him out,
Santos demanded he sign a new three-year contract in
which he played the third season free of charge. Ten years
later he faced the same scenario all over again.

Badly burned the first time, Pelé had diversified his
interests. He now owned a dairy farm, a trucking company,
an import-export business and even a radio station. Yet his
interest in a rubber manufacturing company called Fiolax
had been enough to threaten the end of his entire empire.
Even though a minor stockholder, he had somehow signed
notes guaranteeing a bank loan and agreeing to be responsible for all its liabilities. Fiolax had hit trouble after
breaching government import laws. Pelé was personally
liable for $2 million.

Women proved equally dangerous. When his first marriage failed, a rudderless Pelé fell foul of the blonde
ambition of a one time 'glamour model' called Xuxa.
Her affair with him made her famous. She repaid the
favour by selling their sex secrets and telling Brazilians
Pelé liked his love-making accompanied by Marvin Gaye's
'Sexual Healing'. The final humiliation came after Xuxa
switched her attentions to Pelé's successor as Brazil's
ultimate sporting God, Ayrton Senna.

When she fell pregnant, the Formula One champion
rubbed salt in the wounds with a comment that 'if it
is a girl I will send it to France, a boy I will send it to
Switzerland, if it is black I will send it to Pelé'. (Xuxa's
knack for embarrassing Brazil's icons continues into the

183

Ronaldo era. She extracted a confession from him that he regularly wets the bed. 'Pee-in-the-bed' became his predictable nickname in Italy.)

In each case Pelé would shake his head and rue his naivety. 'I am a simple country boy,' he would mutter. Of course he was far from this. He may see the game differently from the governors, councillors and deputies hovering in his cabinet office, but Pelé was never above a bit of Machiavellian manoeuvring.

Garrincha, the naive 'Joy of the People', disliked the way Pelé dominated the headlines at his expense. Pelé has always denied it, but there are also those who wonder whether he was the invisible force that finally put paid to João Saldanha. In Rio the respected *Jornal do Brasil* journalist Oldemario Touguinho had told me that Pelé had undermined Saldanha's position in the dressing room after one of the ill-fated warm-up matches against Argentina in March 1970. Members of the squad had begun to question openly the coach's grasp of the finer points of the game. During a heated argument they turned to the dignified figure sitting quietly in the corner to adjudicate. It was the only occasion on which Pelé publicly criticized Saldanha's tactics. 'And everybody clapped their hands,' said Touguinho. It may have been coincidence that soon afterwards Saldanha began talking of dropping Pelé and the coach was removed from the job.

What is in no doubt is that Saldanha's attacks on Pelé became increasingly wild in the weeks after his departure. Having at first claimed he was short-sighted – which was technically true – Saldanha went on television to say Pelé was unfit and suffering from a 'very serious disease'. Pelé was so worried he went to Antonio do Passo, the head of the CBD's technical committee, to ask whether medical evidence was being withheld from him. 'For a while he had me believing I was suffering from cancer,' a deeply upset Pelé said later. He never truly forgave Saldanha for his behaviour. Saldanha, in contrast, never forgot how formidable an opponent Pelé could be on and off the pitch.

If you had to nominate his finest piece of political opportunism, however, you would more than likely choose the nifty footwork he displayed at the very end of his career in Brazil. He had never needed it more. When he played his final game for Santos on 4 October 1974, all Brazil watched and waved a tear-stained goodbye. When, just eight months later, he announced he was coming out of retirement to join the New York Cosmos, those same adoring millions felt personally betrayed.

Phil Woosman, the Welshman at the head of the North American Soccer League, had been pursuing Pelé since 1971. By 1974, with financial clouds hanging over him once more, he couldn't resist Woosnam's offer. When the news broke, however, Pelé was pilloried. The humble humanitarian hero had revealed himself as being all too human. Many Brazilians felt let down at the news that even he had a price – although they did not know it yet. He was labelled mercenary and worse in the press. By the time the negotiations were complete, however, Pelé had once more transformed himself into the hero of the people.

In his negotiations with Warner Communications, Pelé played to win. First he negotiated a contract worth $4.5 million. Then he demanded an exchange programme by which American and Brazilian sports coaches would share expertise. Brazilian trainers would school young

Americans in football while their trainers would teach swimming, basketball and athletics in Brazil. In addition he persuaded Warners to sponsor a soccer school for the poor children of Santos. By the time details of the package had been unveiled to the Brazilian public, Pelé's move to America was being hailed as the greatest export deal in Brazilian history.

When Pelé made his debut against Dallas, the match was shown live on Brazilian television. The cameras spent almost as much time on the banners reading 'OBRIGADO BRASIL – THANK YOU BRAZIL' as they did on the football.

He went on to play four fabulously successful seasons in front of 60,000 crowds in New York. When he finally retired for good even President Carter felt moved to encomium, thanking him on behalf of the American people 'for the smiles he put on children's faces, the thrills he gave the fans of this nation and the dimensions he added to American sports'. He went on: 'Pelé has elevated the game of soccer to heights never before attained in America and only Pelé, with his status, incomparable talent and beloved compassion could have accomplished such a mission.'

Arnold Palmer and Jack Nicklaus had blazed a trail in golf, but their sport meant little in Paraguay or Biafra. Mohammed Ali was the most famous man on earth, but his politics made him an uneasy property for commercial sponsors. Pelé filled the void. In many ways he was the first truly global, truly commercial sports star. Where he led, the Jordans, Ronaldos and Agassis of today would follow. None of them have matched him and no one ever will.

*   *   *

Yet in the summer of 1969, as the qualification games for the 1970 World Cup loomed, even Pelé still had something to prove. At Goodison Park against the Portuguese in 1966 he had been carried off the pitch by Mario Americo and an assistant on the coaching team. He had returned to witness the last rites of that campaign with a heavily strapped leg, an ineffectual shadow of himself. His body may have healed after the brutality of 1966, but his pride remained wounded. 'I wanted to put to rest, once and for all, the idea that I couldn't enter a World Cup series without getting hurt.' He was also acutely aware of his place in history.

What better way to cement his status than to win permanent ownership of the Jules Rimet Trophy? Encouraged by the fact that the games were being played in a country where he was idolized, that he had – in Tostão – the best international partner he had yet found and that the CBD under Havelange had finally conceded the root causes of the *fracasso* of Goodison Park, he reconsidered his decision to retire from international football.

No one was happier than FIFA and the television companies who had paid eye-popping sums to transmit the first colour pictures of a World Cup finals by satellite. In the absence of a Eusebio, a Cruyff or a George Best, Pelé provided the glamour figure the tournament needed.

Yet the World Cup's greatest asset was also its greatest liability. The chaotic weeks leading up to the opening ceremony had offered a stream of evidence vindicating those who had opposed the choice of Mexico as hosts back at the FIFA Congress of 1964. Mexico had triumphed over Argentina partly because of its relative political and economic stability. Relative seemed the appropriate word in May 1970 as strikes and terrorist bombings nudged the country towards the edge of anarchy. Only two years after American athletes Tommy Smith and John Carlos had used the Mexico Olympics as a platform for the Black Panthers, real fears existed that the tournament could be hijacked for the sake of internal propaganda.

Pelé had to be guarded round the clock after a group of captured, Cuban-trained guerrillas tipped Mexican police off about a plot to kidnap him before the tournament kicked off. In retrospect, it was little wonder Pelé laughed at the Nazis' POW camp security years later in *Escape To Victory*. Compared to the Suites Caribes, Stalagluft 17 must have seemed like a break in Acapulco.

At the Suites Caribes, a former Brazilian swimming champion, Major Jeronimo Guarani, kept his Mexican troops at their posts twenty-four hours a day. The front gates were guarded by an extra two Mexican police cars and a handful of plain-clothes agents. Journalists were told the official FIFA Press Cards were insufficient to gain entry. An additional card was issued to those deemed reputable and safe.

In their frustration, some Brazilian papers began concocting dramatic tales from the other side of the wire. According to one, Pelé was moved to a different room every night to avoid kidnapping. According to another, he was forbidden from even appearing on the hotel's most popular verandah overlooking the Avenida Lopez Mateus.

When he emerged to train at the nearby Clube Providentia, however, there was no hiding the seriousness with which the threats were being taken. Security guards circled him as he climbed on and off the bus. Pelé would have to pass autographs and even answers to journalists' questions back through his minders.

'My job is thankless but he is a *patrimonio*, a property,' Major Guarani shrugged when asked whether this was not overkill. 'He is a symbol of Brazil.' Whenever journalists got too close to Pelé, he joked, all he had to do was shout that Medici's SNI secret police were on their way and they would soon scatter.

Inside the camp, however, Pelé seemed to have closed his mind to everything but football. Even to those who had watched him in previous campaigns, he had never seemed so determined. 'He is always saying that we need to win and that we shouldn't be scared about breaking a leg to do so. It seems it is the last thing Pelé wants to do in his life as a player,' said Mario Americo, the huge, Kojak-like masseur who had served on the three previous World Cup squads. 'Pelé seems to be a child waiting for Santa Claus.'

If Christmas began against Czechoslovakia, it lasted for sixteen days that will live in the memory of football fans for ever. Each of us carries our memories of Pelé from that tournament. To me, at least, his multi-faceted genius was encapsulated by three moments on the road to the Final.

Against Czechoslovakia he was like a kid playing in his school's first eleven trial. His energy and his hunger for the ball was endless. He would run back deep into his own half to pick up possession. From there he would repeatedly set off on his inimitable drives forward. Pelé's runs were not so much dribbles *à la* Best or Maradona, they were full-steam sprints with the ball seemingly magnetically attached to a point six inches or so ahead of him. Whatever

189

the spell the Czechs too were under it. Time and again Pelé took the ball the length of the field before laying it off to Tostão or Rivellino. Just as the Czechs had got used to it, he switched tack.

To the rest of the world, his half-way line goal attempt was simply proof of his divinity. ('Now I really have seen everything,' said the BBC's Coleman.) As far as Pelé was concerned, however, he had played his hand too soon. He may have silenced Saldanha – 'So much for myopia,' as he said later – but he had also tried and wasted a tactic he had planned in advance. He had intended using the long shot after watching many of the European goalkeepers stray off their lines. 'I wished I'd saved it for a more difficult adversary,' he chided himself.

The second defining moment came against England when he set up Jairzinho for his goal. Pelé later admitted that, in what seemed like a split second to mere mortals, he had had time to think first about shooting, then spot that Banks, Labone and Cooper had moved to cover his shot, then reassess the situation so as to feed Jairzinho with an unmissable opportunity instead. His extraordinary gift for 'seeing' the game around him – I'm surprised no one ever called it PeléVision – had never been wielded so lethally.

The third – and most significant of all – came after Félix and Piazza had conspired to summon up the ghosts of the Maracanã against Uruguay. Pelé personally rallied a side suddenly staring failure in the face. He ran first to the distraught Félix then, it seemed, to every other player on the pitch, including a visibly shaken Gérson. It revealed a reality perhaps best summed up by the great Brazilian football writer Armando Nogueira. 'For the first time Pelé and Brazil share the same destiny,' Nogueira said while in Mexico. 'In the past there were always two entities. Their objectives may have been similar but they moved towards them separately. In the past he was never a leader, not even at Santos. Now Brazil and Pelé are integrated. He is leading this team to their destiny.'

His destiny was decided at the Azteca on that wet, sunny Sunday afternoon.

'Cinema! Cinema!'
Brazil v. Italy, Mexico City, 21 June 1970

After three weeks devoted to the twists and turns of football's greatest event, the vast majority of the 600 million worldwide audience who gathered around their television sets that afternoon were clear where their support lay.

In the heart of Italy, however, one man felt deeply confused. Inside his private chambers at the Vatican, Pope Paul VI was torn between the nation of his birth and the world's largest Catholic country. According to the *Jornal do Brasil*, the pontiff would spend the ninety minutes of the Final fighting to suppress his desires to cheer for either side. He must have been one of the few, football-loving men on earth who failed to show his emotions on an afternoon of extraordinary drama.

For FIFA – and the world – the Final provided the classic confrontation it craved, a match as multi-layered as the Azteca itself. South America v. Europe, New World against Old, the exuberance of Brazil's samba football against the calculating coldness of the *azurri* and their *catenaccio* defence. It was a battle for football's soul and ownership

191

of its most cherished trophy. Secretly, even the Pope must have been praying for a Brazilian win.

Italy had progressed to the Final with their customary, insidious efficiency. Their intentions had been obvious from the moment coach Feruccio Valcareggi announced his squad. The *azurri* arrived in Mexico with three goalkeepers, sixteen defenders and midfield players and only three recognized strikers, one of these the uncapped Gori of Cagliari. No one was in any doubt their attack would be built around the muscular Sardinian assassin Luigi Riva and their game would be built around their infamous defensive system.

In their group matches Italy had been an all too familiar bundle of paranoia and professionalism. The eleventh-minute goal Angelo Domenghini had scored to give them their only win over Sweden in the opening match had been the solitary goal in their three group games as well. If the 0–0 draw with Uruguay had been the most predictable scoreline of the entire tournament, the goalless draw they fought out with Israel was the polar opposite. When the draw had been made Italy had been expected to overwhelm the group's minnows. Instead they barely bothered to come out of their shell in the most sterile and cynical of all their performances. A point was all they needed. Why risk it?

It took a goal from Gonzalez of Mexico to stir them into action against the hosts in the quarter-final. Over the next three hours of football, the world rubbed its eyes as the defensive Dr Jekylls of the tournament were transformed into free-scoring Mr Hydes.

Domenghini got his second of the tournament after a deflection, before Riva finally showed his abilities with two goals. Rivera's fourth broke the Mexican hearts. The long-suffering Italian fans had barely recovered from the shock by the time their semi-final against West Germany was turning into the most thrillingly unpredictable game of the tournament.

At first the game had seemed a classic piece of *catenaccio* smash and grab. The bustling Roberto Boninsegna had given Italy the lead in the ninth minute and for the remaining eighty-three minutes Italy did what it did best by closing the game down. With the imperious Beckenbauer out injured, the Germans seemed to have no answer. Then, as the Peruvian referee added two minutes of stoppage time, in an uncanny echo of the 1966 Final against England, Karl-Heinz Schnelliger brought the Germans back from the dead. Extra-time was a switchback of emotion with first Gerd Muller putting the Germans ahead, only for Tarcisio Burgnich to equalize. Then Luigi Riva scored Italy's third before Muller again levelled it at 3–3. Gianni Rivera, on as a substitute for his great rival Mazzola, closed the match with minutes to go. At the end all twenty-two players lay prostrate on the lush Azteca pitch. The eleven Italians knew they had just two full rest days to recover.

The Brazilians were forced to uproot themselves from the Suites Caribes for Mexico City. Pressmen who travelled with them could not help being impressed by their cool, calm demeanours as they made the climb to an even higher altitude.

Their tactics were finalized at a series of meetings on the Saturday night and early Sunday morning. Zagalo had already explained his plan to use Jairzinho to lure Facchetti out of position on the left side. With the *cobras*, Pelé, Gérson and Carlos Alberto, he had also stressed that Brazil's best hope of all might lie in Italy's sheer exhaustion after their semi-final. His side had finished all their matches the stronger outfit. Never would their stamina prove more useful, he predicted.

The Italian man-to-man marking threw up a series of classic confrontations. Bertini spent much of his time impressing Pelé with his sly repertoire of rib-digs, shin-taps and shirt-pulls. The Brazilian later called him 'an artist in fouling a man without getting caught'. Bertini's art even extended to his complaints to the referee. Whenever Pelé went down under his tackling, he would run to the East German referee, Herr Rudi Glockner, and scream 'Cinema! Cinema!'

Gérson, typically, had proclaimed that the Italians were terrified of playing his side. They were certainly terrified of Pelé. When Rivellino's cross drifted into his path in the thirtieth minute, a lifetime of experience went into wrongfooting and utterly dumbfounding the Italian defence. Burgnich was soon deputized to take over the least enviable job in the world, with only marginally improved luck.

Having inspired them, Pelé was shattered to see Clodoaldo, Félix and Brito conspire to throw an equalizer away.

The period following Boninsegna's goal was, to Pelé's mind at least, the most dangerous of the entire campaign. If Italy had been able to overcome their natural caution and gone for his side's jugular, he confessed later, history might have turned out differently. 'If the Italians had capitalized on our momentary demoralization,' he explained, 'I might have wondered if we had come this far only to lose.'

Pelé's rare attack of insecurity deepened when, with thirty seconds of the first half seemingly still to play, Glockner blew for the interval just as he was placing the ball once more in Albertosi's net. 'Were we going to be victimized by a referee from Europe?' At half-time, Pelé thanked the heavens for allowing him and his team to 'recover our spirits and morale'.

In the second half it was Gérson who embodied that spirit and morale best. His patience in waiting for an opening had been exemplary. The great Scot Bill Shankly later told his countryman Hugh McIlvaney how he had watched Gérson hang back in the first half. 'He discovered before half-time he could move up and put Italy in trouble, but he knew if he did too much of it they would see what was happening and try to find a solution at the interval.'

The sort of improvizations Gérson, Carlos Alberto and Pelé could introduce with a quick, on-field conference proved beyond Facchetti and the inflexible Italian system. Gérson ran riot, with Pelé his most sophisticated supporter.

After Gérson's goal had flown in, Pelé helped Jairzinho to one of the afternoon's many records. He brought the curtain down on his World Cup career with the kind of selflessness he had shown throughout the tournament. When he received the ball in the Italian penalty area from Jairzinho, Pelé would have been within his rights to shoot. No one would have begrudged him a final farewell flourish to his World Cup career. Instead he completed the most perfect passing movement of the game with a friendly, rolled pass into the path of Carlos Alberto. His friend would never stop thanking him for it.

When the final whistle went Pelé was hoisted aloft by the

sea of fans that invaded the pitch. Before they reached him he made sure he had taken his shirt off. 'I had no intention of being strangled by some delirious fan,' he explained afterwards.

Amid the lunacy of the dressing room he sought solitude in the shower where he offered a little prayer. He recalled later how his mind was filled with thoughts of the friends and family who had helped him on the long road from Três Corações. His mind was so active, he admitted, 'I thought of so many things that in truth I don't remember exactly what I thought.'

Finally I get in to see Pelé at around six. By now the ante-room has thinned out. The last of the official delegations has delivered its honours and left. My presence has become a source of curiosity to the small assortment of politicians that remain. When they discover I have come from London there is only one question they want answered. 'How much do MPs earn in England?' The answer leaves them deeply unimpressed. 'It's OK, OK,' says one.

Originally I was told Pelé would have to leave at 3.30 p.m. His private jet was booked to leave ten minutes later. Two and a half hours later, I am becoming desperate. Finally the baby-faced doorman ushers me in. To my horror the rest of the room follows. It seems Pelé has agreed to have his picture taken with all the remaining politicians. Once they are appeased I am his – until, that is, he runs to catch the plane already warming up its engines at a nearby airfield.

Among the group is the shiny-suited character who had bewailed his chances of re-election. He is now grinning from ear to ear. With his photograph safely taken, he even shakes my hand and thanks me as he leaves. When one of the group gets a little too close Pelé makes a joke about a newspaper photograph of the Argentines Claudio Caniggia and Diego Maradona. 'Did you see that picture of Caniggia and Maradona kissing on the lips?' he says. 'Too much,' he laughs. Being seen to behave like an Argentinian is close to death for any Brazilian man, let alone a politician. The man withdraws to a more dignified distance.

By the time the office has cleared, Pelé seems drained. As we talk he tells me that he is heading for Europe within the next few days. Among other things he has meetings with Umbro, the sportswear manufacturers, Michel Platini and Bernie Ecclestone. 'Very clever man,' he says of the Formula One boss. There is something about Pelé that makes you protective of him. 'Very ruthless man too,' I am tempted to add, but don't.

He is still a slim and supremely athletic-looking specimen, dapper in a dark jacket and grey slacks. Time too has been kind to his lineless face although he admits he keeps the grey hairs from his head with a pair of tweezers. The most charismatic smile in the history of sport still shines with a megawatt brilliance. Yet for the first time he looked something more than half his fifty-seven years of age. It is in his heavy, faintly haunted eyes that the weariness gives itself away.

I hand him a copy of one of my previous books. I have signed it *Para Pelé, con amor e admiracão*. To Pelé with love and admiration. We both know he will never read it but he thanks me nevertheless. He takes me over to his desk from where he produces boards filled with drawings of the prototype for the multi-purpose sports stadia he hopes to build in major cities all over Brazil. The

Pelezinhos as they have been christened, are impressive, partly open-aired affairs. There are basketball courts as well as football pitches.

'Everything I have and everything I am, I owe to football. The only thing I want as a minister is to repay a little bit of what I received. This is what I am most passionate about,' he says, showing me the elegant blueprints. 'I am not here to do politics, I am independent,' he stresses again. 'That way I will be able to achieve something. My work is to help the children.'

Of course if a more conventional politician talked in such terms you would be tempted to laugh in his face. In Pelé's case, however, his genuine identification with the victims of the poverty from which he himself emerged, is at the very core of his popularity – both in Brazil and around the world. This is the man, who in 1969 after scoring his famous 1,000th goal at the Maracanã, publicly wept as he said, 'Remember the children, remember the poor children'. As Cardoso said himself when he announced the appointment, Pelé is 'a symbol of Brazil that has come up from the roots, that has triumphed.'

He is the first to admit he is no saint. He was sent off far more times than is commonly thought, mainly – it has to be said – for retaliation. Yet at times, like those he is currently passing through, his genuine humanity must seem wasted on the world he inhabits.

Brasília has no shortage of sharks who want to make him look out of his depth. In parliament Pelé has constantly complained about the lack of money coming into his

Ministry. 'There is just one thing that makes me upset in the ministry, our funds are very small and sometimes I need to beg,' he pleads. He has criticized other ministers for not collecting the 4.5 per cent of the sporting lottery that is theirs by rights. One replied condescendingly: 'Pelé you are very new to this, you will not be able to understand.'

'I'm learning a lot about Brazil and politics. Sometimes it is very difficult but it is important for my life,' he shrugs. After the toing and froing of this week, however, even he is despairing.

'Football cannot carry on the way it is, something has got to change,' he says of the refereeing scandal, shaking his head sternly. He says he is determined that power be spread wider than Teixeira and Havelange, from whom he has become increasingly estranged in recent years.

Pelé's war with Havelange has now entered the realms of the personal dogfight. No one is quite sure where it all began but it seems to have its roots in the early 1970s. By 1974, when Pelé refused even Medici's pleas to return to the fold, many believed it was bad blood with Havelange that stopped Pelé from playing in Germany. What is certain is that by the 1994 World Cup, Havelange's proudest achievement, Pelé's increasingly outspoken attacks on the corruption within the Brazilian game were hurting. In a fit of childish pique, Havelange banned Pelé – the most famous footballer in history and the only footballer in history as far as America was concerned – from officiating at the draw.

Since then both men have dug their trenches deeper. Pelé maintains corruption is worse today than ever. Speaking of the CBD's successor, the Confederação Brasileira de Futebol, he said, 'If the CBF had to explain the contracts it made with Pepsi, Umbro and now Nike lots of people would be in prison.'

Havelange says condescendingly that Pelé should stick to organizing the schools and making sure there are enough gymnasia in Brazil. 'I am respected around the world, how can they do this in my own country?' he has been crying as he continues to talk of kicking Brazil out of France 1998. Pelé is learning fast. He simply smiles, calls Havelange's threat 'the reaction of a dictator' and quotes the anti-Christ. 'Some years ago Maradona told me that Havelange was going gaga. I defended him and fought with Maradona. But now I really think he is becoming gaga. Havelange must understand that the dictatorship is over.' The two most powerful men in the history of Brazilian sport seem determined to fight until only one of them is left standing. I know where my money is going.

For all his talk of leaving when he has had enough, Pelé is committed to continuing his work at the Ministry. His enemies know that to damage him they will have to damage Cardoso, with whom Pelé is welded together in destiny. For the President, Pelé is a priceless ally. For Pelé the President offers him a chance to fulfil perhaps his ultimate dream: to become the first black president of Brazil.

In another piece of extraordinary political theatre, the Brazilian senate is in the process of rewriting the constitution so that Cardoso can stand for a second term. The 'one term only' rule had been introduced to protect them from unpopular, or corrupt, politicians. When, in Cardoso, Brazil discovered its equivalent of Kennedy and Tony Blair, it decided to do something about it. If Pelé remains, who knows what rewards lie in wait.

* * *

Pelé says he has no time to do the kind of lengthy, in-depth interview I want to do now. In any case he would like an idea of my questions in advance. Primed for this, I hand a printed collection to his *chef de cabinet*, the grey-suited, grey-haired Luis Felipe de Cavalcanti Albuquerque. I know full well he is too busy to be able to answer them in any detail – if at all. (Without Cavalcanti, it turns out, I would never have made it this far. He had been my most powerful advocate inside the ministry, prompting Pelé at one point to wonder why he was siding with me? 'I am not siding with him, I am siding with the human race,' he had replied.)

Pelé gathers together a few more pieces of correspondence while I talk to the dapper Cavalcanti. Before I know it Pelé is away. Tired he may be, but Pelé is still the fastest thing I have ever seen over three yards. No sooner has he shaken my hand and bidden me a farewell than he is out of a side door and on his way to the private jet.

He will, I discover later, be in Wembley by the weekend.

On the plane the following morning, Pelé's fixed smile stares out from all the papers. In-depth reports of his meeting with Cardoso run from the front to the inside pages. In one quote I read, Pelé says 'things have been going down since 1970'. I will not get the answers to my list of questions but at least he has answered one of them for me. Before I know it he has answered another as well.

As the clouds consume Brasília and its swathes of greenery, I wonder how he will survive the nonsense

201

that goes on in his Ministry and beyond. But then I see another interview with him in which he says: 'Two days ago I made a joke with Cardoso that everyone who becomes a minister will need to have heart surgery. It is good that I am from Três Corações, isn't it?' On the evidence of his life so far, Pelé probably does have three hearts rather than one. Don't bet against him becoming President as well as King of Brazil.

CHAPTER VIII

The Ball Thief

Of all the footballers to have visited the soccer-obsessed city of Belo Horizonte, none have made an impression to compare with that of the former Polish amateur goalkeeper who toured the capital of the state of Minas Gerais in 1980. Tens of thousands crammed themselves into the Praça Israel Pinheiro in the neighbourhood of Mangabeiras to catch a glimpse of Karol Wotjyla, lately installed as Pope John Paul II. He rewarded the faithful with an open-air Mass and a ringing endorsement of the decision their founding fathers had taken eighty-three years earlier. 'What a beautiful horizon,' he said, moved close to tears by the view over the Curra Del Rey mountain range.

On a grisly, grey Friday morning, looking out from high above the Rua Uberaba, that same celebrated vista is lost in a muggy mist. It has been raining for two days and shows every sign of raining for several more. At least the clouds are lifting on the face of Wilson Oliveira Piazza. In his office, he is congratulating himself on finding the typed copy of a favourite line of poetry he thought he had lost for ever.

> To be mineiro is to not say what we do nor what we
>   are going to do,
> Is to pretend that we don't know what we know,
> Is to speak very little and listen a lot,
> Is to pretend to be a fool, but be intelligent,
> Is to sell cheese and to own banks.

He nods, smiles, re-adjusts his spectacles then carries on.

> A mineiro doesn't lasso a cow with a straw,
> Doesn't trip in the wind,
> Doesn't walk in the dark,
> Doesn't walk where it's wet,
> Doesn't talk too long with strangers.

> Only believes in the smoke when he sees the fire,
> Only risks when he is sure,
> Doesn't exchange a bird in his hand for two that
>   are flying.

> To be mineiro is to ask why?
> And be different,
> Is to have a trademark,
> Is to have history.

An hour or so by air from both Rio and Brasília, Belo Horizonte stands in the heart of Minas Gerais, a sweeping, mountainous inland state bigger than Paraguay. As Piazza's poetry reading suggests, its people, the Mineiros, are intensely proud of their country within a country. They are prouder still of the city they regard as the jewel of Brazil.

204

Belo Horizonte's tourist board can drown you in statistics in praise of the place. It will tell you the United Nations voted their city as having the best quality of life in Latin America, that its average temperature is 21° C, that each of its 2.1 million inhabitants has 27 square metres of green space. The irony of all this is that Belo Horizonte – and its people – need no selling at all. Both speak eloquently enough for themselves.

Unlike the awesome, awful sprawl of São Paulo and the magnificent chaos of Rio, it is a city in the conventional sense, with form and shape, a civic centre and a sense of civic pride. Its museums and churches, parks and squares – not to mention its sophisticated nightlife – make it a safer, saner, somehow happier city than any other I encounter on my journey. Even the traffic seems to work.

I arrived in the midst of one of the busiest periods in the city's 100-year history. High-powered political delegations from every major country in North and South America are in Belo Horizonte for the imaginatively titled 'Meeting of the Americas'. On the road in from the gleaming, new airport the sky is thick with military helicopters. One side of the freeway has been closed off to allow motorcades of limousines, military police, motorcyclists and armoured wagons to brush their way past.

The display of military might does little to impress the taxi driver. He offers a smirk and a slow shake of his head. 'It's just a show,' he says reassuringly. Over the coming days I will discover his expression is Mineiro to the core.

*   *   *

With Brito and the late Everaldo, Piazza was one of the unsung heroes of the 1970 side. As part of its derided defence his performances were too easily dismissed outside Brazil. His World Cup was far from flawless. He was, most infamously, at the centre of Cubilla's embarrassingly soft goal in the semi-final. Yet his coolness in operating as what the Brazilians call the fourth *zagueiro*, and the Europeans call a *libero*, was central to the team's triumphs. Watch the videos again and his performances will look all the more accomplished when you realize Mario Zagalo had only converted him from his normal midfield role weeks before the tournament.

Mineiros pride themselves on their hospitality, so Piazza insists on picking me up at the hotel then driving me to his office. Like most of the players I had met, Piazza has weathered well. Indeed he seems a lighter, happier character than I remember him. In 1970 his face seemed to be wrapped in an eternal scowl, as if he had eaten one of the bad Mexican oranges Alf Ramsey feared so much. Today he turns up smiling, despite the pronounced limp he is carrying from his latest footballing wound. 'We say that today we take the field, in the past we played,' he smiles when asked about his standard these days.

He guides us on a mini-tour of the city, emphasizing how prosperous it has become thanks to companies like Fiat who have a key South American operation here. 'Brazil is a great country,' he says at one point. 'But it is still a country of social injustice as a whole. There is still unemployment, people starving,' he goes on, shaking his head as he scans the streets.

As he drives through the bustling streets, it is soon obvious that, in one important respect, at least, Piazza is an untypical Mineiro. 'Mineiros are shy people but there are exceptions who like to talk a lot,' he smiles in the mirror. 'Like myself.'

Piazza's life today is a full one. He owns a string of successful businesses and has recently retired from a senior role on the Minas Gerais' equivalent of the Football Association. His energies are concentrated in his office on the Rua Uberaba from where he runs the organization he created himself almost twenty years ago. AGAP, or to give it its full title, Associação de Garantia ao Atleta Profissional de Minas Gerais, is an independent outfit designed to look after players – and their families – when the glory days come to an end. Its equivalent in England, I suppose, would be the PFA's benevolent fund.

He formed the union back in 1978. Now about 2,000 players, around 10 per cent of Minas Gerais professionals, pay an annual fee of just $34 to be covered by AGAP's services. From offering apprentices advice on contracts to helping retired players apply for jobs outside football, AGAP provides a safety net for those who want it.

The majority do not. Piazza shows me round his office and introduces me to his staff. He shows me a file on a famous Atletico Mineiro player, Alberto Monteiro, whose widow he is helping at the moment. There are newspaper cuttings and gruesomely detailed photographs of Monteiro lying in a squalid room where he had drunk himself to death. 'He was thirty-two years old when he passed away,' Piazza says with a disbelieving shake of his head. 'We are trying to help his wife as much as we can.

'I would be happy if AGAP didn't exist,' he explains, sitting me down in his office a few moments later with a *cafezinho*. 'It would be a sign that we don't have problems. But we have a lamentable maxim here in Brazil: "Football makes the life of a few secure, and the life of many insecure".'

As he sips his coffee and recounts his own, outstanding career, it is soon apparent that Wilson Piazza always knew which group he intended joining.

Piazza was born in the town of Ribeirao Das Neves, Minas Gerais, on 25 February 1943, the son of Jose Piazza and Regina Da Silva Piazza. He describes his childhood as an unremarkable one. His family were modestly comfortable. Piazza was an average student but left school at fifteen for an office job at a tyre company on the Avenida Antonio Carlos. The company had its own football team where he quickly shone.

Piazza was bright and acutely ambitious. He may not have sold cheese but he certainly entertained ideas of working for, if not owning, a bank. He landed a job as a clerk at Banco Mercantil De Minas Gerais and for a while looked set for a commercial career. His true passion, however, was football: 'I wanted to be a professional. Even if I had to play in the worst team in the world, I knew I had to make that dream come true.'

For a time he juggled his two lives, playing football every morning until midday then working at the bank from 1 p.m. until 9 p.m. – or later. Piazza's job was to balance the bank's books at the close of business each day. Some days the figures fitted, some days they did not. 'We could not go home if there was a cruzeiro difference. Sometimes we were there until 11 p.m. or midnight. Once I didn't go home at all and slept in the bank.' He remained at the bank until he was twenty-three and able to live full time off his football. By then he had already emerged as an international in the making.

He was eighteen when he was offered a place as a junior at Esporte Clube Renascença. Though unimposing physically, his determination and intelligence as a ball-winning, creative midfielder soon established him as one of the rising stars in Belo Horizonte. His breakthrough came three years later, when he was transferred to Cruzeiro, a club about to put Mineiro football on the map. Piazza's office is near the club's old ground on the Rua Uberaba. As we drove by there, he pointed out the souvenir shop that is the only relic of the ground's once glorious past. His arrival there coincided with the beginning of a golden age in both Belo Horizonte and Mineiro football.

Since the days of Charlie Miller and Oscar Cox, the story of the Brazilian game had, for all intents and purposes, been the story of the game in Rio and São Paulo. From Porto Alegre in the south to Boa Vista in the far north, the sport was the national passion. Yet, for political, economic and simple geographical reasons, the two big cities ruled. Since the so-called National Championship had begun in 1950, the trophy had never left the big two cities – hardly surprising since it was not open to sides from other states. It would not be until 1971 that a Mineiro side, Atletico, would win a genuinely pan-Brazilian title. Equally the international side was almost exclusively made up of players from the big city clubs.

209

Cruzeiro announced their arrival in 1965, when Belo Horizonte's 110,000 capacity Minerao stadium was opened. They beat Santos, and Pelé, 4–3 in a specially arranged match. A year later they beat Brazil's reigning kings of club football again, this time lifting the Copa Brazil, the nearest to a truly national title, as they did so. Mineiro football was on the map at last.

In 1966, Piazza's clubmate Tostão would be the first player from a Mineiro side to break into the national XI. Where he led, Piazza and other stars like Dirceu and Natal, and later Fontana and Dario, would follow.

Much like Santos, Cruzeiro were bonded by a tight-knit, brotherly atmosphere within the club. The directors' policy of selecting almost exclusively Mineiro players only deepened their devotion to the Cruzeiro cause. 'There was only one player, Raul, who was not Mineiro. So that team in the 1960s was like a family,' Piazza explains.

In the wake of 1966, the national squad was forced to cast its net wider in its search for players capable of making up for the disgrace. Piazza joined Tostão in the first Brazilian national squad assembled post-England under Aimore Moreira in 1967. By the qualification matches in 1969, he had formed a powerful midfield partnership with Gérson. Piazza's intelligence and tenacity looked the perfect complement to Gérson's visionary distribution. His nickname at Cruzeiro was *ladrão de bola*, the ball thief. He supplied the bombardier's bullets.

The energetic young Clodoaldo's emergence at the end of Saldanha's reign had, however, offered Zagalo an even stronger option. When a switch to the centre of defence was suggested after Carlos Alberto, Gérson and Pelé's Rio summit on the eve of the Austria match, Piazza had been reluctant. 'I was a combative player, I liked to be in the action in the middle of the pitch. Suddenly I found myself stuck at the back,' he says. A natural all-rounder, he made the transition comfortably enough in the match against Austria. Yet as Zagalo stuck with the idea of using him as a defender, he felt like a square peg alongside Carlos Alberto and Brito. 'I was used to giving more of myself. At the end of the game it seemed as if I hadn't played, my shirt wasn't wet,' he says. Piazza found himself repeating the phrase the *cachaça*-hazed Garrincha made infamous: 'Is it the end?'

He was, of course, not alone in playing out of position. With the exception of the defence, almost the entire midfield and attack was learning to adapt to a sometimes radical change in their position. To the Brazilian public, however, Piazza's new role seemed the most dramatic conversion since St Paul. It became one of the dominant debates in the press in the days after the squad's departure. Even his mother chimed in with a plea to Zagalo that her boy be restored to his rightful position in midfield.

Piazza's greatest fear was that he would not be able to compete with the Europeans' long-ball game. 'We called it the *jogo aereo*, the air game. I am 1.66 metres (around 5ft 10in) so I thought, "Oh my God, I'm here in the World Cup and they play the *jogo aereo*, they will do what they want".'

Zagalo, however, remained convinced that with Clodoaldo and Piazza, he had the sheet anchors he needed to allow Gérson and Rivellino to play.

*   *   *

211

The psychologist of the 1950s may have been discarded, but experience had taught the senior members of the squad the value of the mental side of the game.

It had been the devout Pelé who had first floated the idea of communal prayer meetings. On the phone to his wife Rosemeri back in Brazil, he had been told how his entire family had been gathering before matches to pray collectively for him and his team-mates. 'Why don't you also pray, all of you?' she had asked him.

Pelé, suffering more than most from homesickness, mentioned it to Carlos Alberto and Rogerio, both of whom thought it was a good idea. Piazza was one of the next to join in.

Not all of the squad were Catholic. Yet soon twenty or so players were holding regular prayer meetings. 'At Guanajuato we would gather under a tree after dinner each evening,' he explains. Each night a different player would offer a different prayer. 'We prayed for the sick, for those in prison, it was not a question of asking God if we could win the Cup,' Piazza smiles. 'Soon we had everybody from the cook to the president of the delegation. There was a spiritual force, it made us feel united as a group and it gave us confidence when we came to the first games.'

Piazza's calming, Mineiro influence would prove priceless in the weeks to come. On the eve of the opening match it deserted him, however. He recalls spending the night before the Czech match playing a card game, *caxeta*, with Carlos Alberto long into the night. 'After months of training you are anxious to begin. I was very nervous, like a bull.' The opening moments of his World Cup did little to ease his anxiety.

Piazza remembers feeling dazed after Petras' early goal.

'It was like if you were punched, not by Mike Tyson, but by a lightweight,' he says.

As Rivellino, Pelé and Jairzinho laid the foundation for a memorable opening win, Piazza felt the nervousness lift. He admits it never returned to haunt him again during the campaign. 'I was scared because I was so relaxed,' he smiles. Such composure was a rare commodity in a team that reflected the breadth of Brazil's colourful, regional character. 'The Carioca is more extroverted, he thinks he is the best, he jokes more,' explains Piazza. 'The Paulista is more hard-working, more conscious about being professional, maybe because in the big city people don't have time to complain, it's only work, work, work. The Mineiro is shy, more hospitable, communicative, they listen more.'

There were moments when the mild-mannered Mineiro influence of Pelé – a son of Minas by dint of his birth in Três Corações – Tostão and himself saved the side from over-confidence, he believes. In the immediate aftermath of the opening 4–1 win the atmosphere in the dressing room had been euphoric. As far as some of the players were concerned, the Cup was as good as in Carlos Alberto's hands. It was Pelé who moored the more excitable temperaments with a little Mineiro wisdom.

'Pelé clapped his hands and made a short speech. He said: "It was good, but we must improve". Then he sat beside me. He knew what kind of person I was. He told me: "Piazza, if we don't say this there will be guys who will think that we are already champions".' Like his fellow Mineiro, Piazza knew there was no smoke until they saw the fire. 'It was Mineiro precaution. He was saying, take care.'

213

If England exposed any defensive deficiencies in Piazza's game, they centred not on his lack of height but his lack of a grounding in the game's black arts. He would never claim to have been an angel. If his memory serves him, he was sent off five times, but always for complaining to referees. As far as he is concerned, his nickname says everything about the way he played. The man was never the ball thief's target. 'I did not kick people,' he says simply.

In the aftermath of Lee's kick on Félix, Piazza had been asked to exact retribution. 'Carlos Alberto said: "We must stop this guy". I told him: "I'm not going to do anything".' Piazza had his own welfare in mind. 'I knew that if I did I would be punished because I never knew how to kick anybody. If you don't know how to do something and you try, it becomes ridiculous.' Carlos Alberto was left to mete out justice instead.

Piazza says he enjoyed the England match more than any other. 'I like a game that demands attention all the time,' he says. When I suggest he left the pitch that day with his first sweat-drenched shirt of the tournament he smiles. 'Yes, it was a good game.'

Piazza reverted to his old midfield role against Rumania. 'I played in Clodoaldo's position, Fontana replaced me as a fourth *zagueiro*,' he says. His energetic intelligence shone through as he linked well with his clubmate Tostão and Paulo Cézar. The win deepened his confidence that even without their stars, Brazil were a force to be reckoned with. 'You cannot be restricted to eleven players. You must have a well-formed group,' he explains. 'We won without Gérson and Rivellino. That was important.'

Piazza shared a room with his Cruzeiro team-mate

Tostão. The two men were friends at Cruzeiro and socialized with their wives, Margot and Vania. 'Our friendship went beyond the four lines of the pitch,' he says. If Piazza had always been an unusually talkative Mineiro, Tostão had not. He preferred not to talk too long to friends as well as strangers. Piazza knew his friend well enough to cope with the silences. 'Sometimes I spoke to the walls,' he smiles. 'Or I went to other rooms. But I was used to Tostão.'

The press offered another alternative, of course. Piazza was among the older, wiser heads free to talk to the journalists allowed into the Suites Caribes. With Gérson and Carlos Alberto he presented a defiant voice. 'We cannot repeat 1966,' he had said in one interview. 'The Brazilian people do not deserve that again, despite the fact that they didn't support us. The people do not deserve defeat.'

Like every other player, he concedes they came closest to defeat against the old enemy Uruguay. Of all the Brazilian side, Piazza was the most painfully aware of the brutality he was about to face in the semi-final. He recalls, to the day, his introduction to the Uruguayan school of macho football. 'The twelth of June 1968, that is when I broke my leg at the Maracanã playing against Uruguay,' he says. 'I admire Uruguay, besides they are bold, brave. If they want to fight with you they fight in your home, in their home. Their game is not like the Argentinian, that is more like Brazil, more technique; Uruguay use more force.'

He admits that he – and his side – played badly in the first half. Like Félix, he is still not willing to take the blame for the blunder that induced 110 million missed heartbeats. He says it was a mistake by Brito that forced

215

him out wide to cover Cubilla. He did not dive in with a tackle because he was sure he could force the attacker further away from the goal by staying on his feet. Like Félix he wishes Cubilla had connected cleanly. 'It was a bad shot,' he says. When he hears Félix's explanation about the pitch markings, he cannot but arch an eyebrow and smile: 'I thought the pitch was perfect.'

Returning to his boxing analogy, he nods when I ask him whether Cubilla's goal was the closest thing Brazil encountered to a Mike Tyson punch. 'Yes,' he says. Yet by the time the team had dragged itself back from the edge of disaster and triumphed, Piazza's inner confidence had reached its zenith. 'When we won that game against Uruguay, I lay in bed that night and thought "We are the champions",' he says simply.

'Everything or nothing'
The celebrations, 22 June 1970

The clerk who once slept with his bank rolls has clearly prospered in the years since he left the Banco de Minas Gerais. As well as financing much of the AGAP operation himself, he owns a successful chain of petrol stations. 'I always had parallel activities besides football,' he says with a canny smile. He tells a story to explain how his Mineiro caution extended itself to his finances.

'While I was working at the bank I had a colleague who was in the cinema at 4 p.m. while I was still working hard. He had a nice car while I walked a lot and took the tram. Today, unfortunately, that man is in a very bad situation,' he says with a shake of his head. 'So there are players that like to have a great car today and will have to walk a lot later in their life,' he smiles. 'I have a very nice car today.'

When the players were searching for representatives to negotiate their fees for playing in Mexico twenty-seven years ago, Piazza was, unsurprisingly, at the head of their list. Piazza, with Carlos Alberto, Gérson, Pelé and Félix, had formed the players' committee who would deal with João Havelange and Antonio do Passo. As Piazza recalls, the final negotiations over the pay structure for the World Cup took place in Rio, shortly before the squad left for Guanajuato in May.

At first the players had asked for a package that would earn them between $1,500 and $2,000 for each game leading to the Final and then another $3,000 or $4,000 if they made it all the way to the Azteca on 21 June. The package would have brought each player between $12,000 and $14,000.

Instead Havelange and do Passo offered a remarkable alternative: a smaller payment for each game leading up to the Final, and a large, lump sum if – and only if – they brought the Jules Rimet Trophy home.

The offer was talked about in a calm and constructive meeting of the players. 'We openly discussed it,' he says. A sense of duty and destiny quickly prevailed. 'Of course we wanted to earn, we were professionals, we wanted to earn the maximum, but we were so conscious that we were trying to recover our reputation after 1966, that it was not so important for us. We wanted to recover the title for Brazil. We knew that there was the political regime and we needed something.'

In the end the players unanimously agreed to accept

Havelange and do Passo's proposal. 'Of course we thought it could be better but we accepted their rule,' says Piazza. 'So for the first games we earned $900 per match. If we lost the Final we kept the $4,500 from the five matches to get there. If we won we got $10,000. So the Final was everything or nothing.'

'I always say football is a fairytale in your life, it's the time of the unreal life,' says Piazza. 'Later you come back to reality, you come back to life.' No period in Piazza's life would match the surreal few days that followed the win over Italy.

The team returned to a nation in the throes of the wildest party in its history. Even the playwright and arch-pessimist Nelson Rodriguez admitted there was 'no longer any need to be ashamed of being a patriot'.

In Brasília, Rio and São Paulo they were driven through vast crowds on top of heavily guarded *bombeiros*, or fire engines. In his autobiography, Pelé described the scenes on the Avenida Brasil in Rio as 'a madhouse'. 'There was pure carnival in the streets, traffic diverted, the avenue jammed with people shouting, singing, dancing, drinking, clogging an artery of traffic and not being bothered by the honking horns nor the edging bumpers.' In the chaos, 44 people were killed and 1,800 injured during the two-day celebrations.

Their countrymen's gratitude for what they had achieved seemed to know no bounds. The CBD had told the players they were free to bring back as many gifts as they could carry through the airport. Brazil's strict customs laws were suspended for the players. (It is perhaps a measure of the importance of the win to the ordinary Brazilian that, when the 1994 World Cup winning side tried to do the same with twelve tons of high-tech merchandise on their return to Rio, they were held at the airport for half a day while the Finance Minister agonized over whether to allow them through. When he finally agreed to waive the duty, public opinion disapproved of the decision by a massive 70 per cent majority.)

As well as the money they had agreed with the CBD, the players were rewarded by their state legislatures and clubs. With Tostão, Piazza returned to a tickertape welcome in Belo Horizonte. The two heroes were each given a section of land by the city's elders as a mark of their gratitude. Only the Cariocas seemed to lose out. Back in Rio Paulo Cézar had complained that all he received for his part in the triumph was a 'filet mignon'. 'In Minas, Tostão and Piazza earned a piece of land, so did Everaldo in Porto Alegre. In Rio they invited us to have dinner and gave us a filet mignon,' he had said. ('It was shit, we didn't earn anything,' he added of the rewards that came his way.)

For Piazza, however, the rewards continued to come – and in the most unexpected ways. It was in 1971 that he was first approached to join the leading opposition political party, the MRB. His fame as a footballer made him an ideal candidate, he was told. He stood for a place on the Camara Municipal, Belo Horizonte's civic legislature and won.

Piazza went to the 1974 World Cup, the only member of the 1970 back four to return. The tough-tackling Luis Pereira of Palmeiras – eventually sent off for attempting to decapitate Neeskens in the ill-tempered Holland match –

219

epitomized the more ruthless, European-style defence Zagalo opted for and Piazza spent the tournament on the bench. By 1977 he had retired to concentrate full-time on politics.

The professional politician seems still to rank somewhere beneath the tax inspector and the death squad commander in Brazilian life. Piazza, like Carlos Alberto and Pelé, seems almost embarrassed to admit to his alternative career. At least Piazza's defence is a little sounder than either of his superstar colleagues.

'There are circumstances where a man does not do what he likes to do, he is pushed, conducted into a situation,' he says, sounding a little like Clint Eastwood trying to justify the circle of bodies lying at his feet. 'But football taught me a lot about politics. In football you work in a team, a group atmosphere and you must think that way.' He must have learned to look after himself as well in the council chamber as he did on the pitch. He went on to serve three terms, and was re-elected in 1976 and 1982. His tenure lasted for sixteen years in all. The senior role he has played on the Minas Gerais ruling football body and his work at AGAP seemed a natural progression from there.

It is clear that Piazza has prospered through his success as a member of the 1970 side. And by now it is clear that none of the team – with the possible exception of Paulo Cézar – is in need of the kind of professional help AGAP provides for the players of today.

Yet Piazza knows better than anyone the rewards available to the Ronaldos and Romarios, Rais and Roberto Carloses of today. As the driving force behind an organization pledged to protect players' welfare, did he share

Paulo Cézar's feeling that he and his team-mates were exploited back in 1970, I wondered?

'No,' he says instantly. 'It's true that it doesn't pay for the meat on the table or my son's school. But sport is important, it is a vehicle that opens up dreams.' He goes on to express a view I have heard before and that seems to sum up, perhaps, how different the footballers of his generation were from today's – off as much as on the field.

'What is more rewarding is being part of the so-called golden age of Brazilian football,' Piazza goes on. 'Despite the fact that Brazil won a fourth World Cup, that team is a part of history. If you go out here in Belo Horizonte, or Rio or São Paulo and say "Give me the names of the players that won in 1994" they don't know. "Now say the team of 1970": they know.

'I have affection and recognition. As a person I feel that is my reward.'

At the end of our morning together, Piazza once more insists on driving me back to the hotel. As we drive through Belo Horizonte he continues chattering away in his un-Mineiro way. He tells me he is the father of two children, a twenty-two-year-old daughter Fabrizia and an eighteen-year-old son, Felipe.

He explains that he has seen little of his former room-mate Tostão in recent years. When Tostão's marriage broke up and he moved out of the family home in the Parque das Mangabeiras, Piazza's wife Margot took Vania's side. Their regular foursomes in Belo Horizonte became a thing of the past. 'It tore us apart a little bit,' he says rather sadly.

221

The likeable Piazza is in no doubt of where he stands in the affection of his countrymen. He is no Pelé, Gérson or Tostão, and he knows it.

On the pitch his contribution was prosaic. Yet in his life away from the game Piazza, of all the players I have met, is the one with the most obvious touch of poetry in his soul. At the end of our time together he tells an old Brazilian story about a hummingbird. It is intended to explain his view of the work he has been involved in since Mexico. In many ways, it sums up his unsung contribution to the triumph just as well. It is, perhaps, the way we should remember him.

'A bird came across a great fire in the forest and saw a hummingbird flying back and forth. Each time the hummingbird filled its beak in the river then flew back to the fire dropping its beads of water on to the flames. The other bird stopped the hummingbird and asked: "I have been watching you a long time. What are you doing? Do you think you can extinguish the fire, are you crazy?" The hummingbird replied: "No, I'm just here doing my part."

'I'm the hummingbird. I'm here doing my part.'

CHAPTER IX

The Recluse of the Rua Curitiba

'Magic and dreams are finished in football.'
Carlos Alberto Parreira, 1994

The Rua Curitiba flows through the heart of Belo Horizonte with all the grace and grandeur of a great river. A teeming epic of a street, it rises in the vibrant heart of the city, a lattice work of noisy, steeply banked alleys crowded with newspaper vendors and shoeshine boys, fresh fruit and cigarette stalls. By the time it has petered out at the foot of a rollercoaster hill, a mile or two later, it has become a tranquil, tree-lined boulevard overlooked by empty old tenement buildings and sophisticated, well-secured, modern apartment blocks. At the end of its eventful journey, only its small, corner cafés and elegant restaurants offer discernible signs of life.

It is somehow fitting that the home of Dr Eduardo

223

Gonçalvez de Andrade stands here amid the stiller waters of one of his home city's most compelling streets. Even when the world knew him as Tostão, he was invariably the deepest and most serene member of the Beautiful Team. His life, however, has been no less dramatic than the Rua Curitiba itself.

Tostão was the great enigma of the 1970 side. At first glance – certainly compared with the ebony-skinned original with whom he formed perhaps the best striking partnership in the history of football – 'The White Pelé' seemed unathletic, underdeveloped, even frail. He showed few glimpses of the spectacular shooting skills of Rivellino or Gérson, even though at his club Cruizeiro he was known for packing a punch in his left foot. Instead he was the most elegant and intelligent member of the team, a provider of darting, sometimes diverting runs, short-range passes and killer finishing touches. He scored two goals in the final stages, but his 'assists' were treble that amount. Tostão even ruffled the immaculate Moore of England, nutmegging him to set up Jairzinho's only goal against the soon-to-be ex-world champions. If Pelé and Gérson represented the soul and the steel of the side, Jairzinho, Clodoaldo and Rivellino its youth and energy, then inside the tousle-haired head of Tostão beat its most sophisticated footballing brain. It was no surprise to read later that he was a qualified doctor.

In the years since 1970, Tostão's life had taken the most obvious turn away from football. The hysteria with which the triumph was greeted in Brazil rested uneasily on his shoulders. Like a quieter, more erudite version of Bruce Wayne, Eduardo Gonçalvez de Andrade laid his superhero alter ego to rest just three years after Mexico. He returned to medicine and Tostão was no more. It is only in recent years that he has picked up his old name and re-emerged, modestly, into the mainstream of Brazilian life as a television analyst on Bandeirantes and a football columnist for two of the country's most respected newspapers, the *Jornal do Brasil* and the *Estada São Paulo*.

By rights then he should have been the most reluctant interviewee of the Beautiful Team. He may not be quite J. D. Salinger, but he is no João Saldanha either. The luck of Brasília had turned, however. Tostão had been polite, even encouraging in his conversations from London. His problem was, he said with evident pride, he was finishing work on a book himself and was busy. While I was in Rio he had learned that he was about to head off for Europe and the Tournoi de France. He was pushed for time but could fit in an hour on a *quid pro quo* basis.

'Anything you could tell me about the England team, I would be grateful.' On an overcast Thursday afternoon, he has invited me to his home for coffee.

As I walk up, then down the Rua Curitiba to Tostão's apartment, I know my journey is now drawing to a close. For Jairzinho's position has hardened. Even though he knows I have spoken to so many of his former team-mates, he still sees the matter as professional rather than personal. He knows I am heading back to Rio before leaving for London but unless there is a professional fee involved, his answer remains no. The figure quoted back to me is $10,000, exactly the fee he received for his contribution to the Final against Italy. I can't help feeling there is a certain sadness to the symmetry.

Of the only other missing member of the team, Piazza's central defence partner Brito, there is disappointing news too. From London he had been full of enthusiasm. He had insisted on being called as soon as I arrived in Rio. No sooner had I set foot there, however, than he had performed a vanishing act.

'He is out fishing,' his wife had explained each day in Rio. The message is still the same more than a week later. By now the fishing trip had turned into an epic reconstruction of Captain Ahab's search for Moby Dick. 'I really don't know when he will be home. He could be gone for days,' Mrs Brito is now lamenting.

In Belo Horizonte Piazza had seemed the ideal person to fill in the gaps. I had been able to glean that, after the ancient one, Félix, Brito had been the second-most senior figure of the side. He was born on 9 August 1939 in Rio where he seems to have settled in the same poor Vila de Penha suburb as Carlos Alberto. Brito, then at Vasco da Gama, had travelled to England in 1966 but had spent his trip on the bench, understudying Feola's gerontophile back four. Four years later Zagalo had built his defence around his muscular, 6ft 2in, 80 kg frame, by now the rock of the defence at Flamengo.

Brito's long, powerful physique and unnatural strength made him the butt of many of the Guanajuato jokes. 'We used to say that man was not descended from monkeys. First Brito was born, then the monkeys and then man,' Piazza had said.

His humour seems to have been only a little more sophisticated. 'If you were taking a photograph he would come and insist on taking it for you,' Piazza told me. 'It would be developed and then it would be only the legs, from the waist downwards. It was his idea of a joke.' Clodoaldo had told me how Brito hid false teeth in Mario Americo's food. 'He was going to eat and suddenly he was shouting "Oh, my God".'

Yet for all his reputation for Carioca craziness, Brito had taken his last chance of World Cup glory as seriously as any member of the squad. At the age of thirty, he was clearly in the best physical condition of his life. 'In the Cooper Tests, he came out as the fittest physically of all of us,' Rivellino had told me. His preparation paid dividends in a campaign in which he was stretched to the limit.

Brito lacked the calculating calmness of a Bobby Moore or the all-round footballing ability of a Franz Beckenbauer. He was responsible for his share of errors. Blame for Petras' opening goal for the Czechs, Sotil's second in the quarter-final against Peru, and, if we are being harsh, Boninsegna's in the Final, could comfortably be laid at his door. Yet talking to his colleagues it was clear that his importance to the side was considerable.

Brito's was the most vocal and physical presence in the Brazilian defence. 'He would call me *chefinho*, little boss. He would shout "Come on *chefinho*",' Piazza had told me. Even Gérson had called him 'a lion' among men.

Perhaps his finest performance came against England. For all the heavy artillery wheeled out against him, Brito held resolute. In the Final too, his strength of personality helped overcome the frequent lapses. No contribution was more important than a wonderful tackle on Boninsegna when Piazza had let him through on goal in the final fifteen minutes. Brito's intervention effectively snuffed out Italy's resistance. Soon Clodoaldo was constructing the *coup de grace* that would end the game in such glorious style.

227

Brito's career seems to have taken a slide afterwards, in part because of his age, in part because of his loosening grip on his temper. Zagalo had been at the Maracanã during the final match of the 1971 Carioca Championship between his Fluminense and Brito's Botafogo. Botafogo had only needed a draw to win the title. They were within a minute of holding out for a 0–0 draw when Lula scored a controversial last-minute goal. In front of 142,000 fans Brito protested to the referee that Marco Antonio had pushed his keeper Urbirajara and that he had been offside. When he refused to cancel the goal, Brito laid him out with a haymaking punch. When Zagalo recalled virtually the entire squad for the Independence Cup tournament in 1972, Brito was the most glaring omission.

Today Brito works for his local authority, in a less grandiose version of what Gérson is doing in Niteroi. He oversees the provision of sports facilities for local schoolchildren. By now I am assuming that fishing is to be a central part of the syllabus.

At the end of the Rua Curitiba, a security guard lets me through the gate and a lift takes me up to the top floor of one of the smartest apartment blocks. The figure that greets me in a baggy black shirt and jeans introduces himself as Eduardo. If I had not known his alternative identity, I would never have guessed it.

Like Ferenc Puskas, Tostão's short, stocky frame was always going to make him look portly in middle age. His hair is thinning and his spectacles thick and bookish. If he looks nothing like a sporting idol, there are no clues of his former life on his walls either. His living room is tasteful and immaculate, decorated with his collection of Brazilian art. The furniture looks French and a collection of impressive cut glass sits on a table. His fastidiousness is an accident of birth, he explains.

Eduardo was born in Belo Horizonte on 25 January 1947. 'Aquarius,' he smiles as he pours coffee from the silver pot his *empregada*, or housemaid, has placed on the table for him. 'I am a very rational person, I analyse things and come to rational conclusions. At the same time I am a critical person, ironic, very quiet, introverted. I speak a little but I don't keep quiet,' he sums up with a sagacious nod.

Eduardo's family was middle class, his father worked in a bank in Belo Horizonte and played amateur football for one of the city's clubs, América. He passed on his love to all four Gonçalvez brothers. 'I grew up in a passionate football atmosphere,' recalls Eduardo.

Eduardo was the shortest of the brothers, but even as a seven-year-old he stood out. Soon he had been christened Tostão, the little coin. Unlike Pelé, he must have liked the name. There are no stories of psychological wounds, only an apologetic smile. 'I can't remember when and why it started.'

By the time he was fourteen, Tostão was playing junior football for Cruzeiro. By the age of sixteen he had signed professional terms at América – his father was no longer on the books. As he passed through his apprenticeship Tostão found time to keep his head in his books. 'I had cultural notions, I liked to read, I liked to study,' he says.

At eighteen, marked out as what he calls a *grande promessa*, Tostão had to choose the direction his life was to take. Until then his opinion of football as a profession had been characteristically white-collar. 'Football was like

229

a paid entertainment,' he says. Blessed with intelligence and a sense of his own God-given ability, he opted to leave his studies, at least for a few years. 'It was worthwhile because I had everything to be a great player. I was aware that it would be for a short time and my future life would be different,' he says.

A natural goalscoring centre-forward, Tostão quickly emerged as the great meteor of the Brazilian game. His intelligence and all-round ability was soon winning him comparisons with Pelé. In 1966 he was called up to the Brazilian squad as the King's prince in waiting. At nineteen, he was little over half the age of some of Feola's veteran squad. He made his World Cup debut as replacement for Pelé in the Hungary match. His baptism was memorable for the explosive left-footshot he fired past the Hungarian keeper Gelei, but eminently forgettable in every other sense. He grimaces at the memory of the humiliations that followed. Tostão lays the blame on the lack of organization and basic physical fitness.

'From the group of 1958 and 1962, the only one who was in condition to play was Pelé. Djalma Santos, Gilmar, Bellini, Orlando, Garrincha, no,' he says, shaking his head. Tostão had heard the stories about Garrincha's alcoholism but still found his disconnection from reality hard to believe. 'They said that Garrincha didn't even know who the opponents were in the Final in 1958. In England Garrincha was in no condition at all and played.'

He left England regretting that Feola had failed to listen to those, himself included, who believed that rather than being his understudy, he should be Pelé's partner. It had been in a warm-up match in Sweden on the way to England that Tostão had sensed he had found a kindred spirit. 'It was a friendly game and we understood each other immediately,' he says. 'He needed a more intelligent player at his side, a player that understood where he was going to be.'

Tostão picks himself up from his chair and walks over to the dining table where he is working on his book. From his carefully laid out piles of cuttings and jottings, he produces a sheet of printed text. He explains he has been writing about Pelé and begins reading a passage. 'I understood why Pelé was the best player in the world. He passed the ball well, he was intelligent, a warrior in the field, growing with each moment. There was no weakness, excess or pain in his football. It was complete simplicity itself. In the field I soon understood the movement of his eyes, his body, his thoughts before the ball arrived.' At the end he adjusts his glasses, smiles, seemingly inwardly pleased with what he has written, then returns the paper to its place in the pile.

It is perhaps his greatest footballing regret that they didn't play together more frequently. 'Today the Brazilian squad meets every month. In my time it was not like that, we played two or three games a year. If I had had the opportunity to play in the same team as him, our partnership would have been richer.' It was not only Tostão's loss, it was the world's too.

Tostão's journey to Mexico was at times unbearably eventful. He was the unquestioned hero of Brazil's qualification campaign under Saldanha. His all-round contribution was as profound as it would be in the finals. During the team's travels around South America and back in the Maracanã in

August 1969, however, it was his phenomenal goalscoring ability that set his countrymen's hearts racing.

He had forced his way into Saldanha's side with his display against England in June that year. Ramsey's men arrived from Mexico with an unbeaten tour record and a quiet confidence that they could strike an early psychological blow against the side already being trumpeted as their most serious rival the following summer. Brazil emerged with the mental edge, after a convincing 2–1 win in which Tostão scored a spectacular winner.

As the ball had broken loose in the English defence, Tostão seemed to pose no threat as he lay prostrate on the pitch. Seeing the ball moving towards him, however, he levered his lower body off the grass with his arms and executed a mid-air scissor-kick that sent the ball crashing home. Back on Fleet Street, photographs of Tostão levitating himself to manufacture a barely believable goalscoring shot was used as chilling evidence of Brazil's rediscovered divinity. Years later Tostão was shown copies of the back-page eulogies he received. 'The people didn't understand how I scored that goal,' he says, a boyish smile breaking across his face. The goal proved a portent of things to come that summer.

From the moment he pounced on the Colombian keeper Lagarcha's parry of a Pelé free kick in the thiry-ninth minute of the opening *elimanatoria* match in Bogotá, Tostão was in the most lethal form of his international career. He scored the second in the 2–0 win in Bogotá and four days later broke the deadlock against the Venezuelans in Caracas. Tostão left the defenders Chico and Freddy floundering before finishing with a cool shot, thirteen minutes from time. In the remaining quarter of an hour he and Pelé ran riot, first Tostão setting up his partner for the second then scoring the third and fourth goals himself.

His form continued back at the Maracanã. He scored two more in the 6–2 win over Colombia but saved his finishing masterclass for the decisive win over Venezuela on 24 August. His hat trick within 24 minutes took his tally to ten in four matches and his team to Mexico. Pelé scored the only goal in the final match against Paraguay. By the end of the month the duo had scored fourteen goals in five games between them.

Tostão's free-scoring performances won him the headlines normally reserved for Pelé. In Europe, where he had only flickered in 1966, the White Pelé became the symbol of the new, revitalized Brazil. Soon he would symbolize the fragility of his nation's confidence instead.

Tostão's career – and so his life – was transformed during a Corinthians v. Cruizeiro match in late September 1969. In a freak accident he was hit in the face by a ball from Corinthians full-back Ditao. Such was the force of the impact he could not see afterwards. In hospital he was diagnosed as having suffered a detached retina.

Drawing on his own connections, Tostão engaged one of Belo Horizonte's most eminent medical figures, Dr Robert Abdalla Moura. On 3 October all Brazil held its breath as Tostão and Dr Moura flew to Houston to undergo potentially risky surgery to the eye. Moura performed the operation himself at the Santa Monica Ophthalmology Center in Houston and returned to Brazil to pronounce himself pleased with the results.

The following months were agonizing for Tostão. In

233

April 1970, on the Friday before he was due to make his comeback against Paraguay in the penultimate warm-up, Tostão woke up in bed in Belo Horizonte with blood streaming from his left eye. At first his bad luck looked like Dario's good fortune. Instead the game ended a goalless draw and both teams were jeered off the pitch. It proved the last time the President's favourite wore the No. 9 shirt and reminded Zagalo how priceless Tostão was to his side.

At first Zagalo had to be convinced of Tostão's importance to the campaign. 'When Zagalo took over he was soon saying that I was a reserve to Pelé. Up front he said he needed a player of speed,' Tostão explains. As the manager watched the team at work in practice in the warm-up matches and began to switch Saldanha's 4–2–4 formation to a more flexible 4–3–3, however, Tostão's importance to the side became clear.

Like Rivellino, Piazza and Jairzinho, Tostão was asked to adapt his natural game to fit into the plan. His sacrifice was, perhaps, the greatest of all. Zagalo asked Tostão to suppress his predatory instincts and act as a sophisticated target man instead. He would spend much of the Mexican campaign with his back to goal, flicking and stroking off a range of simple and subtle passes to Jairzinho and Rivellino, Pelé and Gérson. 'They needed somebody to organize the game up front. I was the pawn,' he smiles.

Yet when he joined the squad at Guanajuato, there were those – Pelé included – who doubted whether he was physically and mentally up to the challenge ahead. Their fears were understandable. Tostão cut a sensitive, secretive figure at the training pitches. Back in Brazil even

President Médici had been expressing his public concern at his fitness. At the sight of a quote-hungry journalist he would hold up his hands and plead 'Please don't ask me about my eye'. Within the camp his insecurity became unsettling. Publicly Pelé expressed confidence that his friend would pull through. Privately he harboured serious doubts. What else was he to think when he saw Tostão unwilling to head a ball in training? 'They were a little bit apprehensive, scared that I was not well,' he nods, pouring some more coffee as he speaks.

Two weeks before the first match he suffered an attack of conjunctivitis. As Dr Abdalla spent a day examining him he offered to withdraw so Zagalo could draft in a replacement. 'I said: "If you are not confident that I can play you should fire me and I would understand".'

Tostão's friendship with Piazza allowed him his peace and quiet in their room. While Piazza made himself scarce, Tostão would spend hours dismantling and studying a large, plastic medical school model of an eye he had been given by Dr Abdalla. The model helped him overcome his fear. 'We are only frightened when we don't know what we are suffering from. I know my problem very well,' he told reporters philosophically at the time. Dr Abdalla remained in Guadalajara and, with Tostão's parents, was a frequent visitor to the Suites Caribes.

As his strength and confidence returned, his patience with the press had seemed to mirror his renewed determination. 'If I give up now, I will never play football again and I will never feel self-confident any more. I cannot give up. Am I a man or a mouse?' he had said, a new defiance in his voice.

Tostão had been the team's touchstone the previous

August. Not a man for idle boasting, when *he* began to talk of Brazil winning his confidence spread through the camp. Even today he can recall the calm certainty he felt in the final days before the opening match. 'It is not something I can explain, it is something deep inside. I am a very intuitive man. I always have a feeling when something good or bad is going to happen and rarely am I wrong.'

Despite the traumas of the preceding months, Tostão fulfilled all his potential in Mexico. He was perhaps the most consistent of all the team. Yet when he puts his own performances in the World Cup under the microscope, his hypercritical mind finds them wanting. As far as he is concerned he made three 'great moves' in the tournament. 'If I left those three moves out I would say I played badly – sincerely.'

He scored two goals against Peru – the first an impudent shot inside Rubinos' near post, the second a scooped shot high into the netting from a dangerous cross-cum-shot by Pelé. Yet he discounts them both. 'The two goals I scored were two simple goals, nothing exceptional,' he says. 'The rest of my contribution was important tactically, very important without doubt, as a pawn.'

He admits the first, the 'nutmeg' of Bobby Moore which led to Jairzinho's goal against England, owed as much to panic as premeditation. He had seen Zagalo warming up his replacement Roberto on the touchline and realized he would have to pull out something special just to remain on the pitch.

'Without doubt it was the most difficult match because

England annulled Brazil's moves. Tactically England were perfect, it became a chess match,' he says. 'Roberto was warming up. I thought "He'll replace me so I must do something now".'

He had already had a shot deflected when he picked up the ball again on the left. His twisting, turning run took him through Moore's legs and away again. His back was turned to the goal, yet his swivelled cross travelled deep into the crowded English area and straight to the feet of Pelé. Pelé sucked in the defence before unloading the decisive pass to Jairzinho. Even the telepathic twosome had never managed quite such a psychic connection. In the elation that followed Jairzinho's goal, however, Tostão was still substituted. 'They had signed the papers, before the goal,' he smiles. 'But there is no doubt the substitution was a stimulus for me to try something different.'

He is far prouder of his crucial contributions in setting up Clodoaldo and Jairzinho's goals in the semifinal against Uruguay. Amid the fireworks of Pelé and Rivellino, Gérson and Jairzinho, the moments are hardly ones that blaze away in the memory. Both were perfectly weighted, inch-accurate through balls rather than moments of extemporized goalscoring. That he should choose these two moments above all others is perhaps the ultimate testimony to his philosophy as a footballer. For Tostão both were triumphs of substance over style.

'Clodoaldo ran and shouted to receive the ball in front of him. I was able to wait a few seconds so he could arrive in the right position,' he says of the first. For the second he had to place a ball in a tiny two-metre space between the advancing Jairzinho and a retreating defender. 'I was very conscious that if I gave the pass in front of the defender he would arrive first. So I gave the pass in front of Jair and behind the defender. When Jair controlled it the defender tried to turn, lost control and Jair went on and scored,' he says.

'I'm more proud about them than the move against England because there it was completely emotional. In the two against Uruguay I had the clear sensation of the consciousness of the move.'

Given the dramas that had befallen him en route to Mexico City, the sensitive Tostão found the Final almost too much to bear. He had been a restless sleeper throughout his career. 'When journalists asked me how I was before an important game, I would say "I'm very well, confident",' he smiles. 'The truth was I was extremely tense, I didn't sleep well because I was preoccupied, thinking.' He admits he barely slept during the stormy night of 20 June.

Tostão's respect for Gérson was enormous. 'Carlos Alberto was the captain, the great leader was Gérson,' says Tostão. Of all the side, he was the player in whom he felt he could confide. 'I liked him very much. We would sit up until three or four o'clock in the morning talking,' he says. The two men sat up late on the night before the Final, each calming the other's nerves.

The Final represented Tostão's ultimate sacrifice. He had been involved in the discussions about how to turn Italy's man-marking system to Brazil's advantage. 'It was the most clear example of the group working together,' he says. As well as the ruse to draw Facchetti out of position, Zagalo and his team sensed that Tostao's ability off the ball might be able to create precious space for his midfield colleagues too.

238

'We agreed that I would play far in front. I would not go back to receive the ball, I should stay with the spare defender, obliging him to stay with me.' The plan worked perfectly during the opening phase of the match as Rosato played the unwitting *consigliere* to his Godfather, shadowing his master's every move. As Tostão buzzed around amongst the back three, Rivellino and Gérson duly discovered the Azteca opening up to them. 'If Rivellino had been on top of his game he would have scored at least two goals from outside the area. I think he put five shots over the bar,' Tostao says with a rueful smile.

The Platonic principles at work within the side had borne remarkable fruit on the way to the Azteca. But perhaps nothing summed up the collective spirit better than Tostão's supremely selfless contribution to the Final. His intelligent runs off the ball kept Rosato and the Italian defence guessing all afternoon. 'My pleasure was to play with the ball but against Italy I was playing without the ball,' he says.

Tostão even appeared in the penalty area to clear the lines at one moment of danger in the second half. We also tend to forget that the famous Carlos Alberto move was begun when Tostão, running himself into the ground in the dying minutes, dispossessed an Italian deep in his own half.

All of us who witnessed it remember the Final for the beauty of that closing phase of play. Gérson and Jairzinho's goals paved the way for a flourish that embodied all the qualities that had made the Brazilians the most admired and loved side in the history of the tournament. Tostão's memories too are dominated by the sheer emotion of its climax. After Jairzinho scored the third goal and he knew the game was safe he admits he could contain his feelings no longer. As the sun poked through, the pitch had begun to dry. Tostão's tears were soon dampening the lush Azteca once more. 'I played the last fifteen minutes crying,' he confesses, wiping the moisture from his eyes as he speaks.

When the final whistle went Tostão became, with Pelé, the focus of the crowd's adulation. The two had turned to each other and embraced. As others ran for cover they were swamped by the throng. Tostão's initial joy soon gave way to fear as Brazilian and Mexican fans ripped his boots, shirt, shorts and socks off him. 'I was in the middle of the pitch. At first it was huge emotion but then I realized I only had my underwear on,' he says. 'I was in panic, the Mexican police rescued me.' He was delivered to a dressing room convulsed by a *crise de choro*, 'a crisis of tears'. It was only hours later that he began to absorb the full impact of what had happened.

With Pelé and the rest he had gone out to the official party at the Hotel Isabel Maria on the Reforma in the centre of Mexico City. Once more the players found themselves besieged by elated Brazilian and Mexican fans and had to virtually fight their way into the party. The popular Brazilian singer Wilson Simonal had been hired to sing. Carlos Alberto led the dancing as the party went on until 1 a.m. on the Monday morning. Pelé, Carlos Alberto and Zagalo were among those who were summoned at one point to talk to President Médici on the telephone. All three struggled to hear a word he was saying.

Tostão stayed only briefly, however. He slipped out without a word and headed back to his room at the hotel. 'I am a reclusive person. I wanted to be alone in my room,' he says simply.

Tostão gave his medal and his No. 9 shirt to Dr Abdalla as a mark of thanks. As he returned to Brazil a national hero, his beloved solitude – and peace of mind – were commodities he would find increasingly hard to come by.

'Forward Brazil'
The Aftermath, Brazil, June/July, 1970

Outside, down on the Rua Curitiba and beyond, a warm, light rain puts a sheen on the streets of early evening Belo Horizonte. In the distance, as the rush hour begins, the horns of the gridlocked commuters build into a cacophony. As if the din is not deafening enough, the air is thick with the sound of helicopter gunships, grazing on the rooftops in another show of military machismo for the visiting politicians.

For Tostão it is all a depressing echo of the way things once were in his country. It was from barracks in Minas Gerais that the tanks had begun rumbling on the morning of 1 April 1964. Dissident army units, hostile to President João Goulart, struck south towards Rio and the Presidential Palacio Laranjeiras. By the end of the day, by now deprived of the support of the generals of the Second and Third Armies in São Paulo and Rio Grande do Sul, Goulart had conceded defeat. The first of a series of military coups that would sweep South America was complete. The generals would rule for the next twenty-one years.

In 1970, the military dictatorship was at the zenith of its power. For all the players may protest otherwise, its influence over the football team ran much deeper than the removal of Saldanha and the Dario affair. Football had become a cornerstone of the military's campaign to present the Brazilian public with a picture of a nation on its way in the world. Spectacular building programmes like the proposed Transamazonia highway and impressive economic statistics like the ten per cent growth rate Brazil now boasted were all very well. To the ordinary Brazilian, however, Pelé, Tostão and the rest were a more tangible monument to Brazilian flair and ambition. They were the greatest export the country had ever produced, the invincible embodiment of Brazil's ascent from Third to First World status.

The win provided Médici and his AERP spin doctors with an unmissable opportunity. Elsewhere in South America, the generals of Argentina would soon be laying out the blueprint for a similar injection of national pride.

Tostão returned to Brazil to discover that the team's win had become Médici's win too. From Mexico City the team was flown direct to Brasília, where they rode in on *bombeiros* protected by tanks and troop-carriers. (In Brasília I was told how one ecstatic fan had run alongside the heavily armed procession in an effort to shake hands with the players. It had been Carlos Alberto who warned him to get back before he was fired on.) Médici opened the doors of his Presidential Palace to the public for the first time then addressed the nation on television.

'I feel profound happiness at seeing the joy of our people in this highest form of patriotism. I identify this victory won in the brotherhood of good sportsmanship with the rise of faith in our fight for the national development,' he told Brazil. 'I identify the success of our [national team] with intelligence and bravery, perseverance and serenity in our technical ability, in physical preparation and moral being. Above all, our players won because they knew how to play for the collective good.'

Tostão watched the situation with a deepening sense of despair. Inside he knew he wanted nothing more to do with faith, brotherhood or the collective good. As a member of a liberal, intellectual family, all his political instincts were opposed to the regime. 'I didn't agree with the dictatorship. I came from a family that criticized that, they were *contestadora*,' he says, his voice hardening for the first time during our afternoon together. 'I knew people that were *assassinated*. I was very angry with the situation.'

In the run up to Mexico he had alluded to his views in an interview. It was a dark age of telephone-tapping and torture, a time when priests were imprisoned and military convoys surrounded newspaper printing plants to pulp dissident editorials. His comments left Tostão, a restless, troubled soul at the best of times, feeling distinctly uneasy. 'Afterwards I was a little bit scared that it could bring me bad consequences,' he admits. His fears were confirmed when he received a phone call in which he was told he would need to 'clarify' what he meant. 'It was anonymous. I don't know whether it was a trick or not.'

Back in Brazil, he was faced with the choice of doing something. During the post-match celebrations in Mexico and the flight back to Brazil, Tostão's elation had been edged with anxiety. 'When we arrived we were received by Médici. I was very angry with the situation in Brazil,' he says, using his hands now to emphasize his points. Sensing he would never get a better opportunity to register his

243

disapproval of the regime, he considered boycotting the official welcome from Médici. His absence would speak louder than any words.

As a member of the eleven that had brought such glory to Brazil, Tostão himself was now untouchable. His friends and family enjoyed no such protection, however. 'I can clearly remember that I was uncomfortable and I didn't feel like going there. But I thought about the repercussions it could cause.'

In the end he dutifully slipped into his official CBD suit, sipped champagne and smiled for the photographers. He has never really forgiven himself. 'I rationalized that one thing had nothing to do with the other, we were professionals in sports and we could not mix that with political problems,' he says, shaking his head still at the memory of the greatest missed opportunity of his footballing career. 'It was a chance I had to protest. I regretted it very much.'

His turmoil only deepened as he watched Médici make political capital of the team's triumph. The military's human rights violations had begun to attract unwanted interest overseas. In 1969 Amnesty International had expressed its concern at the situation. The following year the USA and – albeit obliquely – the Pope added their voice. For the spin doctors of the AERP, the team were the perfect diversion. On television and radio the team's anthem '*Pra Frente Brasil*', Forward Brazil, became the Government's theme song. On billboards and streetcorners, giant posters of Pelé performing a broad-grinned salmon leap were accompanied by the slogan '*Ninguem segura mais este pais*', Nobody can stop this country now.

As if Tostão's pain was not deep enough, '*Marcha do*

Tostão' became one of the Government-inspired songs used to capitalize on the public's pride in the triumph. The song, which opened with a breathless commentary and an elongated cry of '*Goooooooool*', moved millions of his fellow Brazilians to tears. If Tostão ever wept at the song it was out of despair. He would not remain a public figure for much longer.

'If Brazil lose in Mexico, Pelé will come home a prince and not a king. If we win Pelé will come home a demi-God – and Tostão will be his king.' The prediction made by the country's most popular football magazine, *Placar*, pretty much summed up the reality that faced Tostão when he returned to Belo Horizonte. Soon the new king of Brazilian football was distancing himself first from his home city, and then the game itself.

In the months that followed, the little coin became the richest player in the history of Mineiro football. In the run up to Mexico, Tostão had been angered at Cruzeiro's attempts to peg his wages. He drove a hard – and imaginative – bargain when he agreed to stay there. Tostão's deal included a 2,000 cruzeiros novos per month salary, all his income tax paid by the club, a 70,000 lump sum each season, regardless of whether he played or not, a marketing contract with the Minas Gerais Government worth 100,000 and an entire floor in one of Belo Horizonte's most prestigious new apartment buildings. The apartment alone was worth 560,000 cruzeiros novos. The deal totalled a million yet it was not enough to keep him in Minas Gerais.

Vasco da Gama's Amadeu Rodrigues Sequeira, head of one of Brazil's biggest coffee retailers, had run for the vice-presidency of his club on the promise that if elected he would bring the White Pelé to Rio. Sequeira paid the first instalment of his then record $520,000 fee and was the most prominent member of the fundraising effort that followed. Tostão received a tickertape welcome when he arrived in Rio.

Yet Tostão's disillusionment was by now deepening further. Tostão admits he found fame simply unbearable. 'It disturbed me being a person who aroused curiosity,' he says now.

When he once more damaged his eye two years after the World Cup, the doctor's warnings almost came as a relief. The medical men made his decision for him and he retired at the age of twenty-six, in 1973. Even then it took time to rid himself of his other life.

Tostão returned to his studies at the Universidade Federal de Minas Gerais where he decided to devote himself to a medical career. 'I wanted to be a doctor for several reasons. It was a noble and important profession and it was a challenge. But also I have always been a thoughtful person, philosophical. I thought that through medicine I could get to know more about the human being – the body, the mind, life and death,' he explains.

Yet even the academics within the university could not separate Tostão and Eduardo Gonçalvez. He would arrive to find film crews disrupting life in his classrooms. Wherever he went staff preferred to talk of Pelé rather than paediatrics. 'The teachers wanted to talk about football with me instead of talking about the subject that I wanted to discuss in medicine, the nurses wanted to know about football, I would treat a patient and he or she would keep asking me about the game. It all disturbed me, so I had to cut off this relationship,' he says.

A quarter of a century later he feels he has regained some of the freedom he lost. 'Today I'm practically a person,' he smiles.

He remains a solitary, introverted person, however. Tostão is happiest sitting in his eyrie on the Rua Curitiba, composing his syndicated thoughts on football. It was his son who drew him back into football. He went with his family to Italy to watch the 1990 World Cup. 'We went in private. Then I started missing football and wanted to see more,' he says

His renewed interest coincided with his divorce from his wife Vania and a sense of disillusionment with his life as a doctor. He had become one of the most respected members of his university's Faculty of Medical Science and a frequent speaker at graduation ceremonies and a quiet inspiration to his students.

Inevitably politics once more contributed to his unhappiness. Much like Tostão, Brazil had rediscovered its freedom in 1985, after years in the darkness. After a generation of military rule, however, the March election of Tancredo Neves as the nation's first civilian president since the coup of 1964 was far from the end of Brazil's internal problems. Happy though Tostão was to see true democracy restored, he also saw inflation and a chronic lack of public funding undermine all his hard work as a teacher. 'Public education and the university were deteriorating. I was working very hard. I would arrive at 8 a.m. and leave at 10 p.m. and I earned very little. It was frustrating, there was a great deal of tension there.'

When the invitation arrived to be a member of the

television panel on the 1994 World Cup in the USA, he accepted. 'The people liked it and I liked it, it was amusing,' he smiles. He arrived back in Brazil to find he had been offered a full-time contract. For eighteen months he juggled jobs, fitting in as much lecturing as he could while flying to Rio for television appearances.

At the end of 1995, however, he reached a crossroads. 'I said to myself: "I have to decide now".' Since then he has become a pundit on Bandeirantes but it is his writing that stimulates him most. 'Analysing and studying football gives me pleasure,' he says.

Belo Horizonte's name is etched deep in the psyche of English football fans. It was here in 1950 that the USA inflicted the most embarrassing result in the national team's history, a 1–0 defeat in the World Cup finals. The news was telegrammed back to a disbelieving England. In Brazil it was hardly news at all. Interest in English football is barely advanced from then. As Tostão makes fresh coffee in his kitchen, he wants to know about the English side before the forthcoming Tournoi de France. He knows a little of Shearer and Gascoigne, Ince and Seaman, but less of the newer crop of talent. He has heard of David 'Beckman' of Manchester United. Who are the other stars likely to emerge? The name of Paul Scholes, England's only real discovery in the Tournoi as it would turn out, is on no one's lips.

We are soon back on the subject of Brazilian football and the fortunes of his former team-mates. He shrugs his shoulders as if baffled by Jairzinho's unwillingness to talk to me. A genuine concern spreads itself across his face as he asks after Pelé. Tostão fears his footballing soulmate is trying to heal the pain of past criticism that he had at times been disconnected from the wider world of Brazil and its problems. Is his Ministry a means of making amends, he wonders?

Yet he could not agree more wholeheartedly with Pelé's plans to transform the clubs into more accountable, public companies. 'There are clubs that owe $20 million, that don't pay income tax to the Government and they continue buying players. It's a mess,' he says.

'Pelé's ideas are very good. What he is proposing must be done.'

Tostão is approaching the end of his first book. Standing over the carefully collated array of notes and cuttings, he describes a volume that bears little resemblance to the staple biographies that fill our shelves in Europe. His debut will be called *Reflexóes, opinióes e lembranças do futebol*, 'Reflections, opinions and memories of football'. He tells me it is as much an analysis of the history of the game as it is the remarkable story of Tostão. 'The first half will be a collection of chronicles, many of the things we have talked about here today,' he explains. 'The second part is a synthesis with drawings of the evolution of football in the last fifty years.' Even off the pitch, it seems, Tostão sees Brazilian football as a thing of poetry rather than prose.

As he surveys the game today, however, he finds few signs of lyricism. In the three decades since Mexico, he has watched the game become a thing of uniformity, conformity and tactical sterility. 'Today with the globalization of things, you can play the same way in the countryside here in Minas Gerais or in Japan,' he sighs.

Even in Brazil, players and coaches have become

obsessed with energy and efficiency rather than art and beauty. 'I see midfield players who only know how to mark,' he says. 'They do not know how to curve a ball around a defender in the way Rivellino and Gérson, those players knew how to.'

Tostão wonders whether a subtler player like himself would have been allowed to develop in the modern game. 'If players today don't have the physical force and the speed, I don't think they have a place.' He has, at times, despaired for the future of the game he clearly has never fallen out of love with.

'There was this idea that if you play in a beautiful way you lose, if you play in an ugly way you win,' he says, close to anger. 'Teams are not allowed to play only with art as we played in 1970. It is the most foolish thing that can exist, it is stupid,' he says. He apologizes to me in advance. 'I'm sorry about this, but Brazil started to give more value to English football. They wanted to imitate the European teams, there was an overvaluation of discipline, tactics, force, marking. I think the main reason Brazil went twenty-four years without winning a World Cup was because the Brazilian mind changed.'

The 1994 win was a stepping stone, he says. In its current crop of outstanding talent, Ronaldo and Roberto Carlos, Rivaldo and Denilson, Tostão believes Brazil may finally have the makings of a side to restore the game to its golden past. (It also has the lucky ant himself, Mario Zagalo, or Zagallo as he now seems to spell his name, at the helm.) 'I think football is starting to be wonderful again. And I think there is a possibility that this time Brazil will win with a show. I believe it is similar to 1970, I believe it,' he says, pressing his hands together and looking heavenward.

By now Tostão is also casting anxious glances at his watch. His meticulousness extends to his working life. He knows he must spend another few hours with his book. As my time with him draws to a close, I cannot help feeling that my journey is ending in the appropriate place too. I reassure him that I have only two final questions for him.

In the course of my travels around Brazil, I had come to see how absolutely central football is to Brazil's self-image. More than anywhere else on earth, its people see their team as a reflection of their nation's identity and its values. More than anywhere else on earth, winning and losing is a matter of life and death. Why? 'It is I think psychological,' Tostão says. 'Brazil has always been a country that didn't succeed. It is like Nelson Rodriguez used to say, "The people, they're not poor, they lack confidence". In Europe everything is good. It is that thing of the inferiority complex. Every person that has an inferiority complex, in any situation in life, when this person has a chance to show "I'm good at this thing" this person celebrates himself.'

He goes on to describe the way Garrincha would beat a defender and then beat him again – and again if he could. 'It was a celebration of our confidence,' he says. 'It was as if in that moment he was putting aside all the inferiority complex.'

No side has played with a confidence to compare with the Brazil of 1970. No side has been celebrated for doing so. Where then, in his Darwinian dissection of the game, will Tostão rank his side in the evolutionary order? 'I think 1970 was the summit,' he says with all the simplicity that used to exemplify his play. 'The summit of the consecration of the art of playing football.'

He pauses as he muses on what he has just said. 'I think that is why people venerate the team. It represented the ecstasy and beauty of football.' To judge by the satisfied smile, if the phrase is not in his book already it soon will be. Soon we are exchanging handshakes and good wishes. And then I am walking back up a rainy Rua Curitiba, heading for home.

A day after leaving Belo Horizonte, I am back in Rio. I head for the airport and a flight back to London, my journey at an end. Climbing through the clouds that evening, Guanabara Bay and Rio lighting up like the gaudiest birthday cake on earth beneath me, I replay the tape of my interview with Tostão, making a few notes as I go. Hearing him speak so profoundly I am reminded of something I had read much earlier in my journey, by another Brazilian writer Roberto De Matta.

Like Tostão, De Matta believes football reflects Brazil at its self-confident best. 'Although Brazil is bad at lots of things, it is good with the ball. It is a football champion, which is very important,' he wrote. 'After all, it is better to be champion in samba, carnival and football than in wars and sales of rockets.' Tostão, for one, would not disagree with that and nor would I.

As Brazil's endless coast disappears from view, however, it is another line of De Matta's I am drawn to most. No Brazilian felt more proud of the unique qualities of the golden age and the 1970 side in particular. In the team of Tostão and Pelé, Gérson and Jairzinho, Rivellino and Clodoaldo, Carlos Alberto and Everaldo, Piazza, Félix and Brito, he saw: 'art, dignity, genius, luck and bad luck, Gods and demons, freedom and fate, hymns and tears'. On my journey to meet that magnificent eleven I had seen a little of each too.

Magic and dreams are not finished in football. Nor will they ever be while their memory lives on.

INDEX